Waiting for Hitler

Waiting for Hitler

Voices from Britain on the Brink of Invasion

MIDGE GILLIES

HODDER &
STOUGHTON

A CIP catalogue record for this title
is available from the British Library

0 340 83798 5

Typeset in Plantin Light by Hewer Text UK Ltd, Edinburgh
Printed and bound by Clays Ltd, St Ives plc

Hodder Headline's policy is to use papers that are natural, renewable
and recyclable products and made from wood grown in sustainable
forests. The logging and manufacturing processes are expected to
conform to the environmental regulations of the country of origin.

Hodder & Stoughton Ltd
A division of Hodder Headline
338 Euston Road
London NW1 3BH

This book is dedicated, with much love,
to Renee and Donald Gillies

Contents

Prologue

On 7 September 1940 Britain was waiting for invasion.

More than two decades later it was a moment that the makers of *Dad's Army* would capture perfectly in its opening sequence. The British Army, represented by three chipper Union flag arrows, sets off boldly into France until it is forced to shrink back in the face of three swastika-headed serpents weaving their way across Europe. As the Nazis gather on the coast of France, Britain's soldiers beat an undignified retreat back to Britain.

Dad's Army takes its humour from a situation in which a group of disparate men are thrown together with the one aim of saving their country from invasion. In reality, the summer of 1940 offered few laughs. It was a time of uncertainty and rumour, when careless talk cost lives and nothing was quite as it seemed. People who had lived in Britain for most, or all, of their lives were suddenly classified as 'enemy aliens', while everything and everybody came under suspicion.

Hitler's success represented a loss of innocence for the British people: their island status no longer protected them from the threat of invasion as Nazi aeroplanes settled into positions within striking distance of most parts of the country. Ordinary people were asked to take on extraordinary duties; men and women who had spent their whole lives in one town were suddenly catapulted out into the world.

Just as the war offered a new kind of freedom to thousands of Britons, so the world closed in on those left behind on the Home Front. Lives had to be lived in the blackout and in underground shelters. Britons went to ground and looked to nature for clues as to their fate: bad weather kept the invader away, while a full moon guided him to his target.

This is the story of a group of people whose days were marked by the threat of invasion and what happened when the unbearable tension of that summer finally snapped, on the first weekend in September 1940. The Nazis appeared to have readied an invasion fleet and their armies were poised to cross to Britain. The start of the first mass daylight bombing raid on London confirmed what many people now saw as inevitable – that Hitler was on his way.

PART ONE

Spring 1940,
The End of the Phoney War

I

Jenny and Muriel – All Quiet in Norfolk

On 19 March 1940 Alec the tortoise was found dead at home in Norfolk. A family friend concluded that he had woken from hibernation to find there was a war on and promptly died of shock. If this really was the cause of his death, Alec must have been a perceptive beast: in the spring of 1940 Britain was languishing in a twilight zone where the effects of war were discernible only in small inconveniences. Petrol, bacon, butter and sugar were rationed and other commodities such as coal were hard to come by.

The nation groped its way about in a blackout designed to thwart the Nazi bombers who, so far, showed no sign of inflicting 'total war' on their enemy. Instead, the population grumbled about bumping into trees and lampposts, falling off the pavement or, worse, the railway platform. Luminous white paint and torch batteries were soon hard to come by too. People daubed the paint on keyholes and pavement edges; one Essex farmer even gave his black cattle zebra stripes to help drivers avoid any that strayed on to the road. Twice as many people had been killed in traffic accidents as by enemy action since the introduction of the blackout in September 1939.

Many Britons had believed that a gas attack would immediately follow Neville Chamberlain's sombre announcement of war on 3 September 1939 and, as if to confirm this, an air-raid siren sounded almost as soon as he had finished speaking. (It was a false alarm.) Instead, nothing happened and the country settled into an uneasy inertia that became known as the Bore War, the Sitzkrieg and, later, the Phoney War. The gas masks that were carried so assiduously during the autumn of 1939 were now abandoned on the table by the front door. Slipping a gas mask carrier over your shoulder as you went out was something for the over-cautious and those who could not afford to be seen flouting the rules.

After Alec's death, his owners, Muriel and Jenny continued to pursue their outdoor, sociable lives in a remote west Norfolk village. Jenny was twenty-six, Muriel nineteen, and they lived with their widowed mother, Susan. The young women were close, perhaps more so than the seven-year age gap might suggest. In the summer they liked to swim in the sea and play tennis on the courts outside their house. In the cold months they skated on marshland and went for walks in the woods. In the winter of 1939–40 the sea had frozen into salty ridges but this had not prevented them walking the three miles from their home in Snettisham to the sandy beaches that look out on to the bleak Wash. There the North Sea pushes inland to divide Norfolk from Lincolnshire, and thousands of pink-footed geese commute inland to feed off the remains of the sugar-beet harvest.

Jenny and Muriel found village life absorbing: they saw it at close quarters, through the customers who visited the garage and sweet shop they ran with the help of Matthew, the mechanic and handyman. They were also interested in the wider world. At meetings of the Workers' Educational Association they discussed everything from politics to jam-making and H. G. Wells's latest book, *The Holy Terror*, a psychological study of a modern dictator. The sisters also kept a diary for Mass-Observation, an organisation set up in 1937 to study the lives of ordinary people. Muriel and Jenny were proud of their role as chroniclers of wartime Britain, but anxious to keep their pastime a secret from the neighbours they wrote about. As 1940 unfurled, they were to discover that doing anything secret was hazardous.

Like most sisters who live together, they suffered from petty jealousies and irritations. As the elder sibling, Jenny was annoyed that they were regularly mistaken for twins, especially as they did not dress alike. Muriel, too, was keenly aware of their physical differences and could reel them off with the confidence of someone who had spent years measuring them. Jenny's hair was naturally curly, hers was not; they had a similar figure and weighed just over eight stone; their eyes were the same blue, but Jenny's were bigger. Jenny had the larger nose and her complexion was 'made up to look pink', while Muriel's was naturally rosy. Jenny looked like her mother; Muriel resembled the father who had died ten years earlier, leaving thirty-five-year-old Matthew the one constant male figure in their lives. He emerges from their diaries as a long-suffering member of their extended family; someone they relied on in many ways but whom they could not resist teasing. It is easy to imagine Jenny and Muriel sucking their pencils as they composed their diary entries, and Matthew in the corner of their garage, wiping the grease off his hands with a rag and worrying about his soldier brother in France or what was going on at the RAF base nearest to Snettisham.

The sisters' garage was on the coastal route north to Hunstan-ton, or 'sunny Hunny'; its position and their work gave them a keen sense of the region's mood. They knew long before the government's Ministry of Information whether people still carried their gas masks and believed what they heard on the BBC. As the Phoney War turned into something more threatening, Muriel and Jenny were perfectly placed to judge how East Anglians felt about their proximity to mainland Europe. When petrol shortages began to bite and taking a car for a 'spin' became a suspicious activity, their role as custodians of the pumps gave them a position of power that was rare among women.

Snettisham had experienced occasional peaks of excitement before 1940, but it always returned to its natural state of obscurity. Tea-smugglers were caught on its beach in 1737 and in the early twentieth century Queen Alexandra took a fancy to it as a remote bathing spot. She visited it from the rather larger holiday home she shared with her husband, King Edward VII, at nearby Sandring-ham. Queen Alexandra's Bungalow, an ornate flint building with a porch made from an upturned boat, was pulled down on her death in 1925. By 1940 several more modest beach huts squatted on the sand and a middle-aged bachelor lived there all year round. Snettisham, with 1400 inhabitants, had all the trappings of a typical English village: St Mary's Church looked out on to a cricket pitch and the village's ancient chestnut tree provided a shady place for neighbours to linger and gossip. Homes were built from the local carr stone, in a warm butterscotch colour, and known locally as 'gingerbread houses'.

In the spring of 1940 the sisters' world was confined to a triangle bordered by King's Lynn – 'Lynn' for short – a busy market town and port twelve miles to the south, Hunstanton to the north up the coast, whose seasonal kiss-me-quick boldness was tempered by Old World manners, and Norwich, Norfolk's county town, forty-four miles east. The people of Snettisham had a strong sense of place and their own identity within it. At the end of February, when the cobbler pinned up a map of Europe in his shop and customers came in to peer at the foreign place names they heard on their Bakelite wirelesses, they were baffled by the far-off struggle. The frank admission of one villager was echoed all over Britain: 'Well, I did not know Poland was there before. How ever did our government think they were going to help them?'

In peacetime the only strangers Norfolk had encountered were those who travelled to the coast when the sun shone. The war had brought evacuated families from the East End of London. They spoke a different language and often practised a different religion; most had never seen a cow or the seaside and were homesick for noise and bustle. Many wealthy Londoners had already sent their families abroad or disappeared into genteel boarding-houses in remote parts of the country, so it was the poorest who were billeted on families who had room for them: the rich or the childless – two groups least likely to understand their needs. Rumours about them spread quickly. The husband of one woman, who had a couple of young children and came from Shoreditch, was believed to be in jail for arson. A landlady had not known her 'guests' were Jewish until she bumped into them on their way to a religious festival in King's Lynn. From then on she referred to them as 'those Jews', while they retaliated by calling her 'that Christian woman'. The trip to Lynn was the evacuees' first escape from the countryside since they had left London and produced 'an intense pathetic

Fougasse's distinctive posters sprang up
throughout Britain and gave the impression that Hitler
was peering over your shoulder.

longing for a town'. 'We found a Woolworths, what a treat!' they told Jenny.

The war had shrunk the sisters' world. When Muriel saw *Goodbye Mr Chips* at Hunstanton in March it was the first time she had been to the 'flicks' since September, and an outing to Cambridge for a WEA meeting that month was the sisters' only trip to a large town since the outbreak of war. They would have liked to visit Norwich but felt uncomfortable at the idea of being away overnight. Cambridge was a disappointment: most of the brilliant stained-glass in King's College Chapel had been removed as a precaution against a bomb blast and the pair were surprised to see sandbags, which had nearly all been discarded in Snettisham, piled up round the major buildings. Most railway stations were plastered with posters such as the colourful 'Careless Talk Costs Lives' series drawn by the *Punch* cartoonist Cyril Kenneth Bird, who signed his work 'Fougasse'. One showed Hitler and Goering eavesdropping on travellers, but the only titbit the sisters over-heard came from two labourers, lamenting that their sons would soon be snatched away to fight.

The people of Snettisham started to look skywards. In February nine Blenheim bombers 'hedge-hopped' over the marshes, prompting a schoolboy to shout gleefully, 'Here comes Hitler.' A few months later he would be able to tell a Stuka from a Spitfire, a Heinkel from a Hurricane. When Jenny took a tumble on the ice she blamed it on the sudden arrival of an aeroplane with a 'swashtika [sic] under the wings!'. But even this skirmish with the enemy failed to convince their mother that the Germans presented a threat: she gave up hanging her coat, with a stocking stuffed into each pocket, at the end of her bed in case the air-raid siren sounded. Enemy planes were still a novelty, and when one crashed in a nearby field most of the village rushed out to see it; Muriel and a friend took away a bolt and a bullet as souvenirs.

The sisters' lives had changed so little that it was impossible to take seriously the prospect of invasion, even when the evidence pointed to it. In February, Muriel wrote:

This morning we were laying in bed & Mother called out whats that noise. I listened and heard machine gun fire. It was louder and nearer than any I have heard before. We layed in bed and listened and heard burst after burst of guns. This was about eight o'clock. Mother called out 'do you think they are landing on the beach?' She then said 'if they come I shall get under the bed and lay low.' Jenny said 'I think I shall be more of a success with them if I stay in bed!' We all laughed and after a time it stopped and I went to sleep again. Lots of times during the morning we heard it again, and lots of aeroplanes went over, spitfires included.

The threat of a gas attack niggled at the back of their minds, as Muriel reported: 'We decided as we walked there is so many mucky smells in our village, you never would smell a gas attack from some of the other odours in the country. (There's no drainage or sewerage here) . . .' On another occasion Muriel mistook for gas the whiff produced by two hens scratching on a manure heap, and when Jenny visited an elderly couple who had sealed up a room full of books she remarked: 'If they could stay ten minutes in that room, gassing would have been a mild affair.'

The war first impinged on their lives where food was concerned. Susan revived a recipe for Yorkshire teacakes she had used in the Great War because it included no butter. Matthew took three spoonfuls of sugar in his tea and was told to bring his own. Everyone started gardening to ensure Snettisham's supply of fresh fruit and vegetables by the summer; even part of the deer park at Sandringham was ploughed. Meat became scarce and often the butcher could offer only mutton; bacon, when available, was salty and expensive. Once a customer brought the three women a brace of rabbits and Matthew shot pigeons in the wood opposite the garage, which echoed after dark with people chopping and sawing wood to replace the coal that was now impossible to find. 'It does not do to leave any moveable bits of wood for a minute,' Jenny commented ruefully. Most people ignored government pleas not to hoard: Susan and her daughters guarded their sugar reserves jealously, and it was an open secret that a man from Cambridge had filled his holiday bungalow with coal.

Worries about food shortages forced people all over Britain to think carefully about whether they should feed their pets – some owners thought it kinder to put animals down rather than subject them to the aerial bombardment that was expected daily. Tortoises, like Alec, were spared: hibernation made them unobtrusive and when they appeared their demands were minimal. It was harder to make a case for carnivores. 'Much wailing and sobbing because mother had our cat Henry . . . shot,' Muriel confided to her diary. 'Although he has never been a successful cat & had worms and diarrhoea very badly & an insatiable appetite, so Mother said we weren't to cure him again as perhaps we should not have enough food for him soon. Perhaps she is right but it seems a shame. He was so sweet sometimes.' The next day she added, 'Mother said she would have had Happy the old cat shot as well only the man with the gun could not find him. Happy had two abscesses on his head from fighting but as two have cured . . . he is to remain as he does not eat hardly anything.'

Around 400,000 cats and dogs – mainly cats – were killed soon after war was declared and London Zoo destroyed its snakes for fear of them escaping during an air raid. The carnage slowed as owners remembered their pets' practical attributes: cats kept rodents at bay while dogs and birds appeared to possess a preternatural gift for knowing – well ahead of the siren – when bombers were on their way. In 1940 some pet owners claimed, with justification, that their animal could distinguish between enemy and friendly aircraft. The Duchess of Gloucester, who spent the war at a farm in Northamptonshire, said her dogs and ponies showed distress at the approach of enemy planes but were unmoved by Allied aircraft. An advertisement in *The Times* urged readers to buy pheasants as an early-warning system as the birds were said to grow visibly nervous before any human detected the sound of an approaching bomber. Letters to the editor pleaded with Britons to show tolerance to the unfortunate dachshund, who could not help his German name. Vera Brittain pointed out that

'Behind the letter lies the implication . . . that had they been German-bred, ill-treating them wouldn't have mattered.'

Xenophobia was not restricted to dogs. On 10 March Jenny reported: 'New sensational tale! The IRA has been trying to poison our waterworks. Someone found a barrel of poison in a haystack near the reservoir. The boy who told me knows it is true because the boy who told him has a brother in the army and he knows for certain.'

The rumour was probably sparked by news that two IRA bombs had exploded in London injuring twelve people. The blast was a reminder that Britain already had enemies within its shores and coincided with a subtle shift in the public's mood. A few days earlier Muriel had heard her first air-raid siren and described it as '. . . a very weird wail . . . like an ill animal'. That month Jenny noted, 'Things seem very peculiar,' and that the farmer, normally whipped into a frenzy of war production, had not ploughed for two days. Matthew, too, had become obsessed with the paraphernalia of war: he searched the skies for planes and took great pleasure in showing visitors local defence works, searchlights and the aerodrome – the sisters worried that they might be arrested under the Official Secrets Act.

Muriel found the changing landscape depressing: 'It seems so awful to think that all that development and building can be done so quickly for destruction and wars, yet if any social developments and improvements are to be done it takes years and no end of talk first.'

Older inhabitants of Snettisham remembered the Great War and the village's vulnerability to attack. The Wash acted as a huge aerial signpost, much like the Thames in London, and St Mary's Church spire, which at 175 feet was the second tallest in Norfolk, after Norwich Cathedral's, stretched heavenwards like an over-eager pupil demanding to be noticed. In 1915 a zeppelin dropped a bomb in the field close to the church, shattering the glass on the east side. The new windows paid tribute to the parish's forty-four men who had perished in the Great War and reminded the village that, despite its remoteness from the centre of power, its sons could still die in battle.

The National Service (Armed Forces) Act of the previous September made all fit men between the ages of eighteen and forty-one liable for military service. The call-up was slow and systematic. Generally, the youngest joined first and by May 1940 anyone who was twenty-seven or below should have registered, unless they were in a reserved occupation. Over the next few months, Muriel and Jenny heard of customers and neighbours who either had relatives in the British Expeditionary Force (BEF), which had been posted to France, or were in it themselves, as part of the Anglo-French Alliance. The man from the next village who had delivered groceries was found dead in his lorry in France and a customer asked the garage to collect his car from Tewkesbury because he had suddenly been posted across the Channel. Matthew considered sending a pork pie to his brother in the BEF, but Jenny warned that it would not be fit to eat when it arrived. A nearby holiday-camp owner fretted that he had no customers for the summer: in peacetime he had taken all his August bookings by the previous Christmas. To make matters worse his two sons were in uniform: one was serving with the BEF and the other was a merchant seaman, exposed to mines and U-boats. The vicar's son was called up, and Jenny took over his position as secretary of the local WEA between knitting mittens for servicemen. There was general relief when he caught measles, delaying his departure and giving him a few more weeks of civilian life.

The sisters' role at the petrol pumps was becoming uncomfortable: drivers put pressure on them to break the rules. A 'ghastly man', a Cockney, tried to 'wangle' some petrol out of Muriel. 'He adopted a most pugnacious bullying attitude' while his wife and children watched from their car. On another occasion a 'ration coupon swindler' swept up, then sped away when he spotted a police car. Jenny did not record how she recognised him as such but he must have been of a clearly defined type, like the Land Girls, the 'vackies' (evacuees) or the 'conchies' (conscientious objectors). This was a time when labels stuck, and the sisters were anxious not to be squeezed into the wrong pigeonhole. When Muriel was out shopping with Matthew she saw some old school-friends and 'hoped that seeing me with M (he's very fat) and the Oldsmobile – they would not think I'd married a war profiteer!'.

On 14 March the sisters' petrol failed to arrive and they were told that it had been dispatched instead to the RAF. A few days later when supplies appeared the delivery driver told them he was so busy he had to eat his meals as he drove. Muriel wondered how, if there was already a petrol shortage, they would manage if the war lasted several years: '. . . what are we going to sell if we can't get any petrol and how is everyone going to get about? I was talking to a man yesterday who still has 10 gals. buried in the garden!' To confirm her fears, the bank-holiday weekend was deathly quiet: the sisters normally heard cars droning through Snettisham all night, but now there was silence. Their takings for the weekend came to a third of the amount they had earned during the same weekend in the previous year.

Amid this uncertainty and rumour there was an insatiable hunger for accurate, up-to-the-minute news. The nascent television service was shut down 'for the duration', but had had such a limited audience that it was hardly missed. The wireless, which had not existed during the Great War, held sway. Radio programmes were broadcast via the new Home Service, which replaced national and regional networks. The day was punctuated by six news bulletins and families gathered religiously for the nine o'clock news. In the early months of the war, the BBC fell far short of what its audience demanded. The news was remorselessly upbeat and frequently contradictory. Worse, the other programmes were dull. Listeners complained about dreary organ recitals and tedious public announcements.

The one source of entertainment was the clipped, excitable English voice that broadcast from Hamburg and Bremen. It sounded like that of an 'old-fashioned schoolmaster, loaded with sarcasm'. A *Daily Express* columnist had already nicknamed an announcer working from Breslau for the Germans 'Winnie of Warsaw' and on 14 September 1939 published a feature about enemy broadcasting: 'A gent I'd like to meet is moaning period-ically from Zeesen. He speaks English of the haw-haw, dammit-get-out-of-my-way variety, and his strong suit is gentlemanly indignation.' Thus 'haw-haw' originally described upper-class announcers whose identity eluded their British listeners but the name soon became associated solely with William Joyce.

Joyce was born in New York and grew up in Ireland. As a young man he moved to London and joined the British Union of Fascists where he worked closely with Sir Oswald Mosley, who encouraged his fervent anti-Semitic and anti-Communist views. In August 1939, Joyce slipped out of Britain with his wife days before new rules were introduced to detain those sympathetic to Nazism. In Berlin the couple found work as English-language announcers for Reichsrundfunk, Germany's version of the BBC, which broadcast from transmitters in Hamburg, Bremen, Cologne and Zeesen. By 1940, Lord Haw-Haw and his catchphrase, 'Gerrr-many calling! Gerrr-many calling!', were as familiar as Chamberlain and Hitler.

Haw-Haw was Hitler's advance guard, invading British homes and speaking to the occupants in their own language. His distinctive, comical delivery added to his appeal and that he remained a disembodied voice increased his mystique. It did not matter that the 'news' he broadcast had barely half a grain of truth in it, or that he ranted about Jews and Communists: he was neither mealy-mouthed, like the BBC announcers, nor bland, like the interminable organ recitals. At a time of little or no news he was the most interesting thing on the air. A Norfolk schoolboy's comment summed up his new celebrity status: 'I wish Lord Haw-Haw would give a commentary on our skating.'

Jenny switched to a German radio station after the BBC assured its audience that reports of enemy planes over Norfolk were false. She had just spotted a second German aircraft swooping low over the countryside. Muriel tuned in to Germany for other reasons: as BBC reception deteriorated, she found it 'far pleasanter listening to Bremen, it does not fade and is perfectly clear. We are getting quite fond of Der Golden Sieben [she was probably referring to a popular German dance band]'. A secret report by the BBC showed that at the end of January 1940 one in six adults listened to German propaganda regularly, three out of six people occasionally and two never. The majority of the regulars were thought to be intelligent and well-educated, including 30 per cent of the *The Times*'s readership, which carried the German stations' wavelengths and programme schedules.

The traitor Joyce was the first in a line of faceless bogeymen who emerged in 1940 to taunt and worry the British people. Like 'fifth columnists' and spies, Lord Haw-Haw was ubiquitous and omniscient. Snettisham's cobbler claimed that a reliable source had told him who Lord Haw-Haw was and that he had stayed in the village the previous summer. In another version of the story, he had lived in the next village where he had organised meetings for Fascist sympathisers. Garage customers insisted they knew Lord Haw-Haw's identity or that a friend had met him. Jenny wondered whether the broadcaster was having the same effect in other parts of Britain. He was.

Many remember Lord Haw-Haw as little more than a figure of fun, that his broadcasts perked up dreary days and blacked-out nights. This was probably true for most of the population but he upset a significant minority. Muriel reported that Mrs F, an elderly friend, was 'genuinely frightened' by him and said every night that she would not listen to him, but could not resist twiddling the dial until she found his voice.

Haw-Haw's popularity increased as the Phoney War drew to a close. He was said to know what was happening in the tiniest village and his special forte was in telling whether a clock had stopped there. Of course, only the inhabitants knew he was wrong. Some believed he could instruct the Luftwaffe to bomb certain targets or people against whom he had developed a grudge during his time in London. The wife of a former mayor of Shoreditch, for example, was blamed for an air raid because she had berated Lord Haw-Haw for putting up a Fascist poster during the London County Council election of 1937.

As 1940 progressed, the BBC started to fight back with a more interesting, home-grown selection of entertainment. Tommy Handley's *ITMA* (*It's That Man Again*) introduced a series of characters who were as ridiculous as Haw-Haw, but who were on the

right side. In a gentle dig at the Ministry of Information, the fast-
talking Handley became the Minister of Aggravation and Mys-
teries and made his audiences laugh through a mixture of word-
play, satire and plain silliness. Gradually a battalion of characters
from the clattering charlady, Mrs Mopp ('Shall I do yer now,
sir?'), to the sozzled Colonel Chinstrap ('I don't mind if I do') rose
up to see off Haw-Haw.

By the end of March another voice was making an impression.
Muriel recorded in her diary that Mrs F was 'quite recovered from
last Sunday's jitters, and fully confident of victory! Thinks the
Germans nearly beaten! All this change of attitude due to listening
to Churchill's speech last night! It just shows how she is influenced
by the last form of propaganda she has heard.'

2

Ludwig and Hilda – Life as an 'Enemy Alien'

The train jolts to a standstill at the railway station. The soldiers jump down and start to round up the prisoners, who are tired and bewildered; some of the older men are pale after the long journey in cramped conditions behind blacked-out windows. They line up outside the station to cross the town, which has a subdued, out-of-season air. The cafés and restaurants, guest-houses and hotels are empty. A few local people stare, but not unkindly.

Cliffs bear down on the town, which looks out on to a sweeping bay of perfect sand punctuated by brightly painted fishing-boats. The prisoners march to a flat-roofed 1930s building, which squats behind two barbed-wire fences. At regular intervals guards emerge from watch-towers to stamp down the muddy duckboards that lead to their mess room. The new prisoners are allotted numbers and their meagre possessions searched yet again; a guard hands over their files to the camp's intelligence officer. They are led to flimsy plywood huts that wheeze and groan in the wind. Each chooses a bunk bed and huddles under a thin blanket until it is time for the twice daily roll-call, when the camp's several hundred inmates muster in the dining room.

Food is in short supply and it is rumoured that the guards are pilfering rations to sell on the black market. As in any prison, some men know instinctively how to work the system: through ingenuity or, more often, good contacts. These are the prisoners who dine off the best cuts of meat or treats bought in some far-off delicatessen, rather than watery soup and rotting vegetables. For other prisoners Red Cross parcels boost the meagre fare. The technically minded feel the cold less because they have secret, home-made heaters,

which regularly push up the camp's electricity bill, to the con-
sternation of its commander.

Everyone learns how to live at close quarters with the disparate
groups who share the camp: Jews with Nazis, Communists with
Fascists, intellectuals with pastry chefs, trade-union leaders with
capitalists. Everyone worries about the immediate future, not
daring to think more than a week ahead, but keeping this out of
the censored twenty-four-line letters they are allowed to send to
their loved ones twice weekly. With time on their hands, the
intellectuals think and teach. They organise lectures and discussion groups. A camp newsletter, the *Wall*, flourishes briefly before
the authorities decide it might foment unrest. Young men snatch
the chance to resume their studies or to stretch their minds in a way
that is only possible in a confined space: they learn Spanish,
French and Russian, or work with a professor who had taught
at the London School of Economics. The older men play chess or
argue about politics.

The lights go out at 10 p.m. Most climb into bed fully clothed, as
some defence against the cold, and wake to the plaintive cawing of
seagulls wheeling overhead. The air tastes of salt and in bad
weather the sea creeps over the road and seeps into the already
waterlogged camp. Tennis courts, a swimming-pool and football
pitch remind the prisoners of happier times spent among friends
and family.

Ludwig Baruch arrived at the aliens' internment camp in the
winter of 1939. His new home was a former holiday camp at
Seaton, on the south coast of Devon, a few miles from Lyme Regis.
He and his ailing father, Daniel, had been held in various cells and
makeshift prisons since their arrest in Liverpool less than a month
after Britain declared war on Germany. The Baruch family had
already been buffeted by one world war: when Britain and Germany fell out in 1914, Daniel was working as a patent lawyer in
England and engaged to Hedwig, an educated young woman from
a devout Jewish family in Hanover. They abandoned their plans
to honeymoon on the Isle of Wight and Daniel returned to

Hamburg where he enlisted in the army. His war lasted less than a year: in 1915, he collapsed while marching to Poland and was found, barely conscious, in a ditch. He spent the next few years working as the manager of a waste-recycling plant in north Germany. The couple's first son, Ludwig, was born in Hamburg in 1917; two more boys soon followed, and Hedwig struggled to cope with post-war food shortages and tuberculosis.

In 1928 Daniel left his family in Germany to set up a raw-wool business in England for his brother, Louis. Liverpool and Hamburg were similar cities: two ports that looked out over the sea on which their livelihood depended, and whose hinterland was coloured by migrants from all over Europe.

Daniel became convinced that his family's fortunes lay in Liverpool and, amid much bitterness, broke with his brother to set up on his own as a wool merchant in Fazakerley Street. Hedwig and their youngest son, Ury, left Hamburg to join him, but Walter and Ludwig stayed on. Their free time was spent hiking through the pine forests and over the Lüneburger heathland that borders Hamburg and they enjoyed the tail end of German liberalism before Hitler swept to power and Nazism became the overriding dogma. Ludwig made friends easily with the other boys in his class, even though he was the only Jew. Some of his teachers had fought in the Great War and a few boys had lost their fathers to it; one or two students joined the Hitler Youth but Ludwig was never troubled by anti-Semitic taunts. His first experience of oppression was political, rather than racial, and occurred when a teacher ordered him not to wear a shirt that proclaimed support for the Social Democratic Workers' Youth Movement.

Incessant political debate provided the backdrop to Ludwig's early life. He was precociously interested in what went on in the wider world, absorbed in the political cut and thrust of newspapers such as the *Berliner Tageblatt*, the *Hamburger Fremdenblatt* and *Vossische Zeitung*. In September 1930, he and Walter joined their parents and younger brother in Liverpool and watched as if through a telescope the Nazi Party gaining a stranglehold on their country. When Hitler came to power Hedwig wept for days, in the grip of anxiety for her country and race.

Ludwig's political antennae sprang into action when he saw police ruthlessly put down an unemployment demonstration in Liverpool. From then on, he looked out for injustice and found it in the most unlikely place. One day in 1931 he was sent out for firelighters, which came wrapped in a newspaper that told a story as incendiary as his purchase. In the crumpled pages of the *Daily Worker* he read about the 'Invergordon Mutiny' in which sailors on ships off the north-east coast of Scotland had protested at swingeing wage cuts. They had been introduced by a coalition government determined to trim public spending in the face of worldwide depression. Ludwig started to read the paper regularly and joined the Young Communist League (YCL), although he used a pseudonym to protect his parents. Hedwig and Daniel wanted only to blend into their new surroundings but they could not ignore what was happening to the Jewish friends and family they had left in Germany. The large house they had moved to, and from which Hedwig taught German, became a natural staging-post for refugees who had lost their jobs or feared for their lives in Nazi Germany.

All three boys seemed destined for university but Ludwig was headstrong and politically driven. He was regularly in trouble for not wearing school uniform and was finally expelled: as a punishment he had been made to write lines but instead of copying out the given sentence he had transcribed the 'Internationale' in French. His allegiance to Communism made it difficult for him to find work: Daniel called in business favours and pleaded with friends but each potential employer refused to take on his son unless he agreed to leave the YCL. Finally, the Donegal Tweed Company offered him a place in its trimmings department, where he learnt how to prepare pockets and linings for garments. Ludwig was free to follow his political inclinations – which he did with a vengeance.

He joined the Tailors and Garment Workers Union and became a close friend of Harold Martin, a passionate trade-unionist who had spent most of the Great War on the run from the police because of his vehement pacifist views. Ludwig recruited workers to the union and to the YCL, then joined the Communist Party of Great Britain (CPGB). At the Donegal Tweed Company he campaigned for higher wages and paid holidays, and when two brothers were sacked for requesting time off the whole factory walked out in a much-publicised strike. It lasted a week and the workers' demands were met in full. Other factories followed its lead and Ludwig gained a reputation among the police as a Soviet agent and agitator.

He became friends with Jack Jones, then a docker and later leader of the Transport and General Workers Union. Jack remembers him as a small but spirited man, who spoke with a strong German accent. Ludwig might have felt a twinge of jealousy that Jack had been wounded in the Spanish Civil War: the CPGB had decreed that he was more useful to them in Britain. Ludwig also knew Alf Froom, leader of the Tram Workers' Union and editor of its newspaper, *Speed*. Alf had a daughter called Hilda: in her, Ludwig had met his match.

Hilda was steeped in the ideology of the Left. Her father had joined the Communist Party because he felt let down by the Labour Party's tepid support of workers in the General Strike of 1926, and her older brother had been arrested for demonstrating against a rally in support of Oswald Mosley. At seventeen Hilda joined the YCL and raised money for Communists fighting in the Spanish Civil War. Her family's home became a safe-house for refugees fleeing Nazi Germany. She met Ludwig at a birthday party for Tom Mann, an important figure in British trade-unionism who had helped organise the London Dock Strike of 1889 and was a founder of the CPGB.

Technically, Ludwig was still a German citizen and when, in 1936, the German consul in Liverpool told Daniel that his eldest son must enlist in the army, Daniel lied that he had left for the USA. That year, he and Hedwig applied for British citizenship; if they had been successful, their whole family would have become British. However, they were turned down, and again in 1938 – almost certainly due to Ludwig's political activities. Although they sympathised with some of his views, Hedwig and Daniel believed that if they distanced themselves from him politically they might acquire the necessary veneer of respectability. Ludwig moved into a flat a few doors away from his parents; Jack, his wife and baby lived in the rooms below, and Hilda visited often. The couple would roar off on Ludwig's motorbike or borrow Daniel's car to drive to North Wales where they camped and met up with other young people from Liverpool's Left.

On 3 September 1939 British citizenship became a life-changing requirement. That Sunday afternoon, after Neville Chamberlain had proclaimed that 'This country is at war with Germany', Ludwig was told to report to his nearest police station. He was ordered not to use his motorbike or bicycle and to hand over his maps; from now on his every movement was monitored. Fearing that he was about to be interned, he made sure that his books and papers were safe in a secret place. Less than a fortnight earlier the Soviet Union had signed a non-aggression pact with Germany and on 17 September Stalin's army marched into eastern Poland. The Soviet Union's stance provided instant vindication for everyone who had been wary of Communism and its followers; for Britain's Communists it was a bitter blow.

On 15 October Ludwig and Daniel, who was now sixty-three and suffering from a heart complaint, were summoned to appear before magistrates. Hilda and a union secretary were told to wait outside the court while Ludwig was asked a single question, to which he did not know the answer: where was his passport? The police took him back to his flat where he was told to pack some clothes while the officers searched his room. They found nothing. At Dale Street police station he was fingerprinted, photographed and locked up in a blacked-out cell. He was not allowed to telephone anyone but when news of his arrest leaked out, books, newspapers and food poured into the police station. Furious at the way he was being treated he turned to Shakespeare's plays and sonnets for solace. On the second day of his imprisonment he was joined by a middle-aged German sailor, Apel, a member of the Communist Party of Germany. His arrival cheered Ludwig so much that when they were taken with Daniel in a Black Maria to

Lime Street railway station he could see the absurdity of the situation. Their guards, two young soldiers, briefed to watch over the 'dangerous' prisoners, were bemused to discover that their charges were an earnest young trade-unionist, a middle-aged sailor and an ailing wool merchant. Their destination compounded their bafflement: they were making for a Butlin's holiday camp at Clacton-on-Sea, Essex. Hilda and Hedwig waved them off.

Ludwig, who was drawn instinctively to the 'ordinary' man, befriended his guards for the first of what became many times. At Liverpool Street the three prisoners stacked their luggage in a pile and watched it with their guards' rifles while the soldiers went in search of food and drink. At Clacton the prisoners were driven by Rolls-Royce to the camp where a doctor ordered Daniel to be taken on a stretcher to hospital.

The camp had been opened a year earlier but already looked shabby. The pirates' grotto, with its skull and flashing eye-sockets, appeared macabre with no children to squeal at it. Ludwig was one of around three hundred 'aliens' classified as 'Category A' and locked up shortly after the outbreak of war. In 1938 MI5, with the help of Special Branch, had compiled a list of potentially danger-ous foreigners, then sent their details to chief constables in sealed envelopes that were to be opened in the event of war. By the spring of 1938, 30,000 refugees had flooded into Britain. As war seemed inevitable, the need to keep track of them became imperative. Germans or Austrians of 'dubious character' were imprisoned, but the term was open to interpretation and abuse: for some tribunals set up to assess individuals, fighting in the Spanish Civil War and supporting socialism or pacifism offered sufficient justification for internment. As the threat of invasion grew, from mid-1940, the reasons became more arbitrary.

After Ludwig was moved from Clacton to another former holiday camp, Warners in Seaton, he concentrated his thoughts on the tribunal that he felt sure would secure his release. Hilda became his only link with the outside world, the channel through which he dared to pour out his worries and hopes for the future. In return she fed him titbits of news and reassured him that he would soon be free. But letters from one end of England to the other were slow and were sometimes returned to the sender with a harsh warning from the postal censor: 'The communication returned in this cover constitutes a breach of the Defence Regulations. The writer is warned to be careful in future. The communication will be allowed to proceed if the passage or passages referring to movement of ships are omitted, and if it is re-posted to the address in the usual way . . .'

At the end of October Ludwig complained that he had not received a single letter from Hilda. He was desperate to know what was being done to secure his release and urged her to ensure that his trade union had engaged a 'competent solicitor'. He was hungry too:

> I am very sorry if I have to bother you with all sorts of requests, but you are the only contact I have with the outside world. Please send the following things: some cod liver oil or emulsion, tin of treacle, piece of cheese, tasty bread, chocolate, some lard or margarine, a little fruit that keeps, sewing materials, woollen scarf, motor cycle coat for rain, pyjamas and also the things I indicated in last letter particularly the text books and some exercise books. Thank you. (Don't forget warm socks.) I am settling down a little now. I hope the internment won't last long; write, and also send the things I asked for, it would make a lot of difference. I hope you have settled down a little without me, be brave; you are always in my mind. Some day luck will come our way and we will be very happy together. Please be very careful with the money, you never know whether I won't need some when I am released or you may want it yourself. Darling be careful – go to bed early – don't do anything silly – and when you are downhearted think of the lovely times we have spent together. Keep smiling!
>
> Many thousand kisses, yours Ludwig.

He wrote to her with an overcoat and blanket wrapped round his legs against the damp cold that seeped through the plywood walls, having composed the letter in his head during the endless dull hours of that day. In November Hilda's letter arrived, with books, cigarettes and chocolate, all of which he devoured before he replied: 'I am possessed by a peculiar feeling of loneliness, which you can help me to overcome if you write to me about your feelings, attitude and estimation of experiences as far as possible.' He urged her to dress well and to enjoy herself while saving as much money as possible so that she could visit him. 'Please do not forget that we will be married almost as soon as I am free and working again!' he added, and enclosed some of Shakespeare's sonnets. Despite his misery he reminded her to tell the union that whatever happened to him he would remain 'true to the Union principles' and that the 'struggles of the British people will always remain very dear to me'.

Hilda's letters convey a forced joviality mixed with news of the practical steps that were being taken to secure his release. 'All my love and many kisses (to be cashed at an early date),' she ended in November, then added sternly, 'Of course, we must not forget the lads in tougher spots than you.' She told him of her trips to see films, whose titles reveal the obsessions of the time – *Confessions of a Nazi Spy* and *I Was a Spy*, and complained that in the blackout it was 'blooming awful groping to find the way to the tram' but people had learnt to find their way around by smell. Once she had been in Lloyds Bank when the air-raid siren sounded: customers and staff alike had had to shelter in the vaults and someone fused the lights, which exploded with a bang that made them all jump. On another occasion she saw the survivors of a ship sunk by the Germans and was struck by the pain of a man who had lost his wife and their baby girl. His anguish forced her to see the bright side of their own predicament – that Ludwig was not in the forces and that they were not married: 'I would have been in some other damned camp with barbed wire around it . . . They have funny ways of judging enemies – It seems to be whether or not I have a ring on my finger.' She was not embarrassed by her boyfriend's internment, although when children asked where 'Uncle Lou' had gone she said that he was 'at school'.

Ludwig said he jumped with joy when he received his first long letter from Hilda, and added that the nights reminded him of their time together: 'Down here the moon appeared magically bright and spread a very strange and beautiful light over the surrounding hills.' Despite their separation, both were optimistic about the future. Ludwig wrote, 'I am determined that the children that may be born to us shall never have to live in a world like . . . our parents left us to face; this war I feel sure will finish off once and for all those forces which have repeatedly driven millions of people to misery and destruction.' The guards confirmed his belief in the essential goodness of humanity: 'In fact many qualities of character inherent in the British people and particularly the common people have been so heavily underlined and emphasised so as to make this country very dear to me at a time when I felt justly very hurt about my own fate.'

He spent much time talking to the other prisoners and reminded Hilda to send him textbooks on physics, chemistry, maths, French, Russian, Italian and Spanish. In December he attended a celebration of the Jewish festival of Chanukkah – 'But is it not the limit of irony? German-Jewish refugees celebrating the victory over Persian tyranny 2,500 years ago, in an English internment camp.'

Just before Christmas Hilda, who had been saving hard for the train fare, visited Ludwig. She spent a whole day travelling to spend an hour with him. Ludwig had begged his mother not to visit Daniel, who was in hospital near Plymouth, as he feared his heart would give out under the emotional strain. At Seaton, Ludwig and Hilda sat at either side of a wide table, unable even to exchange a kiss. On her return to Liverpool, she wrote:

> You can imagine how merry I am when I cant even waive [*sic*] to you over the barbed wire in case I suddenly invent some kind of semaphore or Morse. It's a good job I have a plain hat or they may think I have concealed earphones – God knows what I might hear! We didn't really appreciate how happy we were together, but I think this parting will make a big difference to us in the future – it will make us appreciate how lucky we are to have each other – it will be like starting all over again with a much deeper understanding and affection for each other.

But even Hilda's irrepressible optimism faltered as the months of separation dragged on. Vera Lynn's 'We'll Meet Again' gave her 'the pip', and although she still went to dances she complained that it was difficult to manoeuvre round a room with someone wearing army boots. She threw all her energy into trying to arrange for Ludwig to appear before a tribunal and wrote to Eleanor Rathbone, an MP who campaigned on behalf of refugees. She wore a locket with Ludwig's picture in it and increasingly found herself defending him.

She also joined Britain's Air Raid Precautions (ARP) network, a group of men and women who ensured their communities were well protected against bombardment. Their duties ranged from filling sandbags to checking that the blackout was properly enforced. During a raid they were expected to direct the rescue services, comfort victims and guide survivors to shelters. They learnt first aid, how to deal with minor fires and to identify poison gas. Once, during a practice, someone said that all Germans should be interned or wiped out; she pointed out that 'German' was not synonymous with 'Nazi', and fulminated to Ludwig:

> I think it is a damned scandal that you, and people like you, are interned and have to share the same accommodation as Nazi-minded people off U-boats, and as they cant distinguish anti-Nazis from Nazis when they capture a crew, they ought [to] give you entirely separate camps. It must be terrible for a person who hates nazi-ism so much as you do to have to share accommodation with them.

Early in 1940 Ludwig was taken to the Oratory School in Brompton Road, Chelsea, where it was decided whether or not aliens should be locked up. There he waited among the children's paintings and the neatly labelled coat-hooks to face the tribunal that would decide his fate. Later that day he returned to Seaton, unaware that it would be several months before he learnt the outcome. Hilda posted him his kitbag so that he could pack and be ready to come home. The daffodil, tulip and crocus bulbs that she had sent him were just starting to appear beneath the barbed wire.

3

Listening to Hitler –
The BBC's Monitoring Service

In the spring of 1940 Britons had many new sounds to adjust to. Easily the most chilling was the wail of the air-raid siren, but perhaps the most bizarre came from a teashop in the centre of a market-garden town in Worcestershire. There, among the restrained chink of china, Adolf Hitler and Benito Mussolini could be heard ranting to their public. Herr Schmidt, an interpreter, tried to convey the gist of the dictators' speeches to the teashop's customers without causing offence. He was not translating from the wireless: George Weidenfeld, a talented mimic and linguist, was using his perfect command of Italian and German to bring alive Hitler, Mussolini and their interpreter to devastating comic effect.

Weidenfeld, who became famous as a publisher, and was also made a life peer, found an audience who appreciated the nuances of his linguistic somersaults in Evesham. Many of the teashop's customers at that time were polyglots in their own right and competed with each other to produce the most polished translation of Petrarch's sonnets or deciphered Egyptian hieroglyphs for fun. Many, also like Weidenfeld, were Jews who had fled Europe just before the Nazi war machine had threatened their lives. They had left behind families they feared they might never see again.

The first of these carefully selected translators arrived in Evesham on a red double-decker bus that had picked them up from London a few days before the outbreak of war. Later recruits were given a voucher with 'Somewhere in the country' printed on it and told to go to Paddington station where a ticket clerk sabotaged the attempt at secrecy by announcing confidently, 'That's Evesham.' Most had answered an advertisement that had appeared in *The Times* in the spring of 1939 for native speakers of European languages. The job, which paid £300 a year, plus board and lodgings, was a lifeline for the many destitute refugees who hung around in the lobbies of London hotels, in their over-long coats and loud ties, hoping to pick up tips on the cheapest lodgings and how to earn money. Before they could take up the linguistic position, which remained unnamed until the last minute, they had to pass an exacting test of their skill in translation. Weidenfeld, who had left his parents in Vienna to come to Britain in August 1938, now sat on a bench beside a Portuguese colonial doctor, a Maltese impresario of circus acts and other Central European intellectuals, some clutching dictionaries. They were asked to transcribe English summaries of a long-winded French radio talk on military manoeuvres in the Alps, followed by a short news bulletin from Radio Paris, with commentary on Hitler's 'rape of Czechoslovakia'. Three weeks later Weidenfeld was interviewed by a bureaucrat and a radio producer, who asked him whether he had ever belonged to an extreme organisation, such as the Nazi or Communist Party, what he thought of the British, whether he was emotionally stable and how he felt about his native Austria. Shortly afterwards he received a letter saying he would be employed as a BBC monitor for three months, or the duration of the National Emergency, whichever was the shorter.

Ewald Osers, a German-educated Czech Jew who had left Prague to study in London, impressed the interviewer with his mastery of German shorthand. Recruits like him and Weidenfeld arrived for their first day's work at the grand entrance to a late Victorian mansion called Wood Norton Hall just outside Evesham, between Cheltenham and Stratford-on-Avon. They were taken through what became known as the Golden Gates to the former home of the Duc d'Orléans, a pretender to the French throne who had scattered fleur-de-lis motifs over the mansion's taps and lavatory cisterns. The BBC had bought the house secretly in 1939 as a bolt-hole to which they could evacuate their operations if war broke out. It offered magisterial views of the Malvern Hills and the river Avon but also, far more importantly, excellent radio reception.

In 1940 Evesham was a tranquil town and the refugees who
drifted past its Norman arches and Tudor buildings might have
wondered whether they had stumbled on to the set of a Shakespeare play. The local people, on whom they were billeted, must
have been equally startled by their exotic guests: at a time when
anything foreign or unusual was viewed with deep suspicion, the
BBC monitors flaunted their unconventionality, particularly in the
way they dressed. The farmers and market gardeners became used
to seeing the 'shaggy White Russian' in his ankle-length overcoat
with the astrakhan collar and galoshes, George Weidenfeld in
riding breeches, the dashing Pole who frequently wore white tie
and tails, and the Scandinavian who regularly appeared naked at
his bedroom window. Even the British-born staff at Wood Norton
were unusual: one woman cycled to work in billowing Adriatic
beach pyjamas, and another rode a horse, which she tethered to the
Golden Gates. The local people kept their distance from the
newcomers, who struggled to understand puns and the quintes-
sentially English characterisations on *ITMA*, and worked odd
hours: they often took time off in the middle of the week when
everyone else was labouring in the fields. Some foreigners preferred their own coffee-house culture to the local pub so sometimes
appeared standoffish, and their precise English caused misunderstandings. Weidenfeld was baffled by his landlady's malapropisms: she described him as 'morose' when she meant 'thoughtful'
and 'resilient' rather than 'responsive'. She also confused 'cataract'
with 'catastrophe'. When a wealthy family invited him to tea the
lady of the house asked him whether he knew the Goerings,
perhaps assuming that everyone was as well connected as she
was and revealing a total misunderstanding of the political situation abroad.

One billet was so bleak that it became known as 'Wuthering
Heights': typists often had to share beds. Ewald Osers was shocked
by some of the unpatriotic remarks he heard at the breakfast table.
Some farmers refused to carry out orders from the Ministry of
Food about which crops to grow, and continued to produce
asparagus for hotel and restaurant customers. When it was sug-

gested that crops might be destroyed ahead of a Nazi invasion they were horrified, commenting, as Osers remembered, 'After all, the Germans would want to eat too, wouldn't they?'

In 1940 the idea of eavesdropping on an enemy – or a potential enemy – was still new. In 1936 the BBC had monitored a few Arab broadcasts after Italy invaded Abyssinia (now Ethiopia) but it was not until the Munich crisis and Germany's assault on Czechoslovakia that the British government recognised that listening to the enemy would provide important information as to their plans. By the time the BBC had advertised in *The Times*, monitoring had become a useful tool in modern warfare. But while the prospect of holding a glass to your enemy's wall was enticing, the BBC still had little idea of what they should be listening for and how to interpret what they heard. The brilliant linguists who had been recruited to listen, in many cases, to their former home countries were given a wide brief. Something as subtle as a sudden change in the type of music played might carry huge significance and even farming news offered vital clues to Germany's food stores or its weather, which was not reported directly but might be of help to aircraft. The monitors knew that their reports might be read by the prime minister and possibly used in making important decisions.

The radio masts that snatched words from Europe's ether were perched on the highest ground in the Wood Norton estate and partly hidden by trees, which also concealed a few leaky wooden huts. Engineers sat in one of these buildings, at a long table facing a row of large black radio sets. They coaxed them into life by twiddling large dials, then fed the broadcasts 'down the line' to Mrs Smith's House (a smaller building near the main mansion – no one ever knew who Mrs Smith was) where around ten monitors sat in the listening room wearing earphones. They were told how to find the radio station they had been allotted and scribbled notes of what was said throughout a programme. When it had finished they reported its content to two supervisors: one was interested in the gist of the broadcast while the 'flash' supervisor wanted to know about anything of immediate value.

Then the monitor hurried to the typing room to dictate his notes to a waiting typist who huddled with him in a cubicle. These women were not 'CTs' (Commercial Types) from the large typing pools but highly proficient and patient secretaries from the BBC's then defunct television department They coaxed a readable text from the monitor's desperate scribblings and ironed out any arcane phrases that had slipped in during translation. Many monitors said that it was in those tense moments that they received their most important lessons in the use of English.

Occasionally even accomplished linguists struggled with specialist vocabulary. Once, Osers was told to monitor a talk for farmers about bulls 'servicing' cows. Bulls' semen was prized in wartime and the lecturer explained in great detail how to avoid wastage. He wrote later: 'My English sexual vocabulary was based more on what one can read on lavatory walls than on scientific animal biology.' A typist, who happened to be a farmer's daughter, sensed that he was floundering and told him to use words he knew – even if they seemed crude – so that she could convert them into the appropriate technical jargon. The exchange caused no embarrassment on either side, Osers reported, as they viewed it on a purely professional level.

The script was then rushed to the supervisor's room to be trimmed and sent by teleprinter to London, where it was decided which ministries or agencies needed to read it. A digest of news bulletins from foreign stations was produced twice a day and split into two sections: the first dealt with German-controlled stations and the second with those in other countries. Throughout 1940 the number of stations in the first category grew at an alarming rate.

The engineers on top of the hill recorded all broadcasts on wax cylinders as back-up or in case a more detailed translation was needed. 'Boys' – the newspaper office term for anyone who ran errands – carried them down in baskets. They were mostly middle-aged men and oblivious to the importance of their task. In wet weather they frequently slid down the muddy slope and the cylinders arrived broken or cracked.

In a typical day, monitors listened to around 1.25 million words spread over three shifts: 8 a.m. to 4 p.m., 4 p.m. to midnight and from midnight to 8 a.m. The two German daytime stations – Deutschlandsender and Hamburg – were monitored carefully in case they made special announcements at unscheduled times. They were popular with the monitors because they often played classical music: you could read a book or a newspaper while you kept an ear open for interruptions. At night the German external service was beamed mainly to America.

At times Wood Norton felt a bit like an Oxbridge college: there were subtle tensions between the monitors and the engineers, and eccentricity was viewed as a natural by-product of brilliance. Women typed, but as a special concession they were allowed to wear dark trousers in the evening. The intensity of the work meant that the more sociable monitors were always looking for a way to escape the claustrophobia of their headphones: they cycled to nearby pubs, played tennis, went boating, picnicked and found a shop that had somehow acquired sufficient sugar to make fudge. They also took full advantage of living in one of Britain's most fertile regions, oozing with fresh fruit and vegetables. Some monitors took part in amateur dramatics and George Weidenfeld's impersonation of Hitler was so convincing that the BBC once asked him to play the Führer on air when a recording of one of his speeches failed to arrive on time. Other monitors doodled cartoons, of which the best might have appeared in *Punch*, if the subject matter had not been so sensitive. In one a government official comments to his colleague: 'I say, there's something deuced fishy about this place "inaudible".'

Anxiety about the friends and families they had left behind gnawed at many monitors, but during the Phoney War at least, the Nazi threat was still distant. When Osers and another monitor worked the first Christmas shift of the war their boss provided them with headphones attached to ten-metre cables so that they could listen to the radio while they played table-tennis.

Early in the morning of 9 April 1940 the atmosphere changed. Frivolity vanished. No one knows which monitor picked up the news that crackled into Evesham from Europe, but soon everyone was scribbling frenziedly. For eleven hours they listened without a break, conscious that they were the first to know: Hitler was coming.

STOP PRESS
WCAB (PHILADELPHIA) CBS (U.S.A.): SHORT WAVE: IN
ENGLISH FOR NORTH AMERICA: 06.25 BST. 9.4 .40.

GERMANY INVADES DENMARK. Sudden German
invasion of Denmark reported by International
News Service . . . Fuehrer's goose-stepping
legions crossed the Danish frontier at . . .
South Jutland at 4.30 this morning. An hour
later, German troops, landing from warships,
entered Copenhagen and began marching
triumphantly through the Danish capital's
streets.

'BRITISH NAVY MAY ACT'.
(Major G. F. Elliott discussing military
significance of Europe's latest news.)
'. . . Before it comes to the armies crashing
in force we may expect to see a desperate
attempt by the British Navy, reinforced by
aeroplanes, to stop or interfere with any
German attempt to land troops in Norway.
German forces in Denmark may possibly become
the target also of Britain.
Britain cannot stand idly by and see the whole
of Scandinavia turned into a German province
and Germans established all along the coast
facing the British Isles. Her existence is at
stake as this proves a serious German bid for
domination of the North.'

Source: BBC Monitoring Service

PART TWO

April – May 1940,
From Norway to Northern France

4

Jenny and Muriel, April – Hitler Catches Two Buses

———◆———

At the beginning of April, Neville Chamberlain told a meeting of Conservatives that Hitler had 'missed the bus', meaning that Germany had left it too late to deal a knock-out blow to France and Britain. It was a curious expression. The ailing prime minister, already gripped by the stomach cancer that would kill him, may have hoped that the homely words would appeal to the man and woman on the Clapham omnibus. Instead, most ordinary people found the image laughable. It was difficult to visualise either Chamberlain or Hitler waiting for a bus and the prime minister's choice of words merely confirmed how out of touch he had become with voters and world politics. Within a month the situation in mainland Europe was so dire that Chamberlain was incapable of rising to speak in the House of Commons without catcalls from Labour MPs of 'the man who missed the bus'.

'Everybody seems very pleased and amused by Mr Chamberlain saying "Hitler missed the bus",' Jenny recorded in her diary. 'When people miss a bus they are normally in good time for the next one.'

The news of Germany's invasion of Scandinavia marked the beginning of a new, more ominous phase in the conflict. As Ed Murrow, the celebrated American radio broadcaster, told listeners on 8 April: 'That something-is-going-to-happen atmosphere that marked the early days of the war has returned.' The knowledge that the German Army was waiting on the other side of the North Sea to board a bus whose destination screen now read 'England via the east coast' sent a shiver of fear through Norfolk. All over Britain people huddled round their wirelesses.

A London author wrote to her American magazine editor:

We gasped over Denmark and Norway. At eight o'clock the next morning, the radio hinted that Norway might be coming to terms with Germany. Deep dejection. At once this was contradicted and we breathed again. Then came the evening when it was announced that there might be important news for us at 10.15. At this hour, the announcer apologised humbly that there wasn't, but he would give us a nice record! His nice record came to an end all too soon. Apologies. Another nice record and so on until 10.45. By that time our hearts were pit-a-patting.

The shock was compounded in Norfolk by the county's proximity to the North Sea and its distance from London: East Anglians felt vulnerable to attack and in danger of being forgotten by the men in Whitehall.

On 9 April, Jenny wrote:

M[atthew] arrived to work in quite a panic about Germany invading Denmark. Had I heard? No I had not. Later M. returned from Lynn and said he saw it on a hoarding that they had invaded Norway as well. So we put on the 1 o'clock news to find out. Went to see a neighbour who is spring cleaning. She had a very odd mac on the linen line which she said she was airing in case she had to flee. She thought if you were a refugee you wanted to look as scruffy as possible and then they would get up a fund for you. No business doing hardly today.

Muriel, too, noted how people around her reacted:

I was astonished to hear via Jenny and M. of the invasion of Norway this morning . . . It seemed such an extraordinary thing for Hitler to do. I suppose he had to do something quick, but I did not realise he was getting so desperate. It worries me as to what he will do next. He seems to get nearer. Jenny thought of packing a bag, also M., but he can't see why it would be any safer the other side of England. Mr T [a customer] came in the afternoon. He says he thinks they will pack their 'go-cart'. He said he would have to take that to put the dog on. I said why not let her go on a lead, but he said she is such a bad walker she would want to come back by the time they got to the next village.

The invasion shook people out of their apathy to the extent that gas masks reappeared. For George Beardmore, who lived in London with his wife, Jean, and baby daughter, the news from Scandinavia brought fears bubbling to the surface that he had so far kept in check. Jean had lost weight in January from worrying about what the war would mean for their family, but news that German troops were on the move prompted her to ask, 'Georgie, it's going to be all right, isn't it?'

George worked in the BBC's engineering department, and although he was technically in a reserved occupation, he was concerned that he might be called up. All over the country people were reassessing their situation and wondering, 'What if . . .' In Snettisham, villagers talked openly about what they would do if the Germans landed. Matthew and another man agreed that they would rather stay in their own home than fight on the streets. Jenny began to read *Mein Kampf* but every time she put it down someone else picked it up to search for clues to Hitler's motives.

The newspapers, straining against censorship, and the confused reports filtering out of Norway, initially presented an almost hysterically upbeat view of the campaign: British submarines had sunk three German ships, Norway was resisting and the Allies were going to her rescue. But the public were not fooled – especially since the same newspapers told them that Holland had cancelled all military leave and that Germany's newly acquired Norwegian airfields would cut by a third the flight time to Britain's Home Fleet at Scapa Flow in the Orkneys. Shortly after the invasion of Norway a secret session of Parliament was called. Many people suspected that the public were not being told the whole story, and doubted that anyone knew exactly what was going on in Norway. The truth, which emerged much later, was that France and Britain had been preparing to seize control of Narvik – the only all-weather port through which Swedish iron ore could pass – when Germany got wind of their plans and invaded Norway and Denmark. Britain was taken by surprise and the two-month struggle for control of Norway revealed the acute weaknesses in the Allies' intelligence and, in particular, Britain's belief that her navy still ruled the waves. Churchill, as first lord of the Admiralty, was lucky not to be blamed for the débâcle.

For many people the invasion of Norway removed any doubt about the wickedness of Hitler's army. As Muriel recorded:

> Mr M [a customer] said that all Germans were dirty swines and the whole lot ought to be exterminated. I have argued with him about that sort of imbecile talk before and I have the idea he was only saying it so I heard to annoy [me] as he knows it makes me wild. M came in the office after he had gone and said 'Mr M is feeling very drastic today. Such silly talk about all Germans ought to be killed. I bet you could kill off a dozen and get rid of all the trouble.' I did not ask him which dozen he would have killed.

Her mother, Susan, ordered two tins of sardines from a travelling salesman in case fish became even scarcer now that Norway was in Nazi hands. When Jenny put away the groceries she discovered a further nine tins of Skipper sardines stashed on the shelf, despite the government's strictures against hoarding. Lord Woolton, minister of Food, tried to reassure the country that Britain had sufficient stocks of bacon and butter to see it through after the fall of Denmark, but a siege mentality had taken hold and shortages concerned everyone. It became an offence to feed bread to wild birds and later exhortations to 'dig for victory' transformed Britain's most traditional 'chocolate-box' villages into intensely farmed vegetable patches. Lettuces and carrots framed Jenny and Muriel's rose garden, the vital ingredients in a range of recipes from jam to curry. They replaced frivolous flowers: pink godetia, yellow snapdragons and glossy red flax now seemed to belong to a bygone age of whimsy and colour.

All over Britain vegetables sprouted in the most unlikely places and government leaflets offered tips on 'Making the Most of a Small Plot'. Housewives clambered on to air-raid-shelter roofs to water their cabbages, and gardens that had been lovingly tended for generations were given over to Brussels sprouts and runner beans. Digging for victory allowed the ordinary person to feel they

" Let's walk through the park and 'ave a look at the vegetables."

In July 1940 *Punch* showed how the campaign to grow more food was
transforming the country into one big allotment

were assisting the war effort and helped to take to their mind off
Germany's intentions. Only occasionally did anyone wonder if it
might all be a waste of time. A retired man asked Jenny why she
was slaving in the garden when she might have to 'leave it to the
Germans any time'. Soon such defeatist comments risked landing
the speaker in jail.

Parks were mutilated in the name of vegetables, and football
matches were played on pitches bordered by sprouting broccoli
and potatoes. So intense was the desire to propagate that in July
Punch ran a cartoon captioned, 'Let's walk through the park and
'ave a look at the vegetables.' In towns, a damp flannel in a saucer
yielded mustard and cress for sandwiches, and windowsills were
cluttered with tomatoes, lettuces, parsley and mint. Vegetables
grew in the moat at the Tower of London. Housewives saved the
water after boiling vegetables to make soup and followed govern-

ment advice on trying unfamiliar products, such as cow's heel, calf's head or pig's trotters. Radio programmes like *Kitchen Front*, among an estimated 1196 wartime broadcasts on food, offered further tips. Slowly, and with much grumbling, the nation adapted to a diet that was low in sugar and fat, and high on portion control. In hounding Britain's merchant fleet Hitler forced the country into an acceptance of healthy eating that early-twenty-first-century doctors can only dream of.

In May, Jenny and Muriel tried imported meat for the first time and decided they would 'go without rather than eat that "muck" '. Their butcher, who had supplied meat to the royal household at Sandringham before the war, was equally disgusted. Jenny decided to buy a couple of rabbits and two goslings to help the family become self-sufficient. They already kept chickens, and added another to the flock, which Muriel named 'Mrs Lewis' after an evacuee who reminded her of a hen with her gaggle of chicks trailing after her. The government encouraged private egg production by lifting a ban on keeping poultry in gardens. Families who kept fewer than twenty chickens were allowed to retain their eggs; if they had more birds they needed a special permit and had to surrender some of their produce. Chickens were an ideal food source, *Woman's Own* told its readers, because they thrived on household waste. It urged women to consider keeping rabbits, too, and even a goat, two more animals, it said, that could exist on food scraps which, even in wartime, humans could not be persuaded to eat.

Britain's island status was proving a double-edged sword: while it offered protection against invasion, the country's reliance on imports meant it risked being starved into submission. The fashion-conscious were also hit by shortages and resorted to raiding the kitchen for gravy browning, which they smeared over their legs to replace stockings. It had to be washed off before bedtime or it marked bed linen, which was now laundered less often as soap was scarce. Jenny and Muriel were unable to find any lisle stockings but, said Muriel, 'I am quite willing to have bare legs all the summer "in the national interest" and have been doing it for yrs in my own interests, and other people call it being mean or showing my legs.' They were the only ones in the village to ignore the injunction, 'Cast not a clout till May is out.' 'No wonder they all suffer from BO,' wrote Muriel. The sisters also decided that, unlike some of the villagers, they would wear their best clothes if they became refugees.

Wool was costly and the most patriotic use for it was in socks for the armed forces; even the Queen was pictured in a knitting circle at Buckingham Palace. Although the campaign to 'make do and mend' was not launched until 1943, fashion editors were already encouraging the idea with imaginative – if not bizarre – suggestions for pepping up a depleted wardrobe that used household waste. *Picture Post* portrayed a model sporting a necklace of discarded corks and declared that beer-bottle caps, film spools and brass hooks would be just as elegant. The *Daily Mail* advised on trimming last season's hats. Some milliners designed headwear reinforced with a lightweight steel cap or 'anti-concussion bandeau of aerated rubber', which claimed to protect the wearer's brain and ear-drums from bomb blasts. It never took off, and headscarves became popular as women took on jobs that required their hair to be safely tucked away. Winston Churchill's wife, Clementine, wore hers knotted on top of her head.

Merchant ships, who were dodging mines and U-boats, were crammed with essentials and had no room for clothing so skirts were worn narrower and shorter, heels lower. The world grew drab as the colour spectrum, like the rest of Britain, closed down. Black, brown and grey were fashionable, partly because coloured fabric was not available but also because muted shades suited the nation's mood. One author wrote to her American publisher that 'England is gradually turning khaki' as more men and women joined the armed services; she added that the uniforms seemed to be 'chiefly pockets with a bit of man between'. The cosmetics manufacturer Elizabeth Arden said that 'burnt sugar' was the most suitable colour to wear with khaki.

Gas-mask boxes offered a rare outlet for a thwarted sense of individuality and Vera Brittain reported a range of containers, from biscuit tins to a lavish suede bag edged with scarlet leather. For some, war was no reason to lower one's standards, as Naomi Royde Smith, a novelist living in Winchester, pointed out:

> Yet the women of England still face the four hours' imprisonment of a Permanent Wave every day. I was told of a lovely young debutante who had decided 'to have my hair waved for the Invasion' as though it were a party. This seems to me to be neither courage nor bravado but a form of single-minded stupidity coupled with the training and the duty of looking one's best on all occasions, which is the British feminine counterpart of martial virtue.

For most people, though, taking too keen an interest in fashion was viewed as bad taste, given the country's parlous state. Sport was regarded in a similar light. Jenny and Muriel were the only people in Snettisham who continued to play tennis after the Nazi invasion of Denmark and Norway, and many people felt almost superstitiously hesitant about enjoying themselves when the world was on the verge of collapse. Britain stayed at home to listen to the wireless and study maps of Scandinavia and *Jane's Fighting Ships*, which became a bestseller. Cinema managers moaned that in one night alone they had lost £250,000 in takings.

By the end of April, newspapers were shrinking in size, due to the shortage of pulp supplies from Scandinavia, and had adjusted their stance on the battle in Norway: now they were preparing readers for bad news. In explaining away the Allies' poor performance they introduced a new element that cropped up again and again in the months that followed. German sympathisers, according to *The Times*, had been 'hiding for weeks in supposedly non-combatant ships, abusing the hospitality of Norwegian harbours. How long the Nazis had been intriguing with the traitors who did so much to facilitate their entry can only be guessed.' Soon British newspapers were full of stories about this 'fifth column' of Nazi sympathisers who had insinuated their way into the country, and were doing their best to facilitate a German invasion. Apparently the expression was coined by Emilio Mola, one of Franco's generals in the Spanish Civil War, who boasted that he had four columns of soldiers surrounding Madrid but a fifth working for him within the city. In Norway, such spies were said to be led by a man whose name became synonymous with treachery: Vidkun Quisling, head of the Norwegian Fascist Party, declared himself prime minister as soon as the Germans landed. He used the Oslo radio station to tell listeners that mobilisation had been cancelled and urged his countrymen not to resist; meanwhile King Haakon fled with his cabinet to the country's northern mountains. Quisling's role in Norway's defeat was marginal, and the existence of a co-ordinated fifth column in Europe was greatly exaggerated, but the two new expressions were significant in extending the language of fear and mistrust in Britain.

The use of such underhand tactics meant that the enemy might already have arrived in Britain and it became everyone's duty to look out for him. In Snettisham, one of Jenny and Muriel's neighbours was arrested for walking near a military camp with a camera and held until his family could be traced. A grocer's assistant said that several odd men had offered her cigarettes and tobacco at pre-war prices. They were probably older commercial travellers who had taken the place of younger men who had been called up. In peacetime, up to three salesmen a day would visit shops; now Jenny and Muriel were lucky to see three in a week.

In the next village a schoolmaster who had been obsessed with gangsters turned his attention to spies and, egged on by his pupils, strode into the head teacher's office and accused a teaching assistant of being an undercover agent. A 'county' woman of about thirty, Muriel noted, was 'v. cross about all the foreigners in this country. Said all ought to be got rid of, spies 5th column etc. After all they are eating our food, most of which has to be imported.' A throwaway line was often pounced on as the truth. When a man called to Muriel that 'All the cars will be commandeered soon to barricade the beach road to stop Hitler from marching in', an old lady heard him and believed that it had already happened. Muriel took a pragmatic view: 'I have the sort of "don't care if we win or lose" feeling, and is it any good fighting? Is it any good living at all? The sooner we're dead the better feeling.'

On 21 April George Beardmore was also contemplating the
future:

> That word 'invasion' comes glibly off the pen but what does it
> mean apart from the business of war? What will it mean to
> Denmark for instance? The arrival of those packed troop
> carriers, one imagines, tanks, and a staff car with a strutting
> officer getting out of it. Proclamations in two languages posted
> up. Martial law. Curfew. The closing-down of dress-shops
> because they are mostly owned by Jews, and the disappearance
> of the Jews themselves to unknown destinations. Schools given
> the task of teaching German – and possibly with a new type of
> history-book. Loudspeakers. Town Councils given their orders.
> Men who collaborate and others who don't. Neighbour looking
> sideways at neighbour to question the side he's on. Betrayals.
> Public executions perhaps – certainly public trials. A much
> much poorer life-style in which the right foods cannot be
> obtained because they have been shipped off to Germany.
> Husbands taken from their families and lost, perhaps forever.
> More than anything the humiliation that is carried round with
> one, even when asleep, like Christian's burden in *Pilgrim's
> Progress*. Well, some day I may have to make a choice.

Jenny became aware of mounting panic, particularly among
her elderly friends. When she visited a couple in their seventies
to help with the housework she saw two suitcases in the hall. 'I
dare not ask what they were for, but as they never go away I
thought they must be ready to flee.' Another couple in their
sixties kept a case packed and ready in the car and one woman
had sewn five pounds into her corsets 'in case'. Some neighbours were worried by a piece in the *Daily Mail* about the road
from the east coast becoming blocked with refugees; the wife
showed Jenny a picture of a German parachutist and told her
that she would leave her husband to live with her sister in Surrey
if the situation deteriorated.

Bicycles were now highly prized and even the postman was
reduced to making his deliveries in a wheelbarrow. As the petrol

shortage became more severe Jenny tried several times to retrieve the bicycle she had lent to a labourer four months previously. When she approached his house the whole family took cover at a neighbour's.

The sisters were becoming more aware of the men and machines preparing to defend Britain. They were often woken at night by overhead aircraft and two airmen came to 'scrounge' an inner tube from the garage. They stayed chatting for an hour and a half and one asked Muriel if she would go for a walk with him; she thought him too old at thirty-six and suspected he was married. They were disconcerted by a visit from the mother of a boy with whom Jenny had gone out for five years and who had won a commission in the BEF. She upset the sisters by intimating that their work in the garage was neither suitable for young women nor likely to survive in wartime: 'One hears all sorts of things and the motor trade is going down so.'

'This is the first time anyone has suggested I was not good enough. Are we fighting for democracy? Or aren't we?' Jenny wrote in her diary. Muriel was less circumspect, describing the woman as 'the most hateful cat'.

Then, suddenly, things got worse.

On Friday, 10 May, Matthew arrived for work and announced, 'Hitler's caught two buses in the night. He's invaded Holland and Belgium!'

STOP PRESS
INVASION OF HOLLAND AND BELGIUM

Hilversum at 06.45 reported that a large formation of German planes were flying in a westerly direction over Holland . . .

BRUSSELS AT 8.25 General mobilisation decreed.

State of siege declared. Government appealed to Allies to fulfil guarantee. Anglo-French

troops are marching. Belgium protested to
Berlin and sent notes to other countries.

'Belga' states that no German diplomatic
demarche took place before the invasion.
Nothing up to 7.30 today. King to speak shortly.

HILVERSUM, HOLLAND. 8.40

Proclamation by the Queen. After keeping up
strict neutrality since beginning of war
Holland was last night invaded by Germany in
spite of previous guarantees. The Government
will do its duty. We ask you to do the same. Our
conscience is clear.

The Government announced that from 03.00 this
morning German troops had been crossing Dutch
frontier. Bombs dropped on Dutch aerodromes.
Flooding measures effectively carried through.
Six German bombers shot down.

Allies have been informed of situation and
will be giving full co-operation. Holland is
now at war with Germany.

HILVERSUM AT 09.94.

Bridges over Maas and Ijsel destroyed. German
parachute troops some in Dutch uniforms
surrounded and captured.

Source: BBC Monitoring Service

5

Jenny and Muriel, May – Scanning the Skies

———◆◆◆———

In early May Frances Partridge, a pacifist and member of the Bloomsbury Group, wrote from her Wiltshire farmhouse, Ham Spray, 'The perfection of the weather is getting on all our nerves. It is too phenomenal and everything super-normal is unnerving.' In Sissinghurst Castle, Kent, politician and journalist Harold Nicolson and his wife, Vita Sackville-West, marvelled at the lushness of the bluebells and primroses. The hopeful signs of spring made the hailstorm of bad news harder to bear. Shortly before the invasion of Holland, Luxembourg and Belgium Allied forces had withdrawn from southern Norway and billboards shrieked details of bomb attacks in Brussels, Paris and Lyons. Friday 10 May was the start of a shocking weekend.

'Just before nine, we turn on the wireless and it begins to buzz as the juice comes through and then we hear the bells,' Nicolson recorded in his diary. 'Then the pips sound 9.0, and the announcer begins: "This is the Home Service. Here is the Right Honourable Neville Chamberlain MP, who will make a statement." I am puzzled for a moment, and then realise he has resigned.'

Chamberlain's departure was a direct consequence of the débâcle in Norway and came about through a seemingly innocuous motion for the House of Commons to adjourn. The debate that raged through 7 and 8 May 1940 has been described as the 'most dramatic and the most far-reaching in its consequences of any parliamentary debate of the twentieth century'. At its end Britain had a new prime minister and a new spirit.

The debate gave MPs a chance to vent their frustration over Chamberlain's appeasement policy and his limp handling of the first few months of the war. Margery Allingham, who wrote detective novels from an Essex village, put into words what many felt when she said that discovering Chamberlain had 'nothing particular up his sleeve' was like realising that 'the man driving the charabanc in which you were careering down an S-bend mountain road, with a wall on one side and a chasm on the other, was slightly tight and not a brilliant driver at the best'.

In searching for a replacement, MPs reached back to earlier crisis points in Britain's history. Admiral of the Fleet Sir Roger Keyes rose to speak in full naval uniform with six rows of medals on his chest. He seethed with fury at the failure of the Royal Navy and the British Army to achieve any of their objectives in Norway and reminded the House, 'One hundred and forty years ago Nelson said, "I am of the opinion that the boldest measures are the safest", and that still holds good today.'

The well-known Conservative backbencher Leo Amery was so carried away with the moment, and the crescendo of applause from other MPs, that he used the more dramatic of the two endings he had prepared for his speech. Quoting Oliver Cromwell when he dismissed the Long Parliament over three hundred years earlier he said, 'You have sat too long here for any good you have been doing. Depart, I say, and let us have done with you. In the name of God, go.'

The government ended the debate with a majority of eighty-one, which in peacetime would have been sustainable, but with Hitler's forces driving through Europe, the House and the country wanted a strong leader. It was painfully clear that Chamberlain was not that man. The foreign secretary, Lord Halifax, was the obvious candidate but declined. He knew that his status as a peer was a huge disadvantage, that Churchill desperately wanted to be prime minister and that his no-half-measures style was well suited to those desperate days. He might also have felt – as many did – that a Churchill government would not last long and that he could step in once his rival had been ousted – or even that he would wield more influence in the cabinet with Churchill as his leader than if he were struggling to control a man with thwarted ambitions. Churchill became prime minister at 6 p.m. on Friday,

10 May. He was sixty-five, an untested leader in charge of an uneasy coalition of MPs. Ordinary people knew him as a maverick politician who had changed political party twice and had supported the Duke of Windsor's desire to marry Wallis Simpson while remaining king.

The people of Snettisham were too caught up in events across the North Sea to comment on their new prime minister. On the evening that he went to Buckingham Palace more than half of the customers at Jenny and Muriel's garage mentioned the threat of a German invasion. The fate of the Low Countries – Holland, Belgium and Luxembourg – crystallised the fears of people living in Norfolk. Plans to flee, drawn up in the early days of the war, were reviewed. 'I think everyone else, although frightened of the hell it is going to be, feels relief at thoughts of getting it [the invasion] over,' Muriel wrote. 'The sooner the better, as it has to come. I wish I didn't live in Norfolk though, it seems only a stone's throw from Holland.'

Frances Partridge wrote that she 'felt a grip of fear and excitement mixed, as if a giant's hand had seized me round the waist where I stood by the telephone, picked me up and dropped me again'.

When society photographer Cecil Beaton heard that the Nazis had invaded the Low Countries he wrote simply that 'Hell had broken loose.' Chips Channon, Tory MP for Southend, described 10 May as 'Perhaps the darkest day in English history.' In Margery Allingham's Essex village someone compared Germany's advance to dry rot: one board in the structure of Europe had given way so that a penknife working at the house meant the shutters and wainscots 'crunched and crumbled and came apart in one's hands in the short afternoons between one news bulletin and the next'. The dramatic headlines were difficult to take in and she commented that newspapers now looked like 'theatrical props from a spy drama'. In parts of East Anglia there was much sympathy for the Dutch: they shared the same sea, and centuries before, many Dutch farmers had settled there, and introduced names such as DeWitt, DeMusset and Nooteboom. Allingham felt the Dutch and

East Anglians shared the same, taciturn demeanour: neither was 'primarily charming and entertaining like most foreigners', she wrote.

Hitler had taken a giant step forward, and his armaments in Holland and France rattled window-frames in Essex and at Virginia Woolf's cottage in Sussex, just as the Kaiser's weapons had twenty-five years earlier. But, unlike the previous war, the enemy now had sophisticated aeroplanes that could fly greater distances either to bomb cities or land an invading army. Each country that the Germans occupied gave them airfields nearer Britain so that their planes could reach parts of the country that had previously been seen as safe havens. In the past an invasion threat had been limited to the southern coast but now, given enough landing space, the enemy might appear anywhere inland that could be reached from Holland or Norway.

Britons reached for their atlases, hoping to find comfort in France's mighty Maginot Line. The chain of fortresses abutted the Franco-German border with a series of partly subterranean forts linked by underground tunnels, a railway line and power stations, which allowed its guards to live in their bunkers for weeks. But anyone searching for a protective serpent twisting around France's borders would have been shocked to discover that the Maginot Line left exposed several hundred kilometres of France's northern border.

Belgium, Britons recalled from school history lessons, was the 'crossroads of Europe' and any army that wanted to wage war with the Continent must hold it. They consoled themselves that King Albert I had fought bravely with the Allies in the First World War and that his son, Leopold III, seemed a fitting successor. In the 1920s he had been a dashing prince, handsome in pinstriped suits or gold-braided uniforms. Sympathy for him increased when, a year into his reign, his beautiful wife, Astrid, niece of King Gustav of Sweden, died in a car accident. Leopold had been driving and was left to bring up three children alone. Belgium was in good hands.

★　　★　　★

Early on the morning of Sunday, 12 May, police knocked at the doors of all German- or Austrian-born men aged between sixteen and sixty who were living in parts of Britain, from the Isle of Wight to Inverness, considered most vulnerable to invading forces. About three thousand 'enemy aliens' were interned and the movements of other foreigners were strictly curtailed: they were forced to report to their local police station each day, not allowed to use a car and had to observe a curfew between 8 p.m. and 6 a.m.

By the following Thursday the threat of invasion was so acute that all army officers were told to report to Wellington Barracks in Chelsea. In Snettisham, Matthew was suddenly gripped by the fear that he would be called up; it was the first time Jenny had seen him waver in his confidence about Britain's chances. He started to work on the cars they kept in the garage, which had not been used for some time, making sure that the radiators and petrol tanks were full so that they could leave at a moment's notice. He said he would bring his gun to work every day, but Jenny suggested that instead he should keep a bottle of water in his pocket to tip into the invaders' petrol tanks – it would be simpler than shooting them and they would be two miles away before they realised that their fuel had been tampered with.

Other villagers revealed their plans. A man of seventy had saved forty pounds in silver to take with him if he 'bolted' and other neighbours had hidden valuables. Jenny had gathered together a few useful possessions at the start of the war but as the immediate threat receded, and shortages meant she could not afford to hoard everyday items, they had become jumbled with the normal debris of life. Both sisters now made sure that their bank books were in their handbags at all times. A great-aunt felt so uncertain about their future that she decided to make the girls a settlement while she was still alive; even Muriel, at nineteen, considered writing her will. 'Everyone here is wondering if we stay put or hop it if they land,' she wrote.

A neighbour admitted buying a wireless and binoculars so that he would be among the first to know when the invasion started. The elderly, with clear memories of the last war, were most jumpy.

Although Muriel slept well on the Sunday after the invasion of Holland, she knew that others were tortured by the prospect of an army descending on them:

> Mrs F said all night she was sure she could hear Germans landing on the beach, and every time the tiles creaked she imagined one with a parachute landing on the roof. Mr and Mrs F will talk about the war all the time, what Mr did in last war, how he would invade England etc etc Mrs is quite [sure] we shall be invaded, all the time she keeps wondering what the Nazis will do to us when they come, and what we ought to do when we see them.

The Whitsun bank holiday was cancelled so that war work, which meant anything from building aeroplanes to tending the fields, continued. People were told to avoid unnecessary travel, and evacuated children, who had expected to return home for the weekend, remained with their foster-families. The abandoned holiday was disastrous for the garage and Whit Monday was the slowest the sisters could remember. The threat of invasion dominated conversation, rumour and counter-rumour swirling round Snettisham – there was a fifth columnist in the village under constant surveillance, a German plane had landed and garages were forbidden to sell petrol. Jenny and Muriel were painfully aware of how suitable East Anglia's flat terrain was for tanks, how close it was to the Low Countries and how convenient a base it would make for an attack on London and the Midlands. The Wednesday after the invasion of Holland Muriel wrote: 'The Germans get nearer. I shall not be at all surprised to hear they have attempted to land any day. My great-aunt (78) said this morning "I'm expecting to hear they're in London any time now." M. says he is going to join the parachute catchers tonight.'

The 'parachute catchers' were the Local Defence Volunteers, an organisation that the secretary of state for war, Anthony Eden, had launched in a radio broadcast on 14 May. Before he had even finished speaking, men were on their way to their nearest police station to sign up, and within a day a quarter of a million had applied to join. The organisation was soon known as LDV, which

sceptics said stood for 'Look, Duck and Vanish' or 'Last Desperate Venture', but Churchill – with his unerring feel for language –
replaced the ugly acronym with the more user-friendly 'Home
Guard'. Newspapers referred to its members as the 'parashots',
and all over Britain, men who were the wrong age or in the wrong
profession to enlist in the regular army joined it. George Orwell
and J. B. Priestley spent their days chained to desks at the BBC and
stalked the countryside during the long summer evenings wearing
LDV armbands, as did men with asthma or poor eyesight.

Officially women were not allowed to join the Home Guard but
a handful of female politicians, most notably the Labour MP Edith
Summerskill, tried to reverse the ban. The government had an
ambivalent view of the role women should play in an invasion.
They were anxious that mothers should stay at home with their
families and not hamper the movement of troops by blocking roads
– as was happening to such disastrous effect in Holland and
Belgium. They were also keen for women to play an auxiliary
role in the armed forces but drew the line at them pulling triggers.
Many, though, were ready to use all the skills and weaponry at
their disposal.

A few set up Women's Home Defence groups. One of the
earliest, established in London in the summer of 1940, was called
the Amazon Defence Corps and included Marjorie Foster, who in
1930 became the first woman to win the coveted King's Prize for
which riflemen from all over the British Empire competed. The
groups were set up to prepare women to be as useful as possible in
the event of an invasion, which meant learning to defend themselves. Members were trained in unarmed combat and taught how
to use a tommy-gun. Technically, the groups' status as uniformed
private armies made them illegal but there seems to have been no
attempt to disband them. Press photos show them squinting
through the sights of a rifle balanced on the back of a deckchair
or lobbing beanbags with the languid arm movement more appropriate to a regal wave than hurling a grenade. 'If the Germans
invade Britain they are going to get a rough handling even from the
women,' the caption read. Others made their own self-defence

plans. An elderly woman in Lambeth, south London, told the American journalist Ben Robertson: 'I've got a butcher-knife myself and I'm going to take a German with me to glory.'

Other plans were more ambitious. As early as March 1940 Lady Helena Gleichen, an artist cousin of Queen Mary, had decided that the Germans might attack deepest Herefordshire and that she needed her own army. She had seen fighting at close quarters during the Great War as a member of the Red Cross ambulance service in France and an X-ray section on the Italian front. The Italian government had awarded her a medal for military valour and she was created an OBE on her return to Britain. But she was haunted by her experience of war, which she wrote about and painted. One image shows the aftermath of a gas attack in which dead soldiers stand slumped over the side of their trenches, rifles at the ready, their mules tethered to nearby trees.

In the spring of 1940 Lady Helena was in her early seventies but strode round her estate, Hellens, near Much Marcle in pork-pie hat and riding habit, puffing at a cigarette, with one of her many dogs snapping at her heels. Her favourite meal included caviar, Gentleman's Relish, salmon and half a bottle of champagne. To protect her house from parachutists she marshalled eighty of her staff and tenants, gave each man a neatly trimmed calico armband with 'Much Marcle Watcher' written on it in ink and drilled them in front of her mansion. She was keen for her soldiers to have proper weapons and marched into the battalion headquarters of the Shropshire Light Infantry at Ross-on-Wye to demand eighty rifles and some ammunition. She is reported to have added, 'I could do with some machine guns, too, if you have any to spare.' When her request was turned down she fell back on Hellens's collection of antique weapons. In the evenings she lectured her army on tactics, drawing on her own shooting skills – she had once stopped a charging bull with a carefully aimed bullet.

Lady Helena's private army was probably much younger than most Home Guard members. While Anthony Eden asked for men between the ages of seventeen and sixty-five to enlist, recruits frequently lied and one joined up at the age of eighty-four, having fought in the Sudan during Queen Victoria's reign. By the summer of 1940 an estimated 35 per cent of the Home Guard were Great War veterans. Alan Brooke, later Field Marshal Lord Alanbrooke, had just returned from France and assumed his former job as commander-in-chief, Southern Command, when he confided to his diary after attending an LDV conference: 'Why do we in this country turn to all the old men when we require a new volunteer force? Old men spell delay and chaos!'

Their uniforms were slow to arrive and usually of the one-size-fits-all variety. When the Second Isle of Ely Battalion in Cambridgeshire turned out for their first parade in a ragbag of ill-fitting suits and carrying a few token rifles someone in the crowd shouted, 'It won't matter now if Hitler does come, for when he sees this lot he'll just die o' laughing.'

At first the Home Guard was desperately short of guns and armed themselves with a battery of such unlikely weapons as pickaxe handles, rifles from the Indian Mutiny, held at the Zoological Gardens in Manchester, pikes from the props department at Drury Lane and a sentry-box from Norwich Museum. Blunt instruments traditionally reserved for burglars were now made ready for invaders as they rummaged through umbrella-stands for old golf clubs, hockey- and walking-sticks, or unearthed long-forgotten assegais and machetes from a colonial past. Units improvised and employed local materials: in London's docklands a platoon made 'hand grenades' from potatoes laced with razor blades, but elsewhere guards had little more than packets of pepper, iron tubing and short lengths of lead cabling. The primitive, home-made quality of the weapons seemed all the bleaker because of the enemy's well-known sleek, and highly mechanised, firepower.

The Home Guard was an obvious – and enduring – butt for jokes. Every unit had its own cast of comic characters and seemed bent on following a script dictated by class distinction and local rivalry. *Dad's Army*, first broadcast in 1968, was a sitcom waiting to happen. When Matthew was sworn in as a Home Guard in Norfolk the mayor, who seems to have shared some of Captain

Mainwaring's blustering leadership skills, asserted tactlessly that ex-servicemen made better soldiers than youngsters. His words prompted the young men in the audience to storm out in a huff. Two days later Matthew and his mates had quit the 'parashooters' because he said, with no hint of irony, the mayor was trying to run it 'like the army'. He also complained that the mayor had let a 'Fascist chap' join who moaned about suits being made by a 'Jew firm and [that] there was nothing to defend now Mosley was locked up'. Sir Oswald Mosley, leader of the British Union of Fascists, had been interned a few days before, on 23 May, and was being held in Brixton Prison. Muriel and Jenny's aunt, too, sounds oddly like Pike's mother who, in the the television series, fussed over her mollycoddled son and Sergeant Wilson, her amiable upper-class companion. The sisters' aunt was similarly unable to grasp that the nation's safety might be more important than her own petty worries. When her husband stayed out all night with the Home Guard without telling her she moaned to her nieces, 'Why, Hitler's a gentleman compared with your uncle.'

Even as the Home Guard was scanning the skies with borrowed binoculars and opera glasses, cartoonists and comedians were sharpening their jokes. In Robb Wilton's monologue, 'Home Guard (The Day War Broke Out)' his missus asks what he, as a member of the Home Guard, is meant to do: 'I said, "I'm supposed to stop Hitler's army landing." She said, "What? *You?*" I said, "No . . . there's Charlie Evans, Dick Roberts . . ." I said, "There's seven or eight of us, altogether." '

A cartoon in the *Tatler* showed an ancient member of the Home Guard leaping excitedly at the sight of a rare bird: 'A spotted titmarsh, by Gad!' he exclaims, while a German paratrooper lands behind him.

George Beardmore, the BBC engineer, was among those drilling with broomsticks in place of rifles and believed that the Home Guard was 'likely to serve no useful purpose whatever should Germans appear in Upper Regent Street'. But for most volunteers the Home Guard fulfilled a vital role: it made them feel of use in the defence of their country.

"A SPOTTED TITMARSH, BY GAD!"

Members of the Home Guard, many of whom were old and poorly armed, were seen as no match for the wily German parachutist, as in this cartoon from the *Tatler*, 17 July 1940.

The Home Guard was born out of fears that the Germans would arrive by air, which in 1940 was still a novel concept. Britain's failure to expel the Nazis from Norway and the speed with which the Low Countries had succumbed to the invader showed that this was a different kind of war. It was no longer sufficient to rule the waves or to rely on Britain's island status. On the coast Martello towers squatted as reminders of an earlier Napoleonic threat. Nowhere was safe. Britons were tormented by visions of planes with black crosses on their sides disgorging scores of Nazi storm-troopers. People all over the country worried about how much space a German troop carrier needed to land – a report in *The Times* suggested a Junkers 52 required at least 300 yards. Cricket clubs and the owners of sports grounds were told to report to their regional commissioner to find out what they could do to prevent the enemy alighting on their neatly trimmed lawns. Letters to *The Times* urged the government to arm golfers, and one journalist recommended that players should keep a gun in their golf bag.

The concept of the German storm-trooper descending from the sky was so vividly etched on many people's imagination that it led to a nationwide optical illusion on the stormy Thursday following the invasion of Holland. Such was the hysteria about aerial attack that several people mistook silver barrage balloons lit up by flashes of lightning for parachutists. The sightings gained credibility because the *Evening Standard* had reported that some Germans wore sky-blue uniforms and used transparent parachutes that allowed them to drift to earth invisibly.

Two reports from the Low Countries caused particular alarm in Britain. The first was that the parachutists who floated down on the unsuspecting Dutch were disguised in a variety of dress, and the second was that their arrival was made so much easier by the presence of Nazi spies who had burrowed deep into the Dutch community. Both revelations led to one conclusion: it was now hard to tell the enemy from one's neighbour. Hitler might already have arrived in Britain.

Stories about Germans in disguise were circulating as soon as

news of Holland's collapse reached Britain. At first the paratroop-
ers were said to be dressed as workmen but as the tales were retold
the costumes became more elaborate. The *Daily Express* informed
its readers that the Germans had come down in police uniforms to
plop straight on to Dutch roads where they immediately began to
direct the traffic. By 21 May the Dutch foreign minister told a
London press conference that his country had been attacked by
parachutists disguised as nuns, Red Cross nurses, monks and tram
conductors. In another account they carried collapsible bicycles.
The choice of disguise – clergy and nurses – emphasised Nazi
cunning, treachery and perversion, but no one seems to have
considered how cumbersome it would have been to parachute in a
billowing skirt and wimple or whether it would not have been
simpler to change into the disguise once you had landed. After the
rumour took hold it became impossible to look a nun in the eye
without searching for signs of stubble or other clues to her true
identity. The children's writer Noël Streatfeild confided to her
brother, 'The wireless broadcast a description of how the parachutists will be dressed, and in spite of the fact that the country is
grimly determined to exterminate the lot, everybody died with
laughter. One of the comforts of war seems to be that when one
horror piles on another there comes a point when a great deal of
what is happening makes the public laugh.'

A report from the Air Ministry confirmed this image of the Nazi
paratrooper as a ruthless killer. It warned that German parachutists descended with their arms in the air to give the impression that
they were surrendering but were in fact holding a grenade in each
hand. The truth was that parachutists always descend with their
arms in the air because they need to cling to the cords above for
support and to guide the parachute. There is no guarantee that
they will land on their feet and rolling over with a grenade in each
hand would be lethal.

The publicity given to German parachutists meant that every
member of the Home Guard wanted to 'bag one'. However, this
zealousness spelt danger for RAF pilots forced to bail out over
Britain where they risked being fired at. As a precautionary

measure the Home Guard were told to shoot at parachutists only when they descended in groups of more than six; this was considered a safe number since no British bomber carried more. Matthew bragged that as a member of the Home Guard he was allowed to shoot anyone on the spot, an irony that did not escape Jenny: 'It's a funny thing, but if we want any of our pets destroying we have to pay someone else to do it and yet he is actually quite prepared to kill a man.'

Snettisham was full of rumours about spies, Fascists and parachutists. The local holiday-camp owner followed instructions on the radio warning him to padlock his garage to stop a parachutist hiding there but his wife argued that a German would shoot him dead if he could not find the key. In June, drivers who did not lock away their cars were ordered not only to remove the key from the ignition but also the rotor arm or main ignition lead to prevent a fifth columnist or parachutist making off with it.

Everyone was tired and fraught, their sleep disrupted by imaginings and strange noises in the night – many of them caused by the Home Guard creeping about. Jenny and Muriel's dog was kept awake by prowlers who turned out to be parashooters guarding the garage.

Towards the end of the month the grocer's roundsman, who was twenty-nine, popped in:

'The news is bad tonight, have your heard it?' We said 'No,' and he told of latest advances then added, 'I think they're going to beat us, don't you?' 'Yes' said the s.m. [schoolmaster]. We said no more and after a few seconds they said, 'We may as well play tennis while we can.' . . . One said the Nazis were v. keen on sports, so he expected we'd still be able to play tennis if they did win. The g.r. [grocer's roundsman] said he expected general mobilisation for all after this, and the s.m. said he expected an invasion here soon. J[enny] said Mr M was saying he should paint a swashticka [*sic*] under the door knocker ready. We all agreed we shouldn't know what to do if they invade. After that we played tennis, very hard exciting play for 2 hrs and forgot all about the war . . .

Much of the anxiety felt and rumour heard in the remote village centred around the garage and petrol supplies, which could mean the difference between fleeing from an invading army or being left to face it. There was talk that the sisters would not be allowed to sell fuel and that the railway would be the sole means of travel. The next rumour suggested that a neighbouring village had run out of petrol and that the nearest supply was at King's Lynn. The sisters fretted about whether their mother would be safer sleeping away from the petrol pumps at their beach hut.

On 28 May invasion came a step nearer. King Leopold of the Belgians went against the advice of his cabinet and surrendered to the German Army. Overnight he became the most hated man in Britain. There was disbelief and outrage at his *volte-face*. In Hammersmith and Dulwich, Belgian refugees were booed in the street. One author wondered where Leopold would hide after the war: 'Does he not realise how small nowadays is the purchasing power of thirty pieces of silver?' she wrote to friends in America. 'Treachery is on the gold standard now.' The kindest thing anyone could find to say about him was that perhaps his mind had become unhinged by the tragedy of his wife's death. Mostly, though, he was 'the traitor king'. Lloyd George ranted in the *London Pictorial*, 'You can rummage in vain through the black annals of the most reprobate kings of the earth to find a blacker and more squalid example of perfidy and poltroonery than that perpetrated by the King of the Belgians.' In Paris, angry crowds decked a statue of Leopold's father with black cloth and wreaths.

The news of Leopold's capitulation reached Britain as the BEF was retreating to the French coast. By the end of the month rumours had escalated to a point at which the invasion was expected that night. As usual at moments of high tension, the sisters played tennis: they stayed out until 9.30 p.m. in a mixed doubles match with the schoolmaster and an elderly gentleman. 'This reminds me of Raleigh or was it Drake?' the twenty-six-year-old schoolmaster mused.

The policeman, the butcher and the water inspector told Jenny and Muriel that they were ready for the invasion. Finally a uniformed general 'in full war paint' appeared and, according to Jenny, adopted a 'bullying attitude':

"Are you prepared to destroy your petrol in defence of our country?" The fuss they all made about a v. small quantity of petrol, you would think they had a main depot on a trunk road to watch. All want to know what I am going to do and where I keep everything, but I'm not telling anybody. I don't trust any of them not to help themselves. They seem to think that petrol supplies are stopped because of expected invasion. Myself I think they are stopped because of financial affairs of certain garages who started rumour and made worse by greediness of car owners.

On Tuesday, 22 May Muriel wrote in her diary: 'News seems v. bad today. I suppose thousands of our men will be trapped in Belgium. It is too ghastly to think about.'

6

Springtime in London

The tulips outside Buckingham Palace at the end of May were a perfect blood red. In the West End of London crowds queued to watch the glorious Technicolor *Gone With the Wind*, and Spencer Tracy's frontier adventure story, *Northwest Passage*. In the first the Americans were fighting each other, and in the second they were fighting the Indians. In Britain, in the late spring of 1940, they were watching from the sidelines.

Apart from the flowers and the colourful American movies, London was a drab place. Everyone was preoccupied. It was almost impossible to lose oneself in a good book. As Mollie Panter-Downes, a British journalist working for the *New Yorker*, wrote, 'The Channel had now shrunk in men's minds to the size of the Thames.' Atrocity stories about the Germans' behaviour in the Great War, their willingness to bayonet babies and crucify prisoners, were dredged up and added to the list of known facts about the Enemy.

London became quiet. The Control of Noise (Defence) Order had silenced unofficial sounds such as factory hooters, whistles and football rattles, leaving all ears pricked for the air-raid siren, which for some reason was pronounced 'sire-een', and often referred to as 'Wailing Willy'. Even the organ that accompanied the roundabout on Hampstead Heath was stopped in case visitors mistook it for an air-raid warning. In mid-June the country's church bells were stilled in readiness for the day when they would ring out news of the Germans' arrival and Bow Bells, which the BBC had used as an interval signal, were replaced with an ominous 'tick-tock'. From now on London's bells came to life only in the centuries-old children's nursery rhyme, 'Oranges and Lemons' –

and even in that they heralded doom, announcing executions at Newgate prison: 'Here comes a chopper to chop off your head!'

The blackout plunged London into a Dickensian darkness. But while its citizens stumbled through the night that was as 'dark as a pocket' they were fully aware that the river Thames was a silvery, welcoming path for German bombers to follow. Taking a short-cut home through the park meant dodging the hidden slit trenches and barbed-wire entanglements. Later in the summer, when Lord Beaverbrook, the influential owner of the *Daily Express* and friend of Churchill who was appointed minister of Aircraft Production, started gathering unwanted aluminium and iron ostensibly to build aeroplanes, park railings disappeared, depriving the fumbling Londoner of yet another clue as to his or her whereabouts. The enforced darkness brought the owl back to Central London, and pedestrians who ventured out late at night found their nerves twanged by the eerie hooting, a portent of doom since Shakespeare's day and alien to city dwellers.

London was disappearing. Well-known landmarks were boxed up to protect them from bomb damage; the American reporter Eric Sevareid recorded that Charles I in Whitehall now looked as if he was on sentry duty. Other historic treasures were squirrelled away. The symbolic Stone of Scone, the 336-pound relic above which every monarch since the fourteenth century (except Edward V and Edward VIII) had sat for their coronation, was taken from the wooden chair in Westminster Abbey and buried nearby. Its exact location was sent to the prime minister of Canada for safe-keeping. Much of the nation's art was evacuated too.

Everywhere there were sandbags. Staff at Westminster Abbey used sixty thousand to protect royal and medieval tombs that could not be moved to safety. All over London the bags sprouted grass and turned green with mould; occasionally women punctured them with their high-heeled shoes or boys worked away at them with pocket knives until their contents leaked out. They were said to be infested with fleas.

As sandbags made the world shrink from the ground upwards, the silver barrage balloons that bobbed over London made its population feel enclosed. The Canadian diplomat Charles Ritchie described them as 'great silver elephants', adding, 'These captive monsters may be seen between their ascents pinned to the ground in the parks or public places – lying exhausted, breathing faintly with the passing puffs of wind.'

Reminders that the Germans might attack at any moment were everywhere. Pillar-boxes carried a square of yellow paint that would change colour when it detected poison gas nearby. Householders were told to keep buckets of sand and stirrup pumps at the ready to douse fires caused by bombs – so far, their main use had been as impromptu litter trays for cats. Notices on the walls of train carriages warned passengers to lie flat on the floor during an aerial attack and not to touch door handles or other pieces of metal if telltale spots appeared on them as this might mean mustard gas had been released.

The refugees who now flooded London were a constant reminder of the German threat to Britain. Ritchie watched 'tough-looking Norwegian seamen with shocks of coarse blond hair, dressed in blue serge suits, lunching at Garland's Hotel – Dutch peasant girls in native costume like coloured photos in the *Geographical* magazine, walking down Cockspur Street carrying their worldly possessions tied up in bundles.' Dutch soldiers in German-looking uniforms 'give one a turn. (Shall we see German soldiers in London streets?)' In Soho, Polish, Dutch and Belgian soldiers gathered to discuss their countries' fate. The arrival of Australian, Canadian and New Zealand troops confirmed that the war was spreading across the globe and that those European countries still free to fight could not win it without help.

London became a waiting room for deposed monarchs. Since most of Europe's royal families were related to one another, they turned automatically to George VI for help. The widowed Queen Wilhelmina of Holland was nearly sixty, a remote but respected monarch who had reigned for over forty years. She had been in her country woodland residence when she heard that the Germans had arrived. She shook her only child, Princess Juliana, awake, whispering, 'They have come.' Although some members of the Dutch cabinet wanted to negotiate with the Germans, Queen Wilhelmina decided her best option was to flee. She phoned George VI, then took her daughter and two tiny granddaughters in a taxi to the docks while bombs dropped all about them. From here they boarded a British destroyer and eventually arrived in Harwich. George VI met their train at Liverpool Street station on Monday, 13 May; Queen Wilhelmina looked dazed and had with her only the clothes she wore and a tin hat that the destroyer's captain had given her.

The Dutch foreign minister, Eelco van Kleffens, escaped by seaplane and landed on Brighton beach. He emerged waving a white flag and convinced the local policeman that he was not a German and should be given enough money to take a train to London. There he joined his queen, who started to broadcast messages of resistance to her beleaguered people. Initially, she was criticised for abandoning them, but her defiant broadcasts meant she avoided the opprobrium that King Leopold had attracted. She was accepted as a member of Britain's extended royal family, and a rumour spread that she snored so loudly that it was easy to tell when she was in your air-raid shelter. There was little fuss in July 1940 when she sent her daughter and two grandchildren to Canada. The little girls were much younger than the British princesses and their father, Prince Bernhard, eventually joined the RAF. Besides, their decision to go abroad for 'the duration' was shared by many well-off British families.

King Haakon VII of Norway's appearance at Buckingham Palace sparked the usual tensions when relatives arrive for an indefinite stay. When his son, Prince Olaf, asked a Master of the Royal Household what would be an appropriate contribution for him to make towards his keep and was told five hundred pounds, he is reported to have said, 'I thought that was rubbish so I paid him fifty.' An even more undignified exchange took place when the king visited the BBC to make a broadcast. As he waited to be taken through to the studio the receptionist asked, '*Where* was it you said you were king of?'

Such high-profile visitors to London demonstrated that the Nazi net was closing and many wondered if the British royal family was planning to leave. Home intelligence reports, commissioned by the government to gauge public morale, noted persistent rumours that Princesses Elizabeth and Margaret, with the government, had gone to Canada. In truth, the princesses stayed at Royal Lodge in Windsor Great Park, and later at Windsor Castle. Officially, they were at 'a house in the country' and their parents travelled to and from Buckingham Palace in an armoured car.

The position of the royal family was made especially sensitive by the king's brother, the Duke of Windsor, who had abdicated in 1936. Since he had left Britain with his American wife, Wallis Simpson, he had drifted round Europe looking for something to do. Before the war he had shown unfortunate Nazi sympathies and had been unwise enough to appear in a photograph with Hitler. As Britain's position looked increasingly hopeless, he was an obvious focus for rumour and intrigue. The intelligence report also suggested that it was thought the Nazis were preparing to install the duke as a puppet king. Clearly a 'proper job' had to be found for him. Although he was keen to return to Britain, Churchill thought this was too risky and had him installed as Governor of the Bahamas.

Just as disconcerting as the refugees pouring into London was the exodus of others. On 17 May the United States embassy advised the four thousand US citizens living in Britain to leave the country immediately and, if possible, to go home via Ireland. US reporter Ben Robertson described the embassy as 'sandbagged like a fort' while inside it was 'as crowded as a beehive'. Its corridors were packed with worried Americans and their families, desperate for one of the last places on the final ship to depart across the Atlantic. Those who were unable to leave, or who wanted to stay, were told to move to remote parts of the country, away from areas of strategic military importance. On 7 June the embassy warned that this might be its countrymen's last chance to get home until after the war. Evidently it felt that the balloon was about to go up.

Most Americans heeded the advice, and when the last train for the last ship to America left Euston station it carried a ragbag of passengers, many of whom had been in Britain for so long that they looked more British than the prime minister. They wore Homburgs, woollens and tweeds, and were loaded with a lifetime's worth of luggage, including dogs and canaries. Those who stayed were mostly members of the press corps, as well as the ambassador, Joseph Kennedy, and other government officials. The journalists were happy to remain, sensing that they were about to cover the biggest story of their lives. Their ambassador, however, was looking for the earliest opportunity to quit a country that he felt had no chance of beating the Germans. Among Kennedy's staff, one clerk had a particular reason for hoping the Germans might arrive sooner rather than later.

Just before 11.30 a.m. on Monday, 20 May, a police inspector from Scotland Yard rapped on the door of a flat at 47 Gloucester Place, just north of Selfridge's, in the West End of London. As he tried the handle of the locked door, a male American voice shouted that he should not come in. The inspector knocked again, to no avail, so he broke down the door – which must have alarmed the landlady, who was hovering in the background. He burst into the room followed by Captain Maxwell Knight, head of MI5's counter-subversion section, officers from Special Branch and a bemused senior diplomat from the American embassy.

Inside, Tyler Kent, a twenty-nine-year-old American, was standing by the bed in his pyjama bottoms. He remained impassive when the visitors produced a search warrant but tried to stop them opening a door that led off his bedroom. In the adjoining room they found a frightened, embarrassed woman wearing a man's striped pyjama top. She said that her name was Irene and explained, somewhat implausibly, that she had dropped by to ask Kent if he would join her for a picnic in Kew Gardens. Kent denied that he possessed anything connected to the American embassy but Special Branch officers discovered a leather suitcase in the wardrobe that contained sheaves of documents and cables stamped 'Secret and Confidential', a box of anti-war slogans, letters, visiting cards and a ledger secured with a gold lock. The police bundled Kent into a car, while Captain Knight and the diplomat followed in a taxi with nearly two thousand classified documents, including correspondence between Winston Churchill and Franklin D. Roosevelt. The two cars made their way back across London to confront Kent's employer, Joseph Kennedy, ambassador to the Court of St James's.

Tyler Kent was a career diplomat whose progress had been blighted by womanising, indiscretion and an arrogance unseemly in one so young. He had been born in Manchuria, where his father was the US consul, and educated at a series of international schools and universities. He had attended Princeton University, the Sorbonne, the University of Madrid and George Washington University, in Washington DC. At some point he had picked up a hatred of Communism and a fervent belief that a Jewish conspiracy was nurturing Bolshevism. He had a natural gift for languages and spoke Russian flawlessly. His well-connected parents hoped he would follow in his father's footsteps but their son's awareness of his own brilliance did not sit well with the required reserve of the diplomatic service. Eventually Kent had found a junior job at the American embassy in Moscow. He resented the work, which he felt was beneath him, and was convinced that his political views were holding him back. In reality, his blatant affair with a married woman on the ship taking him to Russia had already put a brake on his diplomatic prospects. He had started to look for work as a journalist in Moscow when he was posted to the US embassy in London, on 19 September 1939, as a cypher clerk.

Kent was immediately drawn to the White Russian *émigré* circle, who, despite Hitler's pact with Stalin, believed that the Nazi leader was their only hope of overturning Communism and restoring the Russian royal family. Kent became entangled with this bitter, but well-connected group through a surprise phone call from a childhood friend of his mother. She was a member of the London branch of the Russian Red Cross and introduced Kent to two Russian-born women. The first was the pyjama-clad Irene, with whom he began an affair although she was married. The second was Anna Wolkoff, who changed Kent's life and very nearly changed the course of the war.

Anna de Wolkoff, as she liked to call herself, was the daughter of a former admiral in the Russian Imperial Navy. She was thirty-eight and shared Kent's anti-Semitism and hatred of Communism, both of which she blamed for her family's straitened circumstances. Her father ran the Russian tea rooms near London's Natural History Museum and claimed to serve the best caviar in London, although Kent was not convinced. The dingy, down-at-heel café was an obvious place for disgruntled exiles to meet and plot, and an equally obvious place for spies to listen in to their conversations.

Before the war Wolkoff earned a living as a society dressmaker, whose clients included Wallis Simpson. She had visited Germany and claimed to have met Rudolf Hess. She remained brazen in her admiration for the Nazis and their treatment of the Jews, even after the declaration of war. Her work as a dressmaker provided the perfect opportunity to meet members of the British Establishment. Pamela Mitford, she said, had told her the true story behind her sister Unity's 'accident' (infatuated with Hitler, she had shot herself in the head in a failed suicide attempt following Britain's declaration of war). Wolkoff was friendly with Archibald Ramsay, a Conservative MP, who in 1939 had founded the secret Right Club that aimed to avoid war by fighting 'organised Jewry', and ran the club's propaganda machine from her basement flat, just off the Fulham Road. From there she produced anti-war and anti-Semitic stickers and leaflets, which members of the Right Club posted around Kensington. Bizarrely, Wolkoff took her turn at sticking them to lampposts, telephone kiosks and pillar-boxes while wearing the uniform of the Auxiliary Fire Service, of which she was a member. MI5 tapped both Wolkoff and Ramsay's phones for six months and installed a spy in the Right Club in the hope of obtaining a list of its members, but it was only when Wolkoff introduced Kent to Ramsay at the beginning of March 1940 that their enquiries became urgent.

Kent told Ramsay and Wolkoff that he had read telegrams between President Roosevelt and Winston Churchill, then first lord of the Admiralty. That Roosevelt was communicating with

Churchill, rather than the prime minister, Neville Chamberlain, was irregular – and almost certainly unconstitutional. Kent suspected that Roosevelt was positioning America to come to Europe's defence at a time when he faced a powerful anti-war lobby at home led by the all-American hero Charles Lindbergh who had been the first person to fly solo across the Atlantic in a daring adventure that had made him world famous. He copied dozens of papers and smuggled them out of the embassy. Wolkoff persuaded him to hand over copies to her, saying they would provide useful ammunition for Ramsay when he was addressing Parliament. She also sent messages to Lord Haw-Haw – with considerable help from female members of the Right Club, who were in fact MI5 spies. The messages were hardly incendiary, simply claiming that Churchill was not popular and that Lord Ironside, chief of the Imperial General Staff and commander-in-chief of Home Defence, was anti-Jewish. She was arrested two hours before Tyler Kent and both were charged under the Official Secrets and Defence Regulations Acts. Their trials were held *in camera*, and no members of the public were allowed to attend. Wolkoff was sentenced to ten years' imprisonment and Tyler to seven.

Joseph Kennedy was informed of Kent's likely arrest on the Saturday evening before it took place and agreed to waive the clerk's diplomatic immunity. As the full extent of Kent's deceit became evident Kennedy realised how long the British secret services had been watching his embassy without telling him and what this meant for his reputation. A member of his staff had been handing out top-secret documents, which contained proof of how little chance Kennedy gave Britain of beating the Germans and of his belief that 'serious internal trouble' could break out in the country at any time. It was no wonder that he exploded with fury when he confronted Kent after his arrest.

The affair had two effects on the British government: it confirmed its belief in a virulent fifth column and, more importantly, provided it with a chance to discredit Kennedy, and limit the damaging flow of defeatist sentiments he was feeding back to the USA. Churchill was wooing Roosevelt into helping the British cause in any way he could until the American electorate accepted that it should join the Allies. If it became public that he and Roosevelt had been conspiring to this end – even before Churchill was prime minister – Roosevelt would have lost the argument and possibly the presidency, since anti-war feelings were running high among the electorate.

Joseph Kennedy was not a typical ambassador. His style was relaxed – he chewed gum and said what he thought as he did business from behind a huge desk, his feet on the table and a red carnation in his lapel. General Raymond Lee, US assistant chief of Army Intelligence in London, described him as possessing 'the speculator's smartness but also [a] *sharpshooting* and *facile* insensitivity to the great forces which are now playing like sheet lightning over the map of the world'. He was slim with sandy hair, freckles and an easy grin, and wore horn-rimmed glasses with ostentatiously fashionable suits. He arrived at the Court of St James's in 1938, the first Catholic and first Irish American to hold the position of ambassador.

Everything about him was society-page material. His nine children provided the ideal accessories for a photo-call and he ensured his arrival in Britain gained maximum publicity by hitting a hole-in-one at golf. His press relations wobbled slightly when he refused to follow the tradition of wearing knee breeches at Court but his feet-on-the-desk style and skill in public speaking won over journalists. There was one area, however, in which Kennedy misjudged public opinion. While Britain and America were worrying about Hitler's plans, Kennedy cemented his relationship with the German ambassador in London. He believed his friend Lindbergh's assessment of Nazi air superiority and was convinced that Britain stood little chance against it. As early as 1938 he sent his younger children to southern Ireland, away from the German bombardment he expected. By the following year, and before war had been declared, he was regaling guests on the London cocktail circuit with his conviction that Britain could not beat Germany. In spring 1939 he shut up his grand Kensington house and moved to equally grand quarters near Epsom in Surrey. It became a standing joke among American reporters that whenever someone asked where the ambassador was, the answer was always 'somewhere in the country' – meaning he was safely at home. He was one of the few people in London who believed that King Leopold had done the right thing in surrendering and possibly the only one who was unafraid to air this opinion.

His defeatism was so unpalatable that invitations dried up. After he had told George VI that his country would lose the war, the king wrote to him, defending Britain's chances. On a visit home Kennedy lectured the press on why America should stay out of the war; his remarks were reported in Britain, fuelling antipathy towards him. The teetotal ambassador had little time for Churchill, describing him as a 'fine two-handed drinker', and the British government started to bypass him and deal directly with Roosevelt. Many people suspected that he was backing Germany to suit his own financial investments and Lord Vansittart, chief diplomatic adviser to the foreign secretary, described him privately as 'a very foul specimen of double-crosser, a defeatist. He thinks of nothing but his own pocket. I hope that this war will at least see the elimination of his type.' Harold Nicolson attacked him viciously in the *Spectator*, and he was the subject of a similarly cutting gibe that did the rounds among the upper classes: 'I thought my daffodils were yellow until I met Joseph Kennedy.'

Kennedy's defeatism was at odds with the copy filed by the many American reporters swarming into the capital. Although his indiscretions appealed to them as journalists, his negative view of Britain did not tally with their own experience. Ben Robertson was one of over a hundred journalists filing reports from London in the summer of 1940. An experienced reporter from South Carolina, he had covered the White House and the Supreme Court for Associated Press, then moved to Britain, aged thirty-seven, to write for the American daily newspaper *PM*. In 1940 life as a foreign correspondent in Europe was challenging and, to some extent, the journalists hunted in packs. Their reports were heavily censored and the British government did its best to control where they went and what they saw. In America there was an insatiable demand for news from Europe and the journalists were under pressure to find a 'new angle'. Robertson was as keen as the others to file a cutting-edge story but his degree in botany and the fact that he had written a novel marked him out as a more 'sensitive' man.

In June 1940 when he booked into the Waldorf Hotel in Central London Robertson noticed that the staff and guests were endeavouring to carry on as if it was just an ordinary summer. A sign told guests not to adjust the curtains – presumably because of blackout restrictions – and that a telephone operator would inform them of an air raid. For six months he ate in the hotel basement and went to bed unsure if he would wake in the morning. 'From then until late in the autumn I and everyone else in England expected the Germans any minute,' he wrote. The difference between the American ambassador and the foreign correspondent was that the latter was convinced Britain had a fighting chance.

7

Frank O'Brien – The Soldier's Story

'I never thought the French people could be so kind. After the war is over I'm coming back to France for a holiday. Life is really marvellous here, Mary,' wrote Gunner Frank O'Brien, to his sweetheart in Glasgow.

That letter to Mary McFarlane, written in April 1940 when Frank was twenty-three, marked a turning-point in his life. He was enjoying the sunny weather of north-west France and the warmth of the local people. Wine, which at home was associated only with the altar rail, flowed freely and life was good – or as Frank would say, in the French he now spoke, with the intonation of Glasgow's Gorbals area, 'C'est bon'.

For Frank and his mates in the 77th (Highland) Field Regiment, Royal Artillery, the enemy remained a faceless figure whom they had yet to meet in combat. When he joined up in April 1939 he abandoned his home, with his widowed mother and four sisters, and his job as a paint mixer.

The war changed his life in many ways, of which the most obvious was that it took him away from Scotland. When he enlisted he exchanged one cramped, close-knit community for another, all-male, version. In the mid-nineteenth century his grandfather, Patrick, had left Ireland to find work in Glasgow, a bustling city where Catholics had more chance of employment than they did in Belfast. He became a miner at William Dixon's Govan colliery, and Frank grew up in one of the nearby four-storey tenement blocks. Hallside Street, where Frank's family lived, was the product of an industrial age, its honey sandstone blackened by soot and the sky permanently lit by the furnaces that burned at Dixon's ironworks. Desperate mothers would threaten to send unruly children to a 'bad fire at Dixon's Blazes'.

Frank and his six siblings lived in two rooms; his parents – until his father died at forty-six of pneumonia – slept in a 'hole-in-the-wall' bed. There was little privacy in or outside the home: the family shared a toilet on the landing and a washhouse at the back of the tenement. The river Clyde provided the only escape, and when he could afford it Frank took day-trips 'doon the watter' by steamer to Rothesay or Millport. Otherwise, the Glasgow fair in the last two weeks of July or the Italian Club provided the only glimpse of a world outside his tenement block. His friendship with the Italian boys ended abruptly one evening when the club took up a collection for Mussolini.

It was Frank's best friend, Harry Slaven, who came up with the idea that they should join the Territorial Army (TA). They knew they would be called up anyway but if they volunteered they would have more chance of staying together and a greater say in which regiment they joined. On 26 April 1939 they signed up for the 307th Renfrewshire Battery, 77th (Highland) Field Regiment, and quickly became known as the 'Horrible Twins' due to their habit of being late on parade. In the run-up to war the government urged each TA unit to recruit more soldiers than it needed in the hope that each would be able to form a duplicate regiment. When war was declared in September, Frank stayed in the 77th but Harry was transferred to the 128th and went to Montrose. Meanwhile his friend headed south.

Frank was sent to Hampshire for basic training. It was his first visit to England and, initially, he was not impressed. He wrote to Mary that Salisbury Plain was 'the worst place I have ever been in; you were up to the eyes in mud all the time. I was glad to get back to Aldershot.' He had the chance – unheard of for a boy from the Gorbals – to speak to the king when he inspected the regiment at Bordon, Hampshire. 'He was asking me how I liked the Army. I said it was good Sir, and the Queen was lovely. I never thought she was so good looking.'

Then the rumours started.

'They say we are going to France about the New Year to give Hitler a few bombs . . .' he wrote to Mary, in November 1939. Until then he went dancing on Saturday and Wednesday nights and to the cinema. It was the longest he had ever been away from home and he wrote, ecstatically, 'I never enjoyed myself so much in all my life,' adding, by way of reassurance, that he had put Mary's photo above his bed, next to a picture of himself so that they stood side by side – a couple in miniature, if not in life.

He returned to Glasgow for a Christmas visit, when their relationship acquired a greater intensity, heightened by the knowledge that he was about to go abroad. On his return to barracks he wrote, 'I am heartbroken at leaving you, Mary. I didn't realize how much I love you darling until I left you dear . . . I want you to no [*sic*] that it doesn't matter what happens to me, I will always be in love with you darling . . . I only wish this war was over so we could be together again. I am absolutely fed up with everything.' His earlier letters had been signed 'Your friend' but now he sprinkled them with the soldier's acronym HOLLAND – Hope Our Love Lasts And Never Dies.

Frank's return to his regiment left a gaping hole in his mother's life too. She had already lost one son, Philip, five years earlier, aged twenty-seven, to tuberculosis. She had been a cotton weaver but now worked as a part-time cleaner-caretaker at the Presbyterian church near her home. The excitement of travel and camaraderie buoyed Frank's spirits, but all she could do was wait and wonder. When a parcel arrived containing his uniform she assumed he had been killed – until she discovered that he had been issued with new battledress and had posted her the outdated version so that she could re-use the material.

While Frank was away Mary continued to work as a tailoress at Burton's in Buchanan Street and at Woolworth's on Saturdays. In 1940 she was nineteen and lived with her sisters in the south Glasgow suburb of Cathcart. Although she had been born in a tenement close to Hallside Street the family had left the city early in her life. Her father was a foreman bricklayer and moved constantly to wherever there was work. When Mary was small they lived in

Cambuslang, a town east of Glasgow, and it was there that she fell down the stairs and broke her hip. The accident left her with a permanent limp and she spent much of her childhood in hospital; her loss of mobility drove her father to seek out their ground-floor flat in Cathcart. The modern building was genteel compared to the city's grim tenement blocks, with its own bathroom and lavatory and a small garden in front. During the summer, if his work took him to a holiday resort he would rent a house there for his family, they escaped to the rugged Ayrshire coast and to the sedate farming countryside of Newton Stewart. Mary was the second youngest of four girls but her father lavished gifts on her – a sewing machine, a banjo and a piano – perhaps to make up for her years of poor health. She probably met Frank one summer's evening when they were both strolling round Glasgow with friends, but their love of music drew them into close friendship. They enjoyed singing, perhaps especially because it cost nothing – an important consideration in the economically depressed 1930s.

Frank left Southampton in the early hours of a bitterly cold February morning and arrived in France with the BEF, which at its peak numbered 394,165 men. The French General Maurice Gustave Gamelin had overall control of the force, which was about a tenth of the size of the French Army. Frank arrived at Le Havre and was billeted in an old farmhouse. As he moved north the weather improved, and his spirits rose. By the end of February he was stationed near Lille, on the Belgian border.

The soldiers settled down to what the regiment's war diary called 'training and digging'. An uneasy boredom descended on them, occasionally interrupted by visits from 'top brass' such as the Duke of Gloucester, and Viscount Gort, commander-in-chief of the BEF. But the waiting took its toll: at the beginning of March two of Frank's fellow gunners were given fifty-six days' field punishment for being 'drunk on guard'. Two days later the Roman Catholic padre set up a regimental café, the Gunpit, at 3 rue de Roubaix where soldiers could play ping-pong and darts, write home or have a hot meal.

Frank heard about the German invasion of Norway on the

radio: 'Well, darling I'm still enjoying myself but I dont know how long it will last now that Germany and Norway have started fighting and our leave has been stopped . . .' he wrote to Mary on 14 April, 'ÇA NE FAIT RIEN C'EST LA GURRE [*sic*] . . .' Three weeks later he added, 'I'm moving about quite a lot just now so if you dont receive a letter for a while dont get worried darling.'

At home, the ordinary Briton was blissfully unaware of the struggle taking place just across the Channel. But in northern France and Belgium the days that followed were marked by confusion and fear. The regiment's war diary picked up a story that Frank had neither the energy nor the time to tell:

10 [May] 0800 News received that GERMANY had invaded HOL-LAND, BELGIUM and LUXEMBOURG early this morning . . .
11.30 Conference at 4 Div. RA HQ. Numerous air raid warnings & much AA [anti-aircraft] fire. British tps [troops] start moving across the BELGIAN border. Columns passing day & night.
11 [May] Much enemy air activity. Tp movements continue.
12 [May] Enemy parachutists seen landing this area. Double guards & extra precautions in force.
14 [May] Regt moved off from CROIX. Entered BELGIUM at 0536hrs. Route via TOURNAI, RENAIX, NINOVE to billeting area DE HEIDE, NW of BRUSSELS. Heavy traffic congestion on roads by thousands of refugees. Enemy aircraft active, low flying MG [machine-gun] attacks and parachutists being dropped.

On 16 May the 77th Highland Field Regiment entered Brussels at 9 p.m. and was told to hold the canal nearby. Belgian soldiers poured out of their country as the Germans occupied the area north-east of the capital. British troops were unable to fire on the enemy because of the large number of civilians and instead did what damage they could by blowing up canal bridges. 'Enemy sniping and parachutists troublesome,' the war diary stated succinctly.

Two days after it had entered the city, the regiment beat a hasty retreat, changing direction with each new command and squeezing along the roads, which were congested with refugees. No soldier likes to retreat but for the BEF the about-turn was even more devastating after the tumultuous warmth of their reception in Belgium. The cheers and lilac blossom were replaced by makeshift white flags that fluttered from windows and church towers as ordinary people loaded their worldly goods and fled.

Heavy fighting broke out on the river Escaut, and on 21 May Frank's regiment suffered its first casualty when Gunner Wallace was killed. A cook and another soldier died later that day during intense shelling. 'No signs of RAF to deal with situation,' the war diary commented tersely.

On 22 May Frank was back in France and enjoying his first decent night's sleep in nine days. His battery's visit to Belgium had cost the lives of five men, and ten others had been wounded. Forty-eight vehicles, including nine motorcycles, had been destroyed. The skies were filled with terror: on 24 May a German plane – probably a Stuka – had swooped down to strafe them and killed another gunner. The wireless reported that German tanks had swept south through France to take Boulogne, crippling the Allies' lines of communication and forcing the BEF to cut back on its already meagre food rations. It was on the run, the soldiers camping wherever they could, one day hiding in a disused brick factory, the next in the splendour of a château.

The roads were thick with cars, trucks, prams, even a hearse and an ice-cream van, piled high with mattresses as protection from aerial attack and jangling with pots and pans snatched at the last moment. Progress was so slow that sometimes troops took advantage of the German planes: while refugees dived for cover they dashed down the clear road. Dispatch riders wove through the chaos but many were killed in their eagerness to pass on vital instructions. Misunderstandings between the French and British armies intensified as lines of communication stretched to breaking-point: telephone operators abandoned their posts during air raids and officers tried to make sense of the shifting front. The BEF accused the French Army of blocking the roads, and the French muttered about having to take orders from foreigners on their own soil.

German panzer divisions trundled north towards Calais,

whether to create a bridgehead from which to cross to Britain or to head off the BEF no one knew The BEF were ordered to make for Dunkirk. In Britain, Sunday, 26 May, was declared a National Day of Prayer, the first indication for most people that the army was in trouble. The new directives, to immobilise parked cars and put petrol pumps out of commission at night, confirmed the sense of imminent danger. The Archbishop of Canterbury led prayers for 'our soldiers in dire peril in France', which were echoed in places of worship across the country. When the soldiers fighting in France heard that Britons were on their knees, many felt for the first time that their plight must be hopeless. At home nerves tensed in anticipation of bad news. The BBC's live broadcast from the Roman Catholic cathedral in London was suddenly taken off air when a woman interrupted the sermon shouting, 'Peace!' Some listeners feared that saboteurs had taken over the BBC, while others saw the incident as a bad omen. The BBC said that the woman had been overwhelmed by religious fervour and that the interruption carried no political significance.

The Germans were now some twenty-five miles from Britain and closer to London than Jenny and Muriel were in Norfolk. It was possible in the clear weather at the end of May to read, with the help of binoculars, the time on the tower at Calais and to know that Nazis were studying the same clock face. From Dover, too, you could watch Boulogne burn at night and wonder whether you would be the next target. Vice-Admiral Bertram Ramsay, Flag Officer commanding Dover Castle, pondered the stretch of sea that separated him from the several hundred thousand soldiers trapped in northern France. At three minutes to seven, when the National Day of Prayer was closing, Ramsay was told to start Operation Dynamo, a desperate attempt to rescue as many as possible of the BEF from Dunkirk and nearby beaches. From the Dynamo Room, a stone cavern chiselled out of the rock by Napoleonic prisoners, Ramsay gathered a fleet of ships to send across the Channel. In the circumstances, destroyers would be the most effective vessels: their size meant they could rescue thousands at once, and they were well armed to defend themselves. But if they were sunk on the voyage, Britain, at the most vulnerable moment in her history, would be exposed to sea invasion. Also, the beach at Dunkirk shelved gently out to sea, making it impossible for large ships to come within a mile of the shore, even at high tide.

On Monday the Ministry of Shipping began to contact boat-builders and agents to round up all boats with shallow draughts that could be used to collect troops from beaches – pleasure-boats, yachts and Thames launches were thought especially suitable. General Ironside predicted that Operation Dynamo might save around thirty thousand men, which would leave well over three hundred thousand to face the Germans. Ramsay was told that he might be able to evacuate forty-five thousand in a daring mission that would last two days.

At about the time when Operation Dynamo was expected to finish, Frank reached Dunkirk. The day before he and his mates had been ordered to destroy their weapons; all around them lay battered army trucks and disembowelled radios. The BEF was determined to leave behind nothing that might help the enemy but the act of destroying equipment they had been taught to cherish left the soldiers feeling bereft and tarnished. Their vulnerability was reinforced by the rumours that elevated their foe to a super-human force: they heard that the Germans had developed a secret weapon to prevent rifles firing, and a crewless tank that was controlled from the air. For any soldier who doubted the serious-ness of his situation the Germans dropped leaflets showing crude maps of the Allies' position and urging them to surrender.

As the men approached the port of Dunkirk a few sheltered in cellars; the unlucky ones were crushed when the buildings col-lapsed. Others drank themselves into a stupor and stumbled around the sand dunes. Frank and a friend, Vic Mackay, found refuge briefly in a deserted café where they filled their pockets with cigarettes that they could not bear to leave for the Germans. The town was mostly rubble. Tram wires sagged over roads pock-marked with mortar craters, and a thick pall of black smoke from burning oil clouded the sky.

As Frank clambered over the dunes at Dunkirk, what he saw

must have come close to most people's idea of hell. Queues of soldiers snaked towards the sea between the odd tent flying a Union flag, overturned cars and telltale bumps where a rifle butt had disturbed the sand to bury a body. The air was noxious, fumes from the burning oil mixed with the stench of decaying flesh, human and animal. Remnants of wrecked boats poked out of the water, some still blazing after an attack by the Luftwaffe, who made regular raids over their sitting-duck targets. To the soldiers waiting below the assaults appeared to go unchallenged by the RAF, although many British pilots were engaged in bitter battles out to sea. This was the first time many pilots had seen action and they had yet to discover the tactics that would win the Battle of Britain. The truth was that the BEF was not a priority: with its best soldiers waiting on a beach in France, their equipment burnt and smashed, Britain could not afford to leave itself undefended by sending too many planes across the Channel.

On the beaches a strange discipline prevailed. A few soldiers ran amok, but mostly the British tendency to queue held good. Ramsay had arranged for twelve officers and 160 seamen to co-ordinate the evacuation. Until they left Dover they had little idea of what they were being sent to do – having been told to 'travel light', one man packed his tennis shorts. An officer and a few sailors were stationed at intervals along the beach, like patrolling deckchair attendants. On the evening of Monday, 27 May, the senior naval officer at Dunkirk, Captain Tennant, sent a message to Dover asking Ramsay to dispatch every available vessel to the beaches east of the town as the port was on fire and under constant bombardment. The destroyer HMS *Wakeful* was ordered to move from Plymouth to Dover on her way to France. In crossing the Channel, ships had a choice of routes. At thirty-nine miles, Dover to Dunkirk was the most direct but put the ship at risk of attack because the Germans now occupied positions south of Dunkirk. The other, longer routes took the vessel into parts of the North Sea that had been mined by the enemy and also left it vulnerable to U-boats and the Luftwaffe. Once a ship had arrived at Dunkirk its crew faced heavy bombardment from the air while the waiting soldiers scrambled aboard.

There were few places to moor and the breakwater that separated the port from the sea was at first seen as too risky to use as a landing-stage. Instead, the ships lowered their boats to collect the men. However, the sailors and troops were not used to handling small craft and the operation was painfully slow – 'loading ships by the spoonful', according to one officer. By the end of the first full day 7669 troops had returned to Britain.

Some troops who still had their rifles were ordered to return to rearguard action against the advancing Germans – a prospect that must have been awful to contemplate. Frank and Vic volunteered to row men out to the waiting ships, knowing that this would earn them a place on a departing vessel after they had completed a third trip – if they survived. Frank was already exhausted from lack of sleep and food; now he had to negotiate a path through all sorts of debris, from dead bodies to men intent on swimming to the ships and others clinging to bits of wood. The most desperate tried to clamber on to the rowing-boats, despite the risk of capsize.

At home Britain held its breath. Ed Murrow reported that fashionable tea rooms were deserted, Bond Street was empty, and people read the newspaper while they trudged along, almost as if they were sleepwalking. He saw a woman at a bus stop start to cry; she wept silently, not bothering to wipe away the tears. A man in Regent Street carried a sandwich board with three words written in big red letters: 'Watch and pray.'

Spike Milligan, who later wrote about the war years in a series of comic memoirs, had been in the army twenty-four hours when news came through that the BEF was trapped in France. He was stationed on England's south coast, from where he could hear distant explosions and heavy gunfire from across the Channel. 'Sitting in a crude wood O.P. [observation post] heaped with earth at two in the morning with a Ross Rifle with only five rounds made you feel so bloody useless in relation to what was going on the other side,' he wrote later. 'Five rounds of ammo, and that was between the *whole* O.P.'

That afternoon he went for a swim with another soldier:

With the distant booms, the still sea, and just two figures in the landscape, it all seemed very very strange. We swam in silence. Occasionally, a squadron of Spitfires or Hurricanes headed out towards France. I remember so clearly Bombardier Andrews standing up in the water, putting his hands on his hips, and gazing towards where the BEF was fighting for its life. It was the first time I'd seen genuine concern on a British soldier's face. 'I can't see how they're going to get 'em out,' he said. We sat in the warm water for a while. We felt so helpless.

Having completed their third trip from the shore, Frank and Vic heaved themselves aboard *HMS Wakeful* and a sailor snatched Frank's cigarettes. Inexplicably he flung them into the water. Frank's instinct was to look for a place to rest below deck, out of reach of the dive-bombers, but Vic pulled him back, insisting that the hold was the worst place to be if they were torpedoed. Before they slumped in whatever space they could find they had the presence of mind to drag off their heavy army boots in case their ship sank and they had to swim. Eventually *Wakeful* set off for Dover, zigzagging across the Channel to dodge the Luftwaffe's bombs. Like every other ship that took part in the evacuation, it was crammed with soldiers.

The sea that day was mysteriously calm, which helped to foster the impression that – no matter what else had gone wrong in the scrambled retreat to Dunkirk – God had decided to take the BEF's side. A rumour started that a French refugee had spotted a cloud of angels with spears hovering over Dover's White Cliffs. Many people believed that the National Day of Prayer had summoned the heavenly host. Even Spike Milligan commented that the sea was 'like a piece of polished steel . . . I'd never seen a sea so calm. One would say it was miraculous.' He compared the phenomenon to the Angel of Mons, who was said to have appeared in 1914 to save British troops from the Germans who were advancing on them at Mons in Belgium.

Frank and Vic arrived in Dover on Tuesday afternoon. All around them other ships and small boats were packed with standing troops, row upon row of tin hats, interspersed with the occasional peaked cap of a French or Belgian soldier. When the Canadian diplomat Charles Ritchie visited the town a few days later, he described it as an 'extension of the actual war zone'. He saw destroyers limping home, their flags still flying but one with its stern blown off. On one British ship a bearded soldier lay curled up asleep next to his gun; on a French vessel the sailors confirmed a National stereotype by clustering to study a postcard of a naked woman. A tug pulled up and disgorged a group of German prisoners-of-war, pallid after sheltering below deck during the crossing while their countrymen bombed them; the pilots swaggered along the gangplank, while the ordinary soldiers 'huddled like sheep'.

Frank pitied *Wakeful*'s crew, who knew exactly what they were heading back to – some soldiers pressed cigarettes on their rescuers. The troops were given a sandwich and a cup of tea, then put on to a train. The carriages that took the rescued BEF from Dover and other ports on the south coast carried men whose minds were overloaded with vivid images. Virginia Woolf described the first hospital train she saw from her Sussex home as 'laden, not funereal but weighty, as if not to shake bones. Something – what is the word I want – grieving and tender and heavy laden and private – bringing our wounded back carefully through the green fields . . .'

Those in the south of England who listened to the desperate battle across the Channel, thinking or even saying 'Our turn next', now caught a glimpse of the combatants. They were shocked by what they saw and by the contrast with the Tommies smiling out of their newspapers and magazines. These soldiers, who still had French sand on their boots, were burnt brick red by the sun, unshaven and exhausted. Their uniforms were stiff and whitened with seawater, and many had a special demeanour that set them apart as distinctly as their BEF badge. 'Only occasionally did you see one who sat staring without seeing, as though trying to remember something he had seen or perhaps trying to forget something he had seen,' Ed Murrow noted.

Frank and Vic went to Charmouth in Dorset, where their

regiment was regrouping, as far as Frank knew in preparation for returning to France. If Dunkirk had been hell, Charmouth was heaven. Frank was billeted in a house owned by two ladies and given his own room – in itself a huge luxury for a soldier – with an oak bed. Charmouth was a 'lovely seaside place' with a 'marvellous beach' and the townspeople, aware that the soldiers had just returned from Dunkirk, gave them the run of the place. Frank wrote:

> Mary it was terrible. The British army is not finished with Hitler yet; we gave him something to remember us by. The next time we meet victory will be with us. They were bombing us coming across the Channel but none of their bombs hit us. We have got the navy to thank for that. Believe me Mary I'm lucky to be here today. Someone must have been praying for me very hard because I don't know how I escaped so much danger. I'm very lucky, I'll tell you all about it when I come home . . . I'm just dying to see you darling. I still love you very much . . . I better close now and go to sleep darling and dream of you. I'm always thinking about you Mary. I just can't help it darling I love you. I only wish you were here with me now. So cheerio for the present.
>
> Your loving sweetheart, Frank xxxxx

Elsewhere the BEF was resting and trying to recuperate, but many soldiers bore deep psychological scars that were slow to heal, and the population was unsure how to respond. When a Dunkirk veteran appeared in a train the carriage usually fell silent, out of pity and embarrassment. A young woman on holiday at Aberystwyth described the soldiers she saw there as 'desperately exhausted and worn out, they just lay there on the beach, where they had been brought by army coaches. They were so tired that *nobody* heard the bugle call for meals. They just continued to lie there, in the heat of the sun, getting terribly burned.'

It was difficult to know how to deal with what had happened at Dunkirk, which, as Winston Churchill pointed out to the House of Commons on 4 June, had been an evacuation, and evacuations do not win wars. There were recriminations from soldiers, about the lack of RAF cover, the behaviour of the French and of British officers. On the Tuesday that Frank arrived in Dover, 17,804 men were evacuated from France – twice the number saved on the previous day. Operation Dynamo continued for nine days, rather than two, and some 338,266 men were saved, rather than the 45,000 Ramsay had been told to expect.

The evacuation, heroic though it had been, was a disaster in terms of what had had to be left behind. Publicly Churchill described the equipment that had been abandoned or destroyed as luggage that had gone missing. He knew that the BEF had had the pick of the available equipment and now most of it – including 64,000 vehicles and 2472 guns – was rusting in France. Also, more than sixty-eight thousand men had been killed, wounded or captured. Ironside wrote in his diary that the BEF commanders 'know what may come and are perhaps doubtful over the state of their troops both in training and discipline. Anyway, they are tried men and the best we can get now.'

Britain also lost six destroyers, HMS *Wakeful* among them. In the early hours of Thursday, 29 May, after she had rescued Frank and Vic, the ship had been on her way to Dover for the second time. The 640 men she had rescued were resting below when a torpedo struck. The ship snapped in half and sank within fifteen seconds. Just a handful of soldiers and twenty-five crew survived.

The 'myth of the little ships' played a key part in turning the retreat into a sort of victory. The 230 pleasure and fishing craft, yachts and lifeboats which headed for France allowed the ordinary Briton to play a part in a military operation and to do so with a dash of typical English amateurism. Although this motley band rescued a tiny proportion of the overall number, the image of the gallant little boats bobbing up and down while being strafed summed up how many Britons felt. The myth grew and expanded over the years in books and films. In *Mrs Miniver*, which appeared in 1942, the husband, played by Walter Pidgeon, takes his river-boat to Dunkirk in one of the many wartime episodes that shakes this well-off middle-class family out of their complacency. But it was J. B. Priestley, the Yorkshire novelist and playwright, who placed the image in the public's imagination, during the BBC's *Postscripts*, a series of short talks, on Wednesday, 5 June. He focused on the plight of a paddle-steamer, *Gracie Fields*, which he had once taken to the Isle of Wight and which had been sunk during the evacuation: 'But now – look – this little steamer, like all her brave and battered sisters, is immortal. She'll go sailing proudly down the years in the epic of Dunkirk. And our great-grandchildren, when they learn how we began this War by snatching glory out of defeat, and then swept on to victory, may also learn how the little holiday steamers made an excursion to hell and came back glorious.'

In his speech to the House of Commons the day before, Churchill had tried to balance the relief of the BEF's rescue with a realistic assessment of what the next weeks might hold. His tone was grave and reflected the ubiquity of the threat: 'We shall defend our island whatever the cost may be. We shall fight on the beaches, we shall fight on the landing grounds, we shall fight in the fields and in the streets, we shall fight in the hills. We shall never surrender . . .'

When a bombardier who had survived Dunkirk joined Spike Milligan on invasion watch he supplied a less than Churchillian summary of events. Asked what it had been like he replied, 'Like, son? It was a fuck-up, a highly successful fuck-up.'

8

To Fight or Flee?

———————◆◆◆———————

Miss Mildred Ewing had lived in the Hotel San Remo, Crumpington-on-Sea, since the start of the war. She had abandoned her
vast London house and left a caretaker in the basement to watch
over its contents, which were shrouded in dust sheets. She lived in
the hotel with her elderly maid, Sparks, and other white-haired old
ladies who had fled the capital and now sat knitting khaki and
navy-blue comforters 'for the brave boys who were having such a
horrid time'. They all felt that Crumpington-on-Sea was the safest
place in England.

But when the hotel started to shake from the depth charges
exploding in the Channel, and the rumble of guns from France
disturbed the lunchtime quiet, Miss Ewing decided it was time to
find another home and wrote to her nephew, who lived in the
depths of the country, far from the coast. She was among an
exodus of old ladies stepping into hired Daimlers, followed by
maids clutching rugs and jewel cases, who were 'part of the tragic
pattern of speeding cars, trudging people, laden farm carts, that
was spreading out over the face of Europe'.

All went well for Miss Ewing at her nephew's until a German
pilot unloaded his bombs in a nearby wood and shattered the
downstairs windows. This time she decided to move to a secluded
hotel in the Welsh mountains. ' "You'll be just in time to get a good
view of the invasion from Ireland, Aunt Mildred," her nephew
said, with a touch of malice.' When his desperate aunt asked him
where in Britain was safe he answered, 'Nowhere.'

Miss Ewing, the protagonist of a short story by Mollie Panter-
Downes, was typical of an estimated two million people determined to sit out the war in remote parts of the country, far away

from London and the cities, which were expected to bear the brunt of the bombing. George Beardmore, the BBC engineer, who earned extra money tracing people who had disappeared without paying their rates, visited homes where the occupants had left in such a hurry that he often found a cigarette stubbed out hastily in a teacup. In the more sought-after parts of London a crop of 'To Let' signs sprang up. Hotels in Scotland, the West Country, Wales and other distant parts of Britain tempted jittery guests with euphemistic advertisements that stressed their tranquillity and the soothing effect this would have on their nerves. In other words, the hotels were so remote that the occupants were unlikely to be bombed or in any other way bothered by Germans. For those who disapproved of such tactics these retreats were known as 'funk-' or 'bolt-holes'.

The writer Margaret Kennedy, who left her home in Surrey with her three children for what she viewed as the safety of Cornwall, described these expensive hotel guests as 'gluebottoms' because they did nothing but sit on their backsides. She spotted them in hotel lounges and on beaches in hammock chairs where they complained of the inconvenience to which the war had put them and how dull it was outside London.

Kennedy spent much of her time pondering the right thing to do if Britain was invaded. She concluded that it was important to be as mobile as possible and not to be a burden to other people. She drew up a five-point action plan:

1. Keep one hundred pounds in cash safely locked up in the house ready to sew into 'stays'.
2. Each member of the household must have a pair of good strong shoes or boots.
3. Everyone must have their own rucksack packed with a change of linen, waterproof, warm, woolly spare socks, comb, toothbrush and torch. Her rucksack must include sewing materials, simple medicines, sticking plaster and brandy.
4. Prepare iron rations of compressed food.
5. Remember gas masks, ration books, and ID cards.

All over the country housewives formed similar strategies: hiding food and making plans to flee while claiming they felt 'absolutely foolish' in doing so. Many found hiding-places for their silver and crystal, uncertain whether this was a precaution against bombing or looting.

The seemingly unstoppable progress of German tanks across Europe forced Britons to make life-changing decisions. Should they stay put, or move to somewhere safer? And if *they* could not leave, what about their families? Writer and Mass-Observation diarist Naomi Mitchison was convinced that her and her husband's 'bad political records' (they were Labour Party supporters) would make them a target for the Gestapo and considered hiring a herring-boat to take them from their remote home on the west coast of Scotland to America. She was pregnant at the time so did not relish the prospect of the crossing, especially as they would not be able to take much luggage since diesel would take up most of the space.

According to one estimate, as many as ten thousand children went overseas in the first year of the war. Typically, they came from well-to-do families who could afford the fare and had contacts abroad. Canada and the United States of America were the most popular destinations, but it was never an easy decision. Crossing the Atlantic was perilous and parents weighed up the danger of invasion and bombs at home against the risk of a torpedo attack in the open sea. And, in 1940, no one knew how long the war would last and who would win it. Parents sent their children away fully aware that they might never see them again and that they were also saying goodbye to the shared experience of childhood. Winston Churchill was heartily against the 'stampede from this country', which smacked of defeatism, and when Tony Benn's younger brother, who was eleven in 1940, wrote to *The Times* saying he would 'rather be bombed to fragments than leave England', the prime minister sent a letter of congratulations to the boy's father, a Labour MP. Occasionally, children provided a ticket out of a tight situation, as Nancy Mitford pointed out in her novel, *The Pursuit of Love*: 'Pixie is frightened to death and she has found out that going to America is like the children's concert, you can only make it if you have a child in tow.'

Eton College wrote to all parents to correct a rumour that the school was about to be transferred abroad. The logic behind its arguments might not have reassured everyone: its first reason for staying put was that Eton's proximity to both Windsor and London made it an obvious target and as such it was therefore well-equipped with air-raid shelters and ARP services. The school also felt that since the town had several evacuated London children, 'It would be disastrous if the impression gained ground that a district considered suitable for the children of the poorer classes is considered unsuitable for the children of [the] well-to-do.' It said, too, that it did not want to fly in the face of government policy, which opposed moving public schools abroad.

Vera Brittain, the pacifist and author of the First World War memoir, *Testament of Youth,* and her husband George Catlin, a well-connected Labour activist and political academic, were among those who decided that America held fewer dangers than Britain. The couple sent their nine-year-old daughter, who became the politician Shirley Williams, and her older brother to America rather than risk the bombs that were expected to fall on Central London.

The final leave-taking was usually more traumatic for the parents, who were burdened by adult knowledge of what might happen; their offspring were preoccupied with the excitement of the journey ahead and usually had their siblings for company. Also, many were used to the protracted separations that boarding school required. Even so, Vera Brittain's description of parting from her children is heartrending. She describes their 'gallant pathetic courage'. They 'kiss us and leave us as calmly as though they are departing for a weekend visit to a familiar relative. Their eyes are bright; their faces do not change as they go with their guide to meet the unknown adventure. At the entrance to the gangway, they turn and wave cheerfully. Then the tarpaulin flaps behind them, and they are gone.' Shirley was thirteen when she next saw her mother.

For some parents the thought of indefinite separation was too much to bear and their resolve failed at the last minute. Celia Johnson and Peter Fleming faced just such a dilemma. The Old Etonian, brother of James Bond creator Ian, married Celia against his mother's wishes and they remained happily married for nearly forty years. In the summer of 1940 she was starring in a play in London's West End and had yet to appear in *Brief Encounter*. The couple had arranged to send their son, Nicholas, who was eighteen months old, to stay with a friend in New York. Some weeks earlier Peter had paid a whirlwind visit to Norway to report back to the British government on the desperate struggle there and was better placed than most to imagine a Nazi invasion. But even he baulked at sending his only son across the Atlantic and the three, plus their nanny, returned from the port of Liverpool with Nicholas's one-way ticket to America unused.

Once the Nazis were positioned just across the Channel, Churchill agreed reluctantly to the establishment of the Children's Overseas Reception Board (CORB), which arranged for youngsters to travel to Australia, Canada, New Zealand and South Africa. More than two hundred thousand families applied to take part in the scheme, which was forced to close after a fortnight due to overwhelming demand. During July and September some three thousand children found new homes in Commonwealth countries until one stormy night in September ensured that sending children across the Atlantic became a last resort that few parents would risk. The liner *City of Benares* was torpedoed on its way to Canada and only thirteen of the ninety CORB children on board survived. Their accounts of clinging to the ship's wreckage for hours in the dark while, one by one, others slipped into oblivion horrified parents.

German radio reported that the royal family's vast wealth had been sent abroad ahead of their own departure. But to those who knew them, the king and queen demonstrated a breezy determination to put up more of a fight than other European heads of state. The queen told Harold Nicolson that she had lessons each morning in firing a revolver. 'Yes,' she said. 'I shall not go down like the others.' Hugh Dalton, minister for Economic Warfare, visited the king at the end of May and found him outraged at Hitler's determination to 'come here'; he added that he understood 1 August was now the most likely date for an invasion. Winston Churchill once discovered the king at target practice with a rifle in the garden at Buckingham Palace. He told the prime minister that if the Germans came he was determined to shoot one; Churchill replied that he would supply His Majesty with a tommy-gun so that he could kill several.

The capture of a royal-family member would have been a huge coup for the Germans, and a blunder that the British security services did their utmost to prevent. The Duke of Gloucester lived in fear of kidnap, and his wife made contingency plans to rush their baby son to a neighbouring farm where the farmer's wife would tell the Germans that the child was her own.

A special bodyguard was formed to protect the royal family round-the-clock. It was known as the 'Coats Mission' after its leader, Lieutenant Colonel J. S. Coats of the Coldstream Guards, and consisted of a company of soldiers who tailed its charges in motorised coaches and four armoured cars. Coats's job was to whisk the king and queen to safety if he felt they were in danger. He had no written orders but knew that at least three large country homes had been prepared as safe-houses if the royal family suddenly found themselves on the run. Madresfield Court, around two miles east of Great Malvern, had been earmarked previously as a sanctuary for George III at the time of the first Napoleonic invasion scare. The other two, Pitchford Hall, about seven miles south of Shrewsbury, and Newby Hall, four miles south-east of Ripon, Yorkshire, were suitably remote and the last was considerably closer than London to the port of Liverpool The king and queen were told to keep a suitcase packed, just in case.

The only time the Coats Mission was tested was when Norway's King Haakon asked George VI what precautions he had taken against an attack by parachutists. In reply the king pressed a button to summon the bodyguards. When there was no response, an equerry was sent to round them up while a bemused police sergeant assured the king that there had been no raid. Eventually the guards arrived and began to flail in the undergrowth as if to flush out an assassin.

Unlike most people the royal family had a selection of homes in far-flung parts of the country to turn to. George VI persuaded his mother, Queen Mary, to move in with her niece, the Duchess of Beaufort, at Badminton House in Gloucestershire. There, she threw herself into tidying the woods, collecting scrap for the war effort (including a large piece of iron that she put into her Daimler; a little later it was discovered that she had inadvertently purloined a neighbour's plough) and giving lifts to passing soldiers. She had four suitcases ready in case she needed to leave in a hurry: she kept one with her, entrusted her dressers with another two and the fourth stood empty for her jewels to be poured into at the last minute. She had also arranged for a plane to take her to a secret destination in case of invasion. During bombing raids she either sat calmly in the shelter engrossed in a crossword puzzle or remained above ground.

The press portrayed the royal family as doing their bit and suffering the same hardships as the rest of the country. Officially they adhered strictly to rationing, but in reality they could supplement their diet with produce from their estates in Norfolk and Scotland. Windsor Castle's parkland was ploughed in favour of cereal crops, and the pastoral setting became a military base of slit trenches and barbed-wire. The king ordered that shirts and collars should be laundered less frequently and that fewer boilers were to be used, which meant that sometimes hot water did not reach the more distant parts of the castle. Staff switched from lavish livery to an austere quasi-battledress that was more appropriate to their wartime work, such as blacking out the endless windows. The king had an old military greatcoat converted into a pair of trousers, which were so heavy that they stood up unsupported by a human frame, and the queen was seen several times in the same dress.

The great glass cases in Buckingham Palace were turned to face the wall to protect their contents from bomb blast, while priceless oil paintings were removed from their gilt frames. The princesses sketched in replacements: Dick Whittington and his cat filled Charles I's space and Mother Goose waddled in to take over from Queen Henrietta Maria. The contents of the picture gallery at Buckingham Palace were sent to Wales, with some of the paintings from the National Gallery. Other treasures were stored in the cellars at Windsor Castle or in disused crannies of the underground system: five large cases of china ended up at Aldwych.

In terms of value – judged in either financial terms or kudos – nothing could match the Crown Jewels, which were locked away in a place that Tower of London officials still maintain as a closely guarded secret – or perhaps no one remembers what happened to them. According to one account, they were kept in the vaults at Windsor Castle, crammed into a pile of old leather hatboxes. The story has the ring of authenticity because many commoners stuffed their own valuables into underwear drawers or a sock at the bottom of their wardrobe. As the news from France grew more desperate, mystery writer Margery Allingham withdrew eighty pounds from the bank and put the notes into a thick envelope, then had no idea where to hide it. She did not want it lying around the house but needed to be able to find it quickly. Eventually she shoved it down the side of an old chair where it became caught in the springs; she had to unpick the canvas seat to retrieve it. She said she felt like Samuel Pepys burying his money in the garden during the Great Fire of London.

Banks and firms which kept considerable sums of money on their premises – to pay their staff, for example – were also concerned about what to do if the Germans arrived. Banks were told that they could destroy notes but witnesses should be present so that they could obtain replacements once the danger had passed. Other firms were told to bury their money. In both cases the government was keen to avoid fraud, which it was feared might flourish in the general breakdown of law and order that might follow an invasion. The Bank of England also built a sort of ballista at the Old Street site where it printed money. The device, which could hurl Molotov cocktails – a bottle filled with a lethal incendiary mix of petrol and creosote, first used in the Spanish Civil War – over distances of a hundred yards, was nicknamed 'Larwood' after the Nottinghamshire fast bowler.

Safeguarding the nation's wealth was more problematic, and the most audacious of all evacuation plans was so fraught with danger that its failure – or even the discovery of its existence – would have put the whole country at risk. In June 1940 the prime minister called a secret cabinet meeting to discuss what to do with Britain's gold and securities (certificates showing ownership of bonds, stocks and shares). The pragmatic option was to ship it overseas where it could be used to buy arms but the Atlantic crossing was as dangerous for gold bars as it was for displaced children. And if a whiff of the plan leaked out it would have been disastrous for morale. People like Margery Allingham in Essex and Jenny and Muriel in Norfolk were already ensuring they had plenty of cash put by in case the Germans arrived. If the government was discovered to be doing the same thing, but on a grander scale in shipping the nation's assets to Canada, a run on the banks would have followed. Also, moving securities owned by individuals and companies without their permission was legally dubious. The first shipment – £30 million pounds' worth of gold – had been dispatched a few months before war was declared when George VI visited Canada. Over the next two years a total of £470,250,000 was shipped to Canada and the United States – most of it during the summer of 1940 – in a scheme that became known as Operation Fish.

In the Bank of Canada's Ottawa vaults a treasure trove of gold bars and coins dating back to Elizabethan times was stacked in wire cages that reached almost to the ceiling in a subterranean room protected by alarm bells and hidden microphones. A few hundred miles away in Montréal, a convoy of trucks crossed the city at dead of night with a priceless load of securities from the railway station to Sun Life Alliance's twenty-four-storey granite building, which dominated Dominion Square. There, the notes – bound in seventy miles of white tape – disappeared into another underground vault. For the rest of the war, the Royal Canadian Mounted Police guarded it. The only time Britain's assets were put at risk was when a freak thunderstorm flooded the basement. Fortunately the crates had been placed on wooden planks so the securities avoided reduction to an indecipherable mush.

Imminent danger forced Britons to decide which of their possessions was most valuable. For Margery Allingham it was the manuscript of her latest book, which represented six months' work and which she kept in a biscuit tin. When her maid scoured the house for china and silver to hide, Allingham asked whether she should buy some so that they had something worth concealing. When Scottish soldiers were billeted in her house and every road out of her village was blocked with old farm wagons and rolls of barbed-wire, she took the biscuit tin to bed with her. David Low, the *Evening Standard* cartoonist who liked to lampoon the Nazis, buried his drawings in his garden with some money in case he was forced into hiding. A friend of diarist Frances Partridge telephoned to ask whether she thought he should bury his treasured copy of Shakespeare's works. At the end of May Harold Nicolson told his wife to make sure their Buick was in good running order with a full tank of petrol. She must load it with enough food for twenty-four hours, her jewels, his diaries, clothes and anything else that was 'very precious' – 'After all, that's what the French did in 1915 . . . This all sounds very alarming, but it would be foolish to pretend that the danger is inconceivable.'

Chips Channon, under-secretary of state at the Foreign Office, buried his diaries in the churchyard near his Essex home and mused about future generations stumbling across them. Other politicians and military leaders, haunted by accounts of barrow-loads of official documents being piled on to bonfires across the Channel so that they did not fall into German hands, took more drastic action. Soldiers were forbidden to keep diaries, but some civil servants and commanders could not resist the temptation. They were under immense pressure and, unable to share their worries at home, found relief in pouring their thoughts on to paper. Many must have realised that if Britain survived they would have a highly marketable account of a unique period. Once it seemed that their readers might be German, though, their attitude changed.

General Ironside, commander-in-chief of the Home Forces, shipped his sixty volumes of diary to Canada for safe-keeping, and the diplomat Sir Alexander Cadogan was careful not to include in his any information that might help the enemy if they got hold of it. He kept completed volumes locked in a safe at the Foreign Office and arranged for them to be burnt with other secret papers if the Germans landed.

A memo from the BBC suggested that it might be necessary to 'destroy a number of secret documents in order to prevent them falling into the hands of the enemy. This might happen if an enemy invasion had proved so successful that there was a likelihood of London, and therefore Broadcasting House, being captured.' It went on to say that 'recent happenings' abroad

> have shown that events move so rapidly that in such a time of crisis no one has time to think of matters such as the destruction of papers which would, if captured, be of great service to the enemy. Such papers would, presumably, mainly be those containing secret correspondence with Government Departments on matters of policy etc, and engineering papers. . . . there may also be correspondence dealing with individual members of the staff which, if they fell into the hands of the enemy, would cause avoidable suffering to such individuals as well as damage to the national cause.

The memo suggested that the BBC in London and at Wood Norton should install a special incinerator and that heads of departments must gather together any important papers so that, if necessary, they could be destroyed quickly.

Museums and art galleries had been looking for safe places in which to store their treasures months before the outbreak of war. Wales and western England were popular choices because, at least in the early months of the war, they were thought out of range of German bombers. The Public Record Office evacuated about half of its countless, irreplaceable documents from London and moved the rest to the lower storeys of its Chancery Lane headquarters. It considered storing some boxes in underground railway tunnels but it was decided this would be too damp. Another suggestion involved keeping the records in a railway train that would park in a remote siding, ready to move if the Germans approached. Eventually the PRO sent many of its documents to the women's wing of a disused prison at Shepton Mallet in the West Country. Lorries ferried the boxes there with a member of the PRO's staff sitting at the driver's side. Not every member of the team, however, was overawed by the nature of their task: when the vehicle transporting the Domesday Book arrived at the prison ahead of schedule the driver and the PRO employee left the precious cargo unattended while they had a cup of tea.

The National Gallery in Trafalgar Square moved paintings to private houses in Wales and Gloucestershire in an operation that took eleven days and was completed on the day before war was declared. Churchill vetoed the idea of sending them to Canada, saying, 'Hide them in cellars or in caves, but not one picture shall leave this island.' Eventually they were moved by rail into a slate mine at Manod quarry in the mountains above the village of Ffestiniog. The National Library of Wales at Aberystwyth put articles from the British Library into its vaults until it was thought that the Germans would invade Britain from Ireland: Wales looked vulnerable so other items were hidden in caves and a disused quarry near Bristol.

The Tate Gallery, on the river Thames, close to the Houses of Parliament, was seen as particularly vulnerable and before the outbreak of war the trustees found new homes for its priceless collection. Very large sculptures were packed in flame-retardant crates and kept in the gallery with a few paintings, which were stored in a blast-proof area in the basement. Some items, with works from the Museum of London, were taken to Green Park Underground station and later to disused tunnels near Piccadilly Circus. Sir Stanley Spencer's *The Resurrection, Cookham, 1924-7* was, at six yards long, considered too large to move so a brick wall was built in front of it.

Three stately homes offered to take in evacuated art: Eastington Hall in Worcestershire, Muncaster Castle in Cumberland, and

Hellens, Lady Helena Gleichen's home, at Much Marcle in Hereford. Fostering art was one of the least painful options for the owner of a large house, as Lady Helena made clear in a letter to an official at the Tate:

> The authorities are becoming pressing as to how many slum children we can take in. As you may imagine I am not anxious for this, as once the valuable oak panelling becomes inhabited with possible & probable visitors . . . this house . . . becomes no longer habitable for human beings & I am told by a builder that no fumigation or disinfection will ever get them [fleas, perhaps] out of our old panelled house.

Big houses were also turned into makeshift hospitals, maternity wards, convalescent homes, schools or refugee billets. Blenheim Palace in Oxfordshire, Churchill's birthplace, absorbed four hundred boys from Malvern College: the Admiralty had ordered the evacuation so that it could take over the buildings in the event that its own quarters in London were bombed. The boys slept in the opulent state room in which prancing horses looked down from eighteenth-century tapestries, which were partly obscured by panels put up to protect the walls. Lino and matting offered some protection for the sumptuous floors and the boys were told to use pencils rather than pens.

Looking after works of art sometimes meant that the owner of a house had better protection and, if they were lucky, help with the fuel bills. 'I hope that Lady Valda's jewellery and the Head of Marie Antoinette arrived safely,' a representative from the Tate wrote to Lady Helena Gleichen, after ten cases, including a selection of Pre-Raphaelite paintings weighing over two tons, arrived by train from Paddington. Lady Helena asked for a fire pump and a hose that would reach as far as the pond, which was 120 yards from the house, and for extra coal so that the paintings could be kept at a constant temperature of 60° Fahrenheit. The Tate warned her to place the pictures at the edge of the drawing room because the floor was not strong enough in the middle to bear their weight.

Lady Helena soon found the Tate staff, who came with the paintings, a trial. She claimed that with the addition of a Land Girl the house was 'completely full'; she resented the paperwork involved in filling in ration forms, the wear and tear on the bed linen and the cost of the extra laundry and electricity during their night watch. The Tate staff, who had to keep a round-the-clock guard over the paintings, found it difficult to adapt to country life and the extra duties Lady Helena expected of them. They missed their families in London and some had to pay rent in two places. Fights broke out with the villagers, and the local pub proved too great a temptation.

Lady Helena complained frequently to their boss in London, forcing the Tate representative in charge at Hellens to defend his men: 'I tried to explain that all men were not domesticated nor perhaps interested in Gardening, and that so long as the men came to "Hellens" in a fit state to carry out the duties allotted to them, she could neither demand nor expect them to do menial tasks . . .' By May 1940 they were sawing logs for the fire, carrying out odd jobs around the house, driving out the cows from the 'swamp' at the bottom of the garden and acting as valet to Lady Helena's badly wounded nephew, who had recently returned from France. One member of staff wrote that he had been up to his knees in mud, which 'rather takes the crease out of clothes'. Relationships finally broke down when she asked a Tate employee to help bring in the hay. He refused, so Lady Helena 'loudly abused' him in front of three young maids, then sent him back to London.

Other national treasures caused less bother. The historic White Park cattle, milk-white with long, pointed horns, which the government shipped to a range in Texas for safe-keeping, settled in well. The government also bought sixty-five thousand Romney sheep from their marsh home in Kent, one of the closest spots to occupied Europe, sheared off their sought-after fleeces and evacuated them to the West Country.

In the run-up to war it was proposed that between twenty and twenty-five thousand civil servants would leave London for spas and seaside resorts. This was officially known as the 'Black Move' and accommodation in the surrounding area was requisitioned in preparation for a mass exodus that never happened. The idea was dropped when it became clear that nowhere in Britain was safe. Instead, several thousand civil servants were evacuated under a scaled-down version of the plan, known as the 'Yellow Move'. The Admiralty relocated some departments to Bath, and parts of the Air Ministry went to Harrogate and Worcester. But France's experience revealed the drawbacks of cutting off the machinery of government from the heart. It was hugely disruptive, bad for morale and, by the beginning of June, pointless since the German advance meant that nowhere in Britain was immune to air attack. It was decided that the cabinet would only leave London for a new base in Worcestershire if the Nazis invaded. When Cecil Beaton visited 10 Downing Street he noticed a truck of pigeons, which he was told were trained to send a last-minute SOS – presumably if the prime minister had no other means of letting the wider world know that he was surrounded. Churchill told his friend, the minister for Air Production, Lord Beaverbrook, that he had no intention of fleeing to Canada.

National newspapers prepared for a short-term disturbance, such as bomb damage to their presses or offices, and for a more lasting disruption. *The Times* would be printed on the *Evening Standard*'s presses if its building was put temporarily out of action, and the *News of the World* would help with typesetting. In the event of a more serious incident, such as invasion or a debilitating bomb blast, *The Times* would be produced at the Northamptonshire Printing and Publishing Company's plant at Kettering.

The proprietors of the Manchester Guardian and Evening News Ltd went to elaborate lengths to avoid the Nazis taking over their papers – even if they had physical control of its presses. When invasion seemed likely the newspaper group's managing director, John Scott, appointed two new trustees to join the Scott Trust, which had been set up in 1936 to safeguard the paper's independence. Crucially, they both lived abroad and would, in theory, allow the paper to carry on as a 'paper in exile', in much the same way that deposed monarchs rallied their citizens and prepared to rebuild their countries once the Nazis had left. One trustee was a colonial civil servant and the other, Paul Patterson, was publisher of the *Baltimore Sun*. The American paper already had close links with the *Guardian* and its foreign correspondent worked out of the paper's London office. Remarkably, Scott sent the precious trust deed across the Atlantic by ordinary post rather than with a courier.

Scott and the paper's editor, W. P. Crozier, suspected they would be rounded up as soon as the Germans took over. They decided that they would have to go on the run the minute they knew an invasion had taken place. A colleague offered to lend them a boat and Scott asked the advice of an Armenian friend with whom he played bridge at the Reform Club in London. The man, whose own country's history had taught him much about survival, advised him to buy a valuable emerald necklace in London's Hatton Garden, which would provide funds when they were in hiding. Since they would need to move fast there was no point in putting the necklace into the bank so Scott and another trustee took it in turns to look after it. When the threat of invasion receded it was sold back to the original dealer for the same price.

PART THREE

June 1940, 'We're in the Final Now'

9

Jenny and Muriel – 'If the Invader Comes . . .'

———◆◆◆———

Early one morning in June, as the Dunkirk evacuation was drawing to a close, Jenny rushed downstairs to see why the dog was barking so furiously. She and Muriel were convinced she was 'holding Nazis off', but could find no sign of intruders. 'No invasion!' Jenny wrote. It is difficult to tell whether she was relieved or disappointed.

All over Britain nerves tensed as people expected the worst, which sometimes led to tragedy. On an unusually warm evening in mid-June two members of the Home Guard were watching a railway bridge at Gwersyllt, two miles north-west of Wrexham in North Wales. Just before midnight a car approached slowly. A guard stepped on to the road and swung his torch backwards and forwards to indicate that the car should stop so that he could check the occupants' identity cards. When the warning had no effect he jumped back on to the pavement and shouted, 'Halt!' But his voice was lost against the sound of the engine. The motorist, perhaps assuming the two men wanted a lift and wary of strangers in such perilous days, sped on. It was the second car in fifteen minutes to ignore a challenge: on the earlier occasion the other member of the Home Guard, George Jones, had fired two warning shots over the vehicle. Now he threw himself on to the ground again, trained his gun on the car's fast disappearing rear wheels, as he had been taught, and fired.

Walter May, a twenty-three-year-old commercial traveller who worked for Lever Brothers and came from Mitcham, Surrey, was sitting next to the driver. The bullet passed clean through his lower chest. Ten minutes after arriving at hospital he died from shock and severe haemorrhaging. At the inquest the coroner concluded that Jones had killed the passenger 'by misfortune and against his will'. It was one of many unfortunate deaths in the tense summer of 1940.

That month an inquest in Romford recorded a verdict of 'justifiable homicide' after a sentry killed a twenty-year-old driver and injured a passenger. The shooting followed a similar pattern to the Welsh incident: the car was going too fast, failed to stop when torches were flashed at it and the sentry shouted a warning. In July police shot dead a farmer after an all-night siege during which he had fired at a policeman: he had refused to hand over his land for wartime cultivation. Lord North, the Earl of Guildford's heir, and his sister were blown up and Lady North badly injured by a land mine when they wandered into a prohibited area on the south-east coast. The coroner said sternly that the public should know where they could and could not walk. A 'brilliant scientist' and an engineer died from burns after an experiment in a field near Cambridge 'in development of ARP work'.

Rather than providing reassurance, the roadblocks that sprang up round the country, manned by eager volunteers and trained soldiers, added to the nation's jitters. Some, made of concrete blocks, barbed-wire and steel poles, were more considered than others, like the old cart, iron bedstead or car dragged into the middle of the road, which smacked of hopelessness. When a dog went missing in Snettisham its owner refused to look for it on the marshes in case the Home Guard fired at her. The tragedies appeared all the more suspicious because of restrictions on reporting them. Reaction to the siege and the land-mine deaths revealed the authorities' desperation to maintain law and order. Compton Mackenzie, author of *Whisky Galore*, wrote in his memoirs, 'I was faintly perturbed by the nervous state everybody was in. If the Germans were going to stage an invasion they obviously would not be able to do it at once, and by the jitters of some people one might have thought that the Germans would be arriving by the next train at Victoria or Waterloo.' Even so, he found it necessary to draw up a list of civil servants whom he thought might collaborate with the Germans 'if their invasion came off'.

In Norfolk, daily life had an apocalyptic feel. 'The East coast is avoided like a disease,' Jenny wrote. The family's sense of isolation was partly due to their being marooned in the middle of a Coastal Defence Zone, which initially stretched from the Wash to Rye on the south coast and prevented unauthorised visitors venturing within twenty miles of the sea. Also, they were surrounded by RAF bases, which meant German aeroplanes had every reason to visit them. Parents were told that their children could be evacuated to the other side of the country, and state schools closed. The sisters knew two families who had moved to Wales. Petrol was in short supply: it was whispered that only one pump was operating in King's Lynn and that this was protected by an armed guard, that there was no petrol in Norwich and that the army was emptying pumps for its own use. Word spread that cars would soon be banned, and the sisters' telephone rang continuously as customers searched for the fuel they needed to flee. 'I've never known such a panic,' Jenny wrote. Roads were deserted and the sisters closed their garage one Sunday for the first time in twenty years. A strange calm descended on Jenny, who decided 'we were all much happier with less work, less money & the whole beach to ourselves'. Their mother talked incessantly about moving to the west coast, and she and Muriel packed a bag. Muriel hummed and hahed about which coat to pack – winter or summer – as she liked both. She wanted to leave now because 'If we wait until invasion is here we may have to leave this part for a battlefield then we should have to ask someone to shoot the dog. I cannot bear to think of abandoning her to her fate. . .'

Their friend Mrs F was constantly on the lookout for Germans. When the sisters went swimming one evening she became convinced that a boat towing another vessel, with a large, ominous shadow at one end, was an advance party of Nazis. 'Mrs F said she was sure the bulk was a gun and got v. windy,' Muriel wrote 'She went and asked a fisherman who lives on the shore and he said it was his son and a party.'

At sixty-five, Mrs F found it hard to risk optimism and told Muriel, 'We had planned to be so happy this year and to retire and have a good time until we get too feeble, but it is impossible with the war on to be happy. We shall be too old after the war to enjoy ourselves. You will still be young. I cannot stop thinking of the thousands of boys being slaughtered every hour of the day.'

The sisters' days were dictated by petrol deliveries: when supplies ran out at lunchtime they enjoyed their first sea swim of the year and when a hundred gallons arrived at 5 p.m. they rang their most needy customers to let them know. They rose late, watched the seabirds on the marsh and daydreamed. While around them people talked of emigrating to America and New Zealand after the war, because there was no future in Britain, the sisters and a friend fantasised about a South Seas island where they would set up a new civilisation; the friend suggested that each man should have two wives . . .

The weather was beautiful; a commercial traveller moaned that if they had not been at war it would definitely have rained. In practical terms it was harder to enjoy the sun: camping and horse-racing were banned but Jenny and Muriel played tennis defiantly – the schoolmaster had warned that this was unseemly during a national emergency. He also revealed that the postman had urged him to stay away from the sisters as they were obviously fifth columnists – a view that he was disseminating throughout the village. Muriel was 'very amused' at the postman's conclusion, guessing that the accusation was driven more by jealousy over their friendship with the schoolmaster than concern for the country's security. Jenny assumed that the postman had probably jumped to the wrong conclusion after sneaking a look at a postcard from Mass-Observation telling them that its magazine, *Us* – which printed extracts from some of its diarists' work – had ceased publication.

Jenny and Muriel were exactly the sort of people who were accused of being fifth columnists in the summer of 1940. For a start, their behaviour was odd: they swam and played tennis when most people were planning their escape and they corresponded with the remote and unfamiliar Mass-Observation. Other diarists faced similar accusations.

A freelance journalist and Mass-Observation enthusiast who lived with his mother and aunt in the Midlands suspected that neighbours had alerted the authorities because he was Irish. While they waited for him to come home, police quizzed his mother: did he work with chemicals and was he 'temperamental'? Officers searched the house for explosives, stripped the beds, studied his diaries and even peered through the dirty linen. It was a haphazard search in which his car was overlooked but his camera viewed as suspicious, even though it was covered with dust and contained film with a 'develop before' date of July 1939. Another diarist in Huddersfield was accused of being a spy when he jotted down remarks made by a factory's watchman.

Jenny and Muriel's apparent calm was resignation, not apathy. They had lived through the anxious days of Dunkirk knowing that Matthew's brother was stranded in northern France with the BEF. His first-hand experience put just one degree of separation between them and the enemy. When he arrived back in England he quickly became a local hero: he had been wounded, had eaten nothing for four days and arrived in little more than a pair of trousers. The story spread that he had been taken prisoner but managed to escape after stealing a German officer's car. Strangers rang the garage to ask whether the Dunkirk hero, who had been a chauffeur in peacetime, worked there; some claimed that he had once driven them. A cable even arrived at the garage for him.

While the sisters were assimilating the news from France and adapting to the idea that a mass evacuation could be a moral victory, the monitors at Wood Norton were weighed down by the knowledge that worse was to come. Those who regularly tuned in to the French airwaves had already detected the death rattle of yet another ally. When France's prime minister, Charles Reynaud, broadcast just before midnight on 13 June he announced the gravest news with dignity and defiance: 'The spirit of France is not broken. Our race does not allow itself to be crushed by an invasion of which it has seen so many during past centuries. France has always thrown back and defeated the invader. Let the world know all this, the suffering and the pride of France. Let the world know it. Let free men all over the world know what they owe to France . . .'

Anatol Goldberg monitored Reynaud's final speech with a special reverence and years later could still remember his defiant last words: 'Le jour de la résurrection viendra! ["France will rise again!"]' On 16 June, Radio Rennes, broadcasting on a Paris wavelength, announced the resignation of Reynaud's cabinet, and that Marshal Pétain had been asked to form a government. The next day German wireless, amid fanfares and much crowing, relayed Pétain's order to his countrymen to lay down their arms. The broadcast ended with the song, 'Wir fahren gegen Engelland [*sic* – "We're on our way to England"]'. On 22 June monitors heard that in Compiègne Pétain's deputy had signed an armistice with Germany. The Germans had surrendered to the Allies in the town at the end of the First World War and it had been chosen now to cause France the maximum humiliation; the ceremony even took place in the same railway carriage. The agreement gave the Nazis control of two-thirds of the country – north and west France, including Paris, the Channel and Atlantic ports – and left Pétain in charge of the remaining area, which he governed from the resort of Vichy.

The people of Snettisham reacted to the news of France's fall with shock and anger. Like most of Britain, their view of the French Army was based on the Great War when French generals had been among the best in the world and their soldiers among the bravest. The news that they had been outwitted and outman-oeuvred by the Germans was as surprising as it was depressing. On Monday, 17 June Jenny wrote,

> Returned home to lunch and heard that French had given up, but did not feel at all worried or surprised. Everyone else is v. annoyed. M. is going to shoot until he has one cartridge left and then shoot himself and several women say they will poison themselves. Mr and Mrs B took Ronnie to Hunstanton for the half-day because they said the child might be killed tomorrow and should have all he wanted first, no matter what the education

authorities said afterwards. Mr B. advised me not to pay the rates or electricity bills until the last possible minute because the council might be blown up and we should not see anything for our money.

Muriel retreated to their usual haven, the beach. Here she took advantage of the glorious summer weather to read a book lying in a hammock. 'With Paris fallen everything seems sort of "anything may happen anytime",' she wrote in her diary. 'I hardly know what I shall be doing in a week's time at this rate and everyone else talks the same.'

At first many people viewed the collapse of Paris as the beginning of the end. A friend told Muriel that if the war was over 'her life might as well be over. She wasn't going to let Hitler have her money.' She speculated about 'the horrors' the Nazis would commit in Britain and warned Muriel against staying because of the 'atrocities the men will do to all English girls. [She] says she knows for certain that if Hitler wins he will have all English men sterilised and make all English women have German babies. Keeps saying she is glad she is too old but pities me and J.' The schoolmaster regretted saving his money, and his headmaster's wife said she would poison herself 'if we're done'. The sisters' great-aunt told Muriel, 'It's not a bit of good fighting Hitler, we may as well give in now as after we lost a lot more men, I think, dear.'

The journalist Mollie Panter-Downes described the fall of Paris as the culmination of a 'tragic week for the British people'. The other bad news had come a few days earlier, when Italy declared war on Britain. Angry crowds smashed the windows of 'macaroni joints' and delicatessens in London's Soho, while many of those who were spared transformed themselves overnight into Swiss restaurants. Other Italian communities in Glasgow and Manchester were hit by xenophobic outbursts against the 'ice-creamers'.

Mussolini's announcement had been expected, but France's defeat was far more shocking and at first Britons reacted with stunned silence. Londoners stood in the street reading their newspapers, column by column, then passing them on to someone else as they walked quietly away. Events were too awful for comment and the city stumbled around in a dream. On Sunday evenings the BBC played the national anthems of Britain's remaining allies but continued to play 'La Marseillaise' with General de Gaulle's broadcasts from London to give the impression that Britain was not quite as alone as she felt. The 'Information Wanted' column of *The Times* began to fill with requests for news of relatives who had last been seen in Paris, and a few frail British exiles arrived from the Riviera with harrowing tales of three-week sea journeys by cargo ship; King Zog of Albania had spent four days on a small steamer, which delivered him from France to Britain. The shock deepened as the psychological blow translated into practicalities: the Nazis now had access to iron ore from Lorraine, coal from northern France and potash, for glass, soap and fertiliser, from Alsace.

The occupation of France felt like a divorce – a messy one at that. As disbelief faded it was replaced by recrimination. Richard Brown, who designed parts for submarines in Ipswich, Suffolk, wrote in his diary, 'Damn and blast the ruddy French.' Amy Johnson, the pioneering airwoman, wrote to her mother, 'I can't understand the French packing up. I feel they lack leaders and any real sort of inspiring ideals.' Others blamed the collapse on the emasculating effect of French morals. Ben Robertson heard the implausible-sounding rumour that two former French ministers had arrived at Bordeaux with mistresses hidden in their suitcases and the secretary of state for India told him, 'The last minutes of France must have been like lifting up a stone in a wet place – all sorts of grubby creatures must have begun a tremendous scurrying activity.'

Gradually, though, the anger was replaced by a strange relief: Britain had been freed from the need to worry about her allies and would live or die by her own actions. A new saying, reportedly coined by a commissionaire at a service club, became popular: 'We're in the final now and it's going to be played at the home ground.' Britain was the clear underdog, a position with which she felt comfortable – especially since historically she had often suffered a major defeat before emerging as the ultimate victor. This attitude was summed up perfectly by a David Low cartoon in the *Evening*

Taking a dip became a rare pleasure once bathers were banned from many
beaches on the south and east coasts.

Shared political views brought Ludwig Baruch and Hilda Froom together and sustained them through a separation which lasted more than two years.

BBC monitors such as Vladimir Rubinstein and Max Brehm [looking down] were often the first to know that the Nazis had invaded a country

Beefeaters converted the Tower of London's moat in to a giant vegetable patch as part of their commitment to a campaign later known as 'Digging for Victory'.

Jenny was twenty-six in 1940 and helped to run a filling station and shop in rural Norfolk with her sister and their mother.

Although Muriel was seven years younger than her sister Jenny, they were close friends.

Everyday life became fraught with minor inconveniences which most people learnt to live with.

The Home Guard trains on a recreation ground in the South East, whilst in the background four women continue with their game of croquet.

At Osterley Park in Middlesex members of the Home Guard learn how to approach a suspicious car. In real life, drivers who failed to stop were shot dead on at least two occasions.

'Nazis will find our women tough', *The War* magazine reassured readers.

Since women were initially banned from joining the Home Guard, some formed their own Amazon Defence Corps; this one was based in Hillingdon, Middlesex.

Joining the army gave Frank O'Brien his first glimpse of life outside Scotland.

Mary McFarlane received letters from her sweetheart Frank, which provided a vivid insight into a soldier's life and Britain's perilous state.

Refugees from the Channel Islands provided a painful reminder that the Nazis had landed on what was seen as British soil.

British and French troops waiting on the beach at Dunkirk for their chance
to be plucked to safety.

Those who were lucky enough
to find room on a ship still
faced a dangerous journey
across the Channel.

A loaf of bread was one of the few
things a soldier could carry in the
race to leave France. Troops were
forced to abandon vital equipment
which they needed to defend Britain.

The removal of signposts was designed to confuse an invading army; instead it baffled British drivers.

An English 'bobby' walks side-by-side with a German at St Helier on occupied Jersey. For many Britons this image represented their worst nightmare.

Ambulance drivers and stretcher bearers knit and listen to the wireless as they wait to be called to the scene of an air raid.

Standard, which showed a soldier standing on the White Cliffs of Dover shaking his fist at France and saying, 'Very well, alone!'

The knowledge that a swastika was fluttering from the Eiffel Tower seemed all the more galling since in Britain towns and villages were doing their best to hide their identity. Signposts and milestones were uprooted and the names of railway stations were removed in an attempt to fox the enemy when he landed; there were rumours that even tombstones would be wrenched up. Despite these grand gestures the country was littered with identity tags – you just had to look a little harder: shops sold postcards showing – and naming – local scenes and army drivers confirmed their whereabouts from the addresses still to be found in public telephone boxes and local-authority names embossed on man-hole covers.

" *Where am I?* "
" *I'm afraid we're not allowed to tell you.* "

The ordinary man or woman on the street knew not to give a stranger – no matter how needy – any information about their whereabouts in case he was a spy. *Punch*, 24 July 1940.

It was another desperate measure that seemed like a good idea at the time but quickly became the butt of jokes that at least made people chuckle. An English friend of Ed Murrow told him there would be a 'jolly good mix-up' on the roads if the Germans did arrive since they drove on the opposite side and there would be no signposts to guide them. A *Punch* cartoon showed a crossroads at which all place-names had been removed and 'Madame X', a clairvoyant, had set up a stall. In another cartoon, a boy said proudly, 'I'll tell nobody where anywhere is.' In the same July issue, a drawing depicted a man regaining consciousness after being hit by a car and asking, 'Where am I?' to which an apologetic bystander answers, 'I'm afraid we're not allowed to tell you.'

The decision to ring church bells only as a warning that parachutists had landed was not so easily laughed off. Many people – as letters to *The Times* showed – found the sudden silence depressing. Church bells had always heralded the major events in the life of a community: deaths, marriages, baptisms, harvest festivals, Easter and Christmas. Their silencing represented the death of part of England and seemed horribly ominous. The 'muzzling', as one reader of *The Times* described it, was all the more painful since it had been reported that German bells rang out triumphantly when the Nazis entered Paris, and for seven days when France and Germany signed their armistice agreement.

From the practical point of view, a church bell was an unpredictable warning device. To ring one is a far more technical operation than simply tugging at a rope. The bell must be 'set': its mouth must face upwards at the start. This ensures that it will produce the maximum sound, but manoeuvring it into position takes strength and skill. Most non-bellringers would struggle for several minutes to raise the alarm – if, indeed, they managed any more than an ambiguous 'clunk'. Bellringing is dangerous, too, and novices have broken limbs – even their own or someone else's neck – when the rope has escaped their grasp and wrapped itself round someone else in the tower.

Confusion persisted over who should ring the bells and when. As late as August 1940 the *Daily Mail* ran an item pointing out that, although the War Office maintained bells should be rung only when parachutists had been spotted, most people thought they signalled that a wholesale invasion had started. In West Grinstead Tom Lock was the obvious choice to raise the alarm: he was the only bellringer in his section of the Home Guard and also lived conveniently close to St George's Church. He was told to ring only after he had received a written order, which would be delivered by dispatch rider from the lieutenant in charge of his section. It was not a task he relished: the bells at St George's are positioned on the ground floor and a German sniper would easily have been able to pick him off through a window. He said that when he asked how long he should ring, the reply was typical of the Home Guard: 'Oh, just give it a good whacking,' his superior told him.

The use of bells as a warning also led to countless false alarms. Hugh Dalton, minister for Economic Warfare, caused a 'local crisis' at the end of June when he arrived at a village near Oxford to address the Home Guard and rang an outside bell in someone's garden, presumably in an attempt to announce his arrival. In Norfolk, a schoolteacher whom Muriel knew awoke to the sound of bells, unaware that a bomb had made the church tower reverberate: 'She was terrified . . . and thought it was invasion. She was alone with [her] dog which she cuddled as [her] husband had gone to [the]ARP post . . . All she could think was what ought she to do, but [she] did nothing but hugged [the] dog.'

In fact, she did exactly what the government had hoped citizens would do in the face of an invasion: she stayed put. This was the key message in a leaflet sent to all households in mid-June entitled, *If the Invader Comes*. It urged Britons not to believe or to spread rumours, and to take orders only from a British officer – having first ascertained whether he was 'really British or only pretending to be so'. Citizens must 'keep watch' and report anything suspicious to the nearest police station or military officer. They must not give or tell the Germans anything, but hide their maps, food and bicycles, and immobilize their cars (one official recommendation was to puncture the fuel tank with a large nail). 'Remember that transport and petrol will be the invader's main difficulties,' the

Issued by the Ministry of Information *in co-operation with the War Office and the Ministry of Home Security.*

If the
INVADER
comes

WHAT TO DO — AND HOW TO DO IT

THE Germans threaten to invade Great Britain. If they do so they will be driven out by our Navy, our Army and our Air Force. Yet the ordinary men and women of the civilian population will also have their part to play. Hitler's invasions of Poland, Holland and Belgium were greatly helped by the fact that the civilian population was taken by surprise. They did not know what to do when the moment came. *You must not be taken by surprise.* This leaflet tells you what general line you should take. More detailed instructions will be given you when the danger comes nearer. Meanwhile, read these instructions carefully and be prepared to carry them out.

I

When Holland and Belgium were invaded, the civilian population fled from their homes. They crowded on the roads, in cars, in carts, on bicycles and on foot, and so helped the enemy by preventing their own armies from advancing against the invaders. You must not allow that to happen here. Your first rule, therefore, is :—

(1) IF THE GERMANS COME, BY PARACHUTE, AEROPLANE OR SHIP, YOU MUST REMAIN WHERE YOU ARE. THE ORDER IS "STAY PUT ".

If the Commander in Chief decides that the place where you live must be evacuated, he will tell you when and how to leave. Until you receive such orders you must remain where you are. If you run away, you will be exposed to far greater danger because you will be machine-gunned from the air as were civilians in Holland and Belgium, and you will also block the roads by which our own armies will advance to turn the Germans out.

II

There is another method which the Germans adopt in their invasion. They make use of the civilian population in order to create confusion and panic. They spread false rumours and issue false instructions. In order to prevent this, you should obey the second rule, which is as follows :—

(2) DO NOT BELIEVE RUMOURS AND DO NOT SPREAD THEM. WHEN YOU RECEIVE AN ORDER, MAKE QUITE SURE THAT IT IS A TRUE ORDER AND NOT A FAKED ORDER. MOST OF YOU KNOW YOUR POLICEMEN AND YOUR A.R.P. WARDENS BY SIGHT, YOU CAN TRUST THEM. IF YOU KEEP YOUR HEADS, YOU CAN ALSO TELL WHETHER A MILITARY OFFICER IS REALLY BRITISH OR ONLY PRETENDING TO BE SO. IF IN DOUBT ASK THE POLICE-MAN OR THE A.R.P. WARDEN. USE YOUR COMMON SENSE.

The Ministry of Information's leaflet, which was sent to householders in June 1940, warned people not to be 'taken by surprise'.

Issued by the Ministry of   Information on behalf of
the War Office and the Ministry of Home Security

STAY WHERE YOU ARE

IF this island is invaded by sea or air everyone who is not under orders must stay where he or she is. This is not simply advice : it is an order from the Government, and you must obey it just as soldiers obey their orders. Your order is "Stay Put", but remember that this does not apply until invasion comes.

Why must I stay put?

Because in France, Holland and Belgium, the Germans were helped by the people who took flight before them. Great crowds of refugees blocked all roads. The soldiers who could have defended them could not get at the enemy. The enemy used the refugees as a human shield. These refugees were got out on to the roads by rumour and false orders. Do not be caught out in this way. Do not take any notice of any story telling what the enemy has done or where he is. Do not take orders except from the Military, the Police, the Home Guard (L.D.V.) and the A.R.P. authorities or wardens.

What will happen to me if I don't stay put?

If you do not stay put you will stand a very good chance of being killed. The enemy may machine-gun you from the air in order to increase panic, or you may run into enemy forces which have landed behind you. An official German message was captured in Belgium which ran :

"Watch for civilian refugees on the roads. Harass them as much as possible."

Our soldiers will be hurrying to drive back the invader and will not be able to stop and help you. On the contrary, they will

Leaflets urged people to 'stay put' if the invader arrived, rather than blocking the roads as refugees had done on the Continent.

leaflet warned. Householders must help the military in any way but be careful not to block roads – unless told to by the army or the Home Guard. Tantalisingly, workers in factories and shops should 'organise some system by which a sudden attack can be resisted', but the leaflet offered no suggestions as to how this might be achieved. Finally, it urged: 'Think before you act. But think always of your country before you think of yourself.'

Newspapers wrote openly about invasion. An editorial in the *Daily Mirror* of 20 June warned,

> Study, till you know them by heart, the rules for civilians now being sent out as guidance when (and not 'if') invasion comes. 'Stay put' is the most important of these. If you get refugee-ing about the roads you will deserve to be shot by your own men. Remember the French. Remember Paris. The blind evacuation of Paris was the most tragic of the many blunders made by a French Higher Command that has hitherto made nothing else.

Other leaflets followed that told the public *how* to 'stay put' in a list of preparations that conjured up a bleak picture of bombed and burning homes. Britons must prepare their air-raid shelters and dig trenches in their gardens and fields. A notice from the Ministry of Agriculture urged farmers and farm workers to continue to 'plough, sow, cultivate, hoe and harvest', in that order, unless they were in the middle of military action. Some farmers were convinced that the blatant error of suggesting you cultivated *after* you sowed – a mistake as glaring as not knowing the current price of cigarettes – proved the order was fifth-column misinformation.

Most people gave some thought to what they would do if the Germans arrived – even if it was only to sharpen a knife or to have a table leg at the ready. Margery Allingham noticed that 'Ordinary people were thinking extraordinary thoughts just then and were preparing for extraordinary deeds, all in the same private half-ashamed way.' This included 'staunch elderly ladies setting aside their shears and trowels', and others considering what damage they could do with a bowl of lighted kerosene. One woman, who had worked out that her home, six miles from the Thames Estuary, was just eleven minutes' flying time from Dunkirk, kept an unloaded revolver ready to clout a German's head. The American reporter Ben Robertson met a goldsmith's wife in Lambeth, south London, who told him that her neighbours were ready to fight with knives, hammers and shovels; she herself had a butcher's knife with which to 'take one German with me to glory'. Lord Beaverbrook had more sophisticated protection: his personal assistant, chauffeur and valet were taught how to assemble the Sten gun that they took turns to carry in a special briefcase.

All over Britain families were going to ground. They studied their home and – if they had one – garden and tried to envisage the best place to hide from the bombs that were expected daily. They imagined the onslaught on Guernica and Rotterdam and wondered how to protect themselves from something similar.

Many opted for the Anderson shelter, a steel hut with a curved roof that was sunk into the ground to a depth of four feet and from which they emerged, hobbit-like, stiff and tired after a night in their dank dormitory. The shelters were a DIY nightmare to assemble and precipitated an endless battle against damp. A sheet of sacking, saturated with water and hung across the doorway in the belief that it would mitigate the effects of poison gas, contributed to the mustiness, and the eighteen inches of soil piled on top, which soon sprouted flowers and vegetables, gave the impression of an animal's burrow. The shelters were tense, gloomy places where families waited by candlelight to discover whether their ground-level home would survive the raid they could hear overhead. Installing bunk beds and other creature comforts, or renaming it the 'Hans Christian Andersen Shelter', as one young woman did, took the edge off the discomfort. 'Siren-suits', bulky boiler-suits that zipped up the front, became popular and were designed to be slipped on over pyjamas. Churchill often wore his while he worked late in his underground bunker in Whitehall. The Morrison shelter, a steel cage in which families slept inside their homes and which held its own claustrophobic horrors, was not introduced until 1941.

Preparing for bombardment provided a sense of security –

rather like carrying a gas mask. But when the bombing started some people preferred to take their chances. In Snettisham, Muriel's neighbours built an elaborate air-raid shelter but never used it, opting to stay in bed. Others felt fatalistic: if your 'number was up' you would die anyway so why spend your last hours in a draughty shelter when you could be tucked up in your own bed? Occasionally, the irony of war confirmed the logic of this approach: elderly people were blown out of their homes and found unscathed, clutching an eiderdown, while the bodies of children who had sheltered in the safest part of a house were dug out of the rubble. In London, others – Churchill included – could not tear themselves away from the cosmic glitter of a war played out in the skies above them.

Jenny, Muriel and their mother took to their bathroom when the air raids started in early June. Having been up three nights running, the sisters were annoyed to hear the BBC announce confidently that the Luftwaffe had not reached their part of Britain. Both Ipswich and Cambridge were bombed in the second half of June and eight people died shortly after midnight on 19 June in an attack on the latter.

All over the country people attended ARP lectures on what to do in a raid. They practised putting out fires and crawling through smoke-filled rooms, fitted splints and giggled at volunteers who had to pretend that shrapnel was embedded in their buttocks. They learnt that the official position to adopt if caught outside a shelter was to lie prone, face down, with hands over the ears, mouth half open and teeth apart. They must keep away from windows – the corner of a room was safer than the middle – and they were told that resentment was a good antidote to fear. When the time came, most people discovered that they forgot to feel resentment as easily as they failed to leave their mouth open. Housewives ordered stirrup pumps and bought long-handled shovels and buckets for sand to put out fires. They kept their first-aid supplies, including tannic acid for burns, close to their gas masks.

One humid night Muriel lay in bed drifting in and out of sleep.

At first she thought she heard bombs, but then was convinced that the noise was gunfire and that it was drawing closer:

> I thought 'Invasion', I'm sure that the Nazi army is advancing somewhere near. It got nearer and louder and I had visions of them marching up the beach road, and in horrorstruck wonder I could not think what to do. I was in a v. dreamy condition, just going to call J. when a v. loud clap sounded overhead and it came to me in an instant that it was a thunderstorm! Then I saw lightning and the rain poured down. I was by now fully awake, and listened to more and more claps of obvious thunder, and thought how silly of me not to have thought of the most natural cause of loud noise. When I told mother and J about what I thought to be an invasion Mother was v. annoyed and said 'Fancy you thinking we were being invaded and letting us lay in bed without knowing.'

Such night-time alarms added yet another degree of topsy-turviness to their lives. Their mother Susan's main concern was that she might be bombed in a state of undress and, while her daughters were content to sit out the raid in their slippers and dressing-gown, Muriel sometimes with her hair in curlers, she insisted on wearing stockings and knickers under her nightdress and coat. Later she added a hat to her ensemble in case she had to dash out to help someone; she was terrified of dying in her bed or in a state of *déshabillé*. She was not the only one to cling to decorum in the midst of danger: Mrs F told Muriel about 'the performance' she and her husband had had getting dressed before they took cover under a tin bath: she could not find her stockings and he had lost his underpants. During the first night raid he had groped about in the dark, telling her: 'I shouldn't like Hitler to see me in a dirty vest.'

As the raids intensified, Susan's nerves frayed. Towards the end of June she heard heavy gunfire while her daughters were playing tennis, and she 'shuddered and trembled'. The following day Jenny counted nineteen aeroplanes overhead in a raid that lasted until 4 a.m. Each woman found her own talismanic routine for coping with the terror. Susan sipped brandy and darted round the house opening and shutting windows and doors, while the sisters squabbled over their precious chocolate rations. Jenny wandered about the garden, occasionally pausing to sit on a bench, while Muriel put a mat over the bathroom window to allow her enough light to read *The Tumult and the Shouting*, the memoirs of *Daily Herald* foreign correspondent George Slocombe. She sat on an upturned linen basket, which left a dent that annoyed her mother – who spent at least one raid polishing the bathroom floor. A female friend fell into the habit of sitting under the stairs with a cushion on her head and a washing-up bowl balanced on top. Their new night life left them tired, irritable and prone to catnapping.

By the end of June the windows of 135 houses in Snettisham were crisscrossed with sticky-tape to stop shards of glass flying through the air after a blast. Most showed white lattice patterns but occasionally home-owners indulged an artistic tendency and adorned their panes with sun rays and Union flags. Muriel and Jenny decorated one side of the garage's office windows with a pastoral scene of fir trees, rabbits and birds. On the other they re-created a wartime picture of a soldier – or perhaps a member of the Home Guard – in a tin hat firing at a parachutist floating beneath a sky of aeroplanes, searchlights and bombs. Local children loved the display and passers-by stopped to look and smile.

The people of Snettisham were also becoming more ingenious in finding ways to supplement their diet as shortages increased. The sisters made blackcurrant jam: the age-old methods for preserving seasonal foods had been a hobby in peacetime but now assumed a grim urgency. A friend pickled samphire, a fleshy, emerald-green plant that grew in the shallow marshland near the sea and has since become a delicacy. Some countryfolk even resorted to shooting blackbirds. One landlady watched in horror as her fourteen-year-old evacuee devoured two rashers of bacon and four sausages for breakfast. She dared not take him for a walk in case it made him eat twice as much.

But the countryside that offered Muriel and Jenny such scope to pad out their rations was also a constant reminder of the threat of invasion. Hayricks were built in the middle of fields to stop aeroplanes landing, and beaches bristled with concrete and wire defences. In a matter of weeks their surroundings had changed more dramatically than at any other time in their lives and the transformation was masterminded not by farmers or other local people but by a distant general. As commander-in-chief, Home Forces, General William Ironside had set in motion an ambitious strategy designed to turn Britain into a tightly guarded fortress.

Frank's Story – The Soldier's Return

On 17 June Frank O'Brien was back in Dorset after a visit to his home in Glasgow. His return to army life left him miserable but brought with it a rush of affection for Mary: 'I only wish we could be together forever and never have to part,' he wrote from Charmouth. 'I love you with all my heart. I never realised how beautiful you were until I saw you darling in my mother's house, you were lovely. Don't ever change you are so kind and thoughtful.'

A week later he realised he had to settle back into the routine. He was a gregarious soldier, who attracted gentle leg-pulling and who wore his heart on his neatly pressed sleeve. He could not stop telling 'the boys' about his Mary; they replied that he was 'going crazy'. Her prayers made him feel protected and he sewed the St Christopher medal she sent him on to his tunic. In return he posted her the lyrics to 'J'attendrai' and promised to sing it to her on his return. When he had exhausted the English possibilities for telling her how wonderful she was, he resorted to his recently acquired French and closed one letter, 'P.S. It is Pa Bon here without you darling . . .'

By 24 June his battery had moved to Hursley Park in Hampshire, where he and his comrades enjoyed living under canvas in the fine weather. Mary sent him a rosary as a further talisman against danger. By the end of the month Frank's letters had lost their relaxed tone: he had to snatch a few minutes between his shifts on guard duty to write to her.

Forgive me darling for not writing sooner. I'm very busy just now; we are all on guard every day of the week. I only have a few hours at dinnertime to myself and sometimes I can't get it. We are camping just outside Southampton. It's [a] pretty hot time with the Germans trying to bomb us. However, I'm not worried as long as my wee sweetheart is safe in Glasgow. My mother was telling me about the air raid on Glasgow on Tuesday night. Now darling take my advice and keep calm and don't worry yourself, the Germans never got near Glasgow and never will.

A few miles away, on the south coast, General Ironside was implementing a strategy designed to make the Germans' landing as uncomfortable as possible and to give soldiers like Frank a fighting chance.

Ironside was six feet four inches tall and known to his colleagues as 'Tiny'. At sixty, he was younger than Churchill but still much closer in age to Home Guard members – in whom he placed great faith – than other top military leaders. He spoke several languages and had spied for the British in Africa; he was said to have been the model for Richard Hannay, the hero of John Buchan's *The Thirty-Nine Steps*, and had the rare distinction of having met Hitler. In 1940, though, his glory days were behind him.

Ironside believed that the Nazi invasion would roll out in four stages. It would start with widespread bombing, designed to crush morale; next, the Luftwaffe would target ports and shipping to cripple the navy and cut off supplies, then turn their attention to the RAF. Invasion – by sea and air – would follow as parachutists seized airfields and other landing-spaces for the use of troop-carrying planes, which would attack beach defences, allowing their tanks and infantry to arrive by sea.

At first Ironside deemed the coastline between the Wash, in Lincolnshire, and Folkestone in Kent, most vulnerable to attack, but as the Germans consolidated their position in northern France the danger area extended to any part of the south coast within two hundred miles of a German-occupied aerodrome. In theory, though, the attack could come on any stretch of Great Britain's 11,073 miles (17,820 kilometres) of coastline. The prospect of defending every inch of the country's cliffs, creeks and crevices was all the more daunting because the BEF had left its best hardware in

France. Ironside had fifteen divisions of troops, one armoured division, fifty-seven Home Defence battalions and the Home Guard, but a poor array of weapons with which to see off the invader.

He began by transforming the most vulnerable beaches into sandy barriers bristling with concrete, barbed-wire, land mines and expectant troops. In some places desperate measures were taken. A central section of Cromer pier, on the north Norfolk coast, was blown up to prevent the Germans using it as a landing base, but had to be replaced when it became apparent that the lifeboat crew could no longer reach their vessel.

If the Germans made it through this initial defensive 'crust', they would face a series of obstacles, or 'stop lines', designed to irritate and, at best, wreck their tanks. They capitalised on existing features such as railway embankments, rivers and canals. The General Headquarters Anti-tank Line (the GHQ stop line) lay behind these minor obstructions like a surgical brace and supported the country from west to east in a line that stretched from Bristol to Maidstone, skirted south-east round London, then headed north through Cambridge to the Wash and wove a route to the east of Britain's industrial heartland as far as Edinburgh.

These ambitious plans, which would have taken months to complete when an invasion was thought to be – at most – weeks away, transformed Britain's countryside. Their ghostly presence remains today. Concrete cubes, like a giant's stepping-stones, lie at likely crossing-points for tanks, near the river Avon at Malmesbury and on the beach in Bridlington, Yorkshire, for instance. Crumbling pillboxes – partly submerged blocks from which soldiers could fire on the enemy through narrow wall-slits – remain in peaceful Norfolk fields or peep out from the undergrowth in Suffolk; a stable block in Burscough, Lancashire, betrays neat gaps in its brickwork designed for a sniper to rest his rifle, and across the country ugly grey lumps of concrete lie discarded beside major roads that once had to be blocked and guarded.

More than eighteen thousand pillboxes were built in 1940, looking out grimly in the direction from which the enemy was expected to appear. Most were on beaches or formed part of stop lines; others protected factories, airfields and radar stations. Although the War Office issued precise instructions for their design and dimensions, many assumed local characteristics. Materials were in short supply and builders improvised with whatever was to hand, in many cases helping to camouflage the site at the same time. At Druridge in Northumberland a pillbox was made to look like a tumbledown cottage; others were disguised as beach kiosks or even piles of logs. One in Pevensey, Sussex, was covered with earth and stones, and with its two gun slits at either side of a slight mound, it resembles a sleeping Goliath.

Britain changed from the air, too. Artists who had spent their careers striving to reveal hidden truths turned their talents to deceit, camouflaging important sites like factories, RAF bases and military camps so that they disappeared into their surroundings. In an attempt to fool a bomber, fake windows and doors were painted on to the sides of factories in Crewe so that they looked like the nearby terraced houses. Nets, matting and clever shading confused German pilots searching for the large shadows cast by tall factory buildings or the barrels of heavy guns.

Ironside shifted the country's preoccupation from parachutists to tanks and the need to set traps for them – as if they were rampaging wild beasts. Rows of reinforced concrete blocks, with sides between three and five feet high, sprang up on beaches and in stop lines. Their job was to block tanks or to tip them over, exposing their underbelly to enemy fire. There were plans to flood parts of Romney Marsh and rumours persist that the same was planned for the fenland around Ely in Cambridgeshire – a desperate measure indeed, given the centuries-long battle to control rising water levels in the area.

The new defences produced new vocabulary. Sometimes this was as ugly as the construction it described – like the Spigot Mortar (also known as the Blacker Bombard), a concrete cylinder with a gun mounted on top that was soon to be sunk into holes at bridges, road junctions and by the coast. In other cases the new terms reflected an awareness that the defenders needed something magical to defeat a German tank: pyramid-shaped anti-tank blocks were known as 'dragon's teeth' and another design, the 'anti-tank coffin', revealed desperation.

Ironside placed great faith in the Molotov cocktail. He believed that thousands flung from windows by the Home Guard would sort out the tanks. In practice, the device was unpredictable. A platoon commander from the First Isle of Ely Battalion demonstrated their use during a visit by the brigadier. As he remarked that they were foolproof, a private had to point out that a leaky cork had caused the contents to trickle down his back as he threw it and set his 'breeches arse' on fire.

Magazines like the *Sphere* and the *War* encouraged civilians to take on tanks by publishing instructions on how to mix a Molotov cocktail, and showing sketches of ordinary people stopping German tanks as they rolled down British streets with little more than scraps of fabric and native cunning. In one suggestion a man clogs up a tank's tracks by feeding an old blanket into them; the accompanying illustration shows him brandishing it like a matador as the tank passes a pub. In a second drawing, a tank meanders down a typical English high street while a cross-section of a nearby building reveals a suited man on the ground floor tugging at two ropes: sacks of rubbish are piled in the room above him. The commentary reveals that he has weakened the wall so that it will collapse, hurling the debris on to the passing tank. One wonders how much of a threat an unexpected quantity of rubbish would represent to a tank driver who had just crossed the Channel. The third illustration shows villagers setting fire to old carts – 'Fire is a weapon greatly feared by the tank,' the article says reassuringly. A church tower lurks in the background of each picture as if to remind the reader of whose side God is on. An even less sophisticated plan, remembered by one soldier, involved troops placing upturned soup plates on the road so that the Germans would mistake them for mines. When the tank drivers emerged to remove them the British would open fire.

As Germany paused to consolidate her base in France the British government snatched the chance to consider what would happen to ordinary life if the Nazis attacked. In the months that followed, it set up 'invasion committees' to bring order to the chaotic chain of command that began in Whitehall. Each committee made detailed notes on what their district should do in the event of invasion, which read like a cross between preparations for a village fête and a medieval siege.

The parish invasion committee at Barton, a village close to Grantchester, Cambridge, outlined its 'Combined Scheme for Military and Civil Defence' in a style that is all the more chilling for its matter-of-factness. If Barton suffered the devastation of Rotterdam or Dunkirk, the church – the institution and the building – would play a key role. Its tower would be used as an observation point during the day, and the vicarage would become a temporary hospital where all deaths would be logged. The committee earmarked the recreation ground and the space behind the council houses on the north side of the high street as an emergency burial ground. Graves were to be shallow so that bodies could be disinterred and buried properly in calmer times. Burials would be carried out as quickly as possible and preferably at night 'to avoid casualties among the living'. All bodies must be labelled.

The typed memo identifies the village's main sources of water as two ponds, three moats and a brook. Food was to be kept locked in three lofts; the food organiser and three distributors would be the sole keyholders. The committee estimated that, on a normal day, the village had enough food for its 550 inhabitants for two weeks, and emergency rations for another week. The food organiser would also arrange for supplies to be 'salvaged' from any damaged building.

The committee drew up lists of men and women who had not already been assigned duties with the ARP, the police, the Home Guard or as firefighters so that they could help with tasks as they cropped up. There were thirty-six men on the 'green list' and thirty-six women on the 'pink list'. The Women's Institute was in charge of cooking. In this nightmarish vision of 'total war' the two most important tasks were 'To defend the village to the last man and last round or bomb' and to keep open certain routes – even at the expense of saving lives. Its thirty-two Home Guard members were to help the police immobilise cars, to guard food dumps and 'suppress any fifth column activity'. Under the innocuous heading of 'traffic control', the document explains how police and air-raid wardens will rope off 'craters and gas contaminated obstructions' and set up any necessary road diversions. Vehicles, including tractors, will be immobilised but bicycles would only be put out of action 'if there is a risk of their being captured by the enemy'.

Civil defence would be co-ordinated from a building called the Institute or, if this was unavailable, 'Mr Jackson's barn'. Anyone affected by a gas attack should 'apply to the nearest house for facilities for thorough washing with plenty of soap and water'. Those whose houses had been bombed should make contingency arrangements to stay with someone else in the village – preferably not their next-door neighbour since their home was likely to have been damaged by the same blast.

Despite the rush to transform Britain into a fortress, at the end of June Ironside was gripped by a sense of time running out: 'Our defences are advancing, but terribly slowly in view of the imminence of the attack and the resources available to the Germans. Every portion of the coast at which I look seems weaker than the other and the troops less trained and more unhandy . . .'

Like many people he was increasingly worried about the presence of a 'fifth column' made up of Fascists, Bolsheviks and 'alien elements introduced as refugees'. One East Anglian newspaper printed a page in which the fifth column was blank, apart from the words, 'We will tolerate no Fifth Columnists', as a protest against the nebulous threat. In Snettisham a neighbour complained to Jenny and Muriel's mother about the government's internment policy: 'Our wives and children have to stop on this East Coast and be frightened by raid warnings, and then they take the bally enemy alien women and put them on a glorious spot the Isle of Man, why, the Dogger Bank would have been good enough for them.'

Italy's entry into the war meant there was yet another group of aliens to deal with. A friend of Glaswegian Frank O'Brien was among those interned, but he was confident that Willie would be treated well: 'He will have a lovely holiday out of it (I hope),' Frank told Mary.

11

Decio Anzani – The Italian's Story

On 11 June Decio Anzani, a fifty-eight-year-old Mayfair tailor, walked into the bedroom where his daughter slept. It was 6.45 a.m. and outside their house in north London the streets were coming alive. Decio was tall with a high forehead, which gave him the appearance of a schoolmaster to anyone who did not know him well. He woke up Renée, a slim young woman in her early twenties, and told her that he had been arrested and that two police officers were waiting to take him to Hornsey Road police station. 'Don't worry,' he said. 'I shall be back in a day or two.' He must have seemed calm, or perhaps she remembered stories from before her birth when he had been frequently arrested – for stealing a sheet in Paris and for vagrancy in Geneva – and reassured herself that this early-morning call was something her father could handle. Either way she turned over and went back to sleep. For Decio, though, this arrest was different: the police officers' kindness and unhurried manner were far more ominous than any violence. Always the most fastidious of men, he packed a small suitcase containing a toothbrush, pyjamas and a bar of soap, and left his home for the last time.

When he did not return the next day Renée and her mother, Victorine, went to the police station where they heard he had been transferred to a barracks in Knightsbridge. They took the bus across London but Decio had already left. After much to-ing and fro-ing an army representative told them that he and other Italians had been transported to Lingfield Park racecourse, south of London, which was being used as an internment camp.

Decio's experience that fine June morning was repeated all over London and in other parts of the country where Italians had made their home. In the space of a fortnight more than four thousand were arrested. Typically, two plainclothes policemen searched the Italian's home, waited while he packed a suitcase and, if they felt the need, handcuffed him. Often the police appeared reluctant – even embarrassed – at what they had to do. The arrests were touched by small kindnesses: handcuffs concealed under a raincoat to avoid embarrassment in front of the neighbours, allowing the man to finish his breakfast and reassure a weeping wife or mother that their husband or son would be back before they knew it.

In a few cases the rounding-up provided an excuse for outbursts of xenophobia. Mobs smashed shop windows and jeered as police whisked Italians to the nearest cell. 'The ice-creamers' or 'wops', as they were referred to, presented an easy target. The declaration of war by the 'top wop', Mussolini, had left them clearly on the wrong side, but there was another reason why they were treated as scapegoats: they were perceived to be doing much better than most other Britons. At a time of high unemployment, Italians were in work. Many were highly visible as waiters, while others had followed the traditional path of the Italian immigrant and sold ice-cream. Their names graced exotic delicatessens and top London restaurants, such as Bertorelli's and Quaglino's. Not only did they enjoy a regular income, they were surrounded by the choicest food when most of the population was struggling to make a meal of boiled calf's heel or carrot curry. Gracie Fields, the Rochdale singer and comedian, lost some of her popularity when she left Britain for Hollywood with her Italian-born partner, Monty Banks, so that he could avoid internment. Although she returned the following year the public were slow to forgive her.

The diplomat Sir Alexander Cadogan wrote in his diary that he had been part of a discussion about what to do with the 'ice-cream vendors'. 'Drown the brutes is what I should like to do . . .' he concluded. A cartoon in *The Tatler* played on another stereotype: its caption reads, 'A neat device for catching wops' while the accompanying illustration shows an RAF pilot swooping over the sea while yelling through a loudspeaker, 'Waiter! Waiter!' to an

WITH THE FLEET AIR ARM—No. 2

A NEAT DEVICE FOR CATCHING WOPS

BY WING-COMMANDER E. G. OAKLEY BEUTTLER

This picture is so eloquently explanatory that to add even one word would almost savour of painting the lily. However, as there may be some simple folk who have never encountered the Italian waiter, it is necessary to explain that the itching palm put it into the mind of the Fleet Air Arm to adopt this clever device for inducing Dago submarines to break surface. Once a waiter, always a waiter

After Italy's entry into the war some commentators resorted to racial stereotypes to depict their new enemy, as in this cartoon from the *Tatler*, 28 August 1940.

Italian submarine, whose captain, napkin over one arm, pops up replying, 'Si, Signore!' Cafés and restaurants tried to fight back by displaying signs proclaiming their patriotism. The Bertorelli brothers pointed out that they were British citizens and that their sons were serving in the army. An Italian organ-grinder in Leeds carried a placard stating, 'I'm British and the monkey is from India.'

The rounding-up of Italians was the culmination of an internment policy that had accelerated after the fall of the Low Countries. The government was convinced that a determined fifth column had emerged from its underground hiding-places to help Germany to victory there and wanted to stop the same thing happening in Britain. Internment, which began in May with the removal of male enemy aliens living near the south and east coasts, quickly expanded so that by 21 June all enemy aliens, including many women, children and more than fifty thousand Jewish refugees, were living in internment camps scattered around the country.

Ludwig Baruch's father, Daniel, was released on grounds of ill-health; the authorities told him that they did not want him to die in a camp. But Ludwig's two younger brothers, Walter and Ury, who were medical students, were arrested in the middle of lectures, causing a sensation among the other students and outrage from the university authorities. Hilda, Ludwig's girlfriend, whose family doctor had just joined the army, was furious at the injustice of locking them up and wrote, with heavy sarcasm, to Ludwig: 'It is really very sensible to take them away because we are crying out for medical students and nurses . . . I suppose being born in Hamburg, they are much . . . greater enemies to the British people than Unity Mitford or Sir Oswald Mosley!'

Ludwig's mother was interned on the Isle of Man, which, like Seaton, overflowed with suppressed talent. Many of its inmates gave and attended lectures in Russian, Spanish, telegraphy, advertising and first aid, and performed concerts and scenes from *A Midsummer Night's Dream*. Walter and Ury were held on a housing estate near Liverpool, yet another bizarre location that had been hurriedly transformed into a staging-post for aliens. In peacetime the council houses at Huyton would have made perfect homes, but in 1940 they were unfurnished and unfinished. Glimpsed through the barbed-wire fence the camp was like a surreal forerunner of the modern gated-community: a gaggle of bored men, hands in trouser pockets, walked down a row of doll's-house-neat brick buildings guarded by a sentry. Prisoners were told to stuff sacks with straw to sleep on, and as the camp filled many were forced to sleep in tents pitched in a muddy field that quickly became waterlogged.

Despite – or perhaps because of – the boredom and uncertainty, Huyton, like the other large internment camps, became a hotbed of creativity and improvisation. The composer Hans Gál wrote his *Huyton Suite* there, and artists Hugo Dachinger, an Austrian Jew, and Walter Nessler, a German whose radical style had been denounced as degenerate by the Nazis, spent their long days sketching the camp and their fellow inmates. They used whatever scraps of material they could find – discarded wallpaper or copies of old newspapers ranging from *The Times* to the more populist *Reynolds News*. Dachinger appears to have made a brush with his own hair, mixed pigments with toothpaste, and concocted a resin of gelatine from boiled bones, flour and leaves, which he applied to newspaper before he painted on it. One of his paintings shows the canteen where prisoners sit slumped over meagre rations, downcast heads resting on hands. A stove dominates the picture, its pipe rising into the roof and dissecting the newspaper page that the artist has used as a backcloth. Two headlines are clearly visible, of which one is painfully ironic: 'Vitamins Enlisted To Win The War'. The second, 'Air Minister's Recruitment Moves Fast', seems otherworldly in its optimism.

Britain's internment policy was a knee-jerk reaction to its dangerous isolation but it was callous, unfair and deprived the country of some of its finest talent: brilliant scientists, engineers and linguists. A Jewish engineer, an expert in designing machine tools for the aircraft industry, had fled to Britain with his team but languished in an internment camp until Lord Beaverbrook sent two German-speakers to find them. About thirty candidates who had been provisionally selected to work as wireless monitors or in the BBC's foreign-language departments were rejected on security grounds. Some parts of the country suffered more than others. Jewish refugees were naturally drawn to north London with its long-established eastern European community and it was said that bus conductors in West Hampstead would ring their bell and shout, 'Alight here for Finchley Strasse.' In Hampstead, police walked into the library and asked for all Austrians and Germans to make themselves known. In Cambridge, sixty enemy aliens were interned; one academic, who was eventually released, returned to his lodgings to retrieve vital research notes only to be told by his landlady that she had burnt them on the night the police had arrested him, 'just in case'.

At first, internment was a popular measure that seemed sensible in dangerous times. The *Daily Herald*'s attitude was summed up in its headline 'Country Saved From Fifth Column Stab' and some MPs convinced themselves that it was safer for the aliens to be behind barbed-wire than exposed to public anger. But the Ministry of Information's research showed that, rather than reassuring people, internment convinced them that their fears of a rampant fifth column were justified. It offended the intelligentsia, who saw their friends and heroes – artists, authors and philosophers – locked up on spurious grounds. Opinion about the wisdom of the policy shifted as stories emerged of suicides within the camps and the injustice of forcing Jewish refugees to live with Nazi prisoners-of-war.

The next time Renée heard from her father was when a letter arrived demanding to know why they had not replied to his previous two in which he had asked for a change of clothes, coffee and chocolate. They immediately sent him a parcel containing a jacket, shirts, underwear and coffee, but a few days later Decio wrote again, in the same hurt tone, to say that he had heard nothing from them. This time his letter was postmarked the Isle of Man. They sent a second package, containing the same precious items. Then there was silence.

Decio Anzani's life story was studded with romantic episodes.

He was born in Forli, Italy, in 1882, where he was said to have been abandoned on the steps of a foundling hospital. At the age of twenty-one he ducked military service and fled to Lausanne in Switzerland. From then on he flitted round Europe, dodging in and out of France until, like Ludwig Baruch, he became a tailor's cutter. Like Ludwig, too, he had a political agenda. He became a peripatetic anarchist, living with a group of similarly minded young people in Paris, then moving to Belgium and later, with his lover, to London. There, the Italian government and British police followed his moves through a series of informers. He joined an anarchist group and organised protests against the First World War. By 1919, however, he had established a workshop and settled down to a career in tailoring.

The reason for Decio's sudden sobriety was that he had a new love, Victorine, whose early life was only slightly less romantic than his own. She, too, had spent her childhood in an orphanage – in her case in Brussels – and her father was reported to have been a wrestler from Luxembourg. She came to London to escape the war and was working in a café on Old Compton Street in Soho when she met Decio. She was nineteen; he was thirty-four. He used stealth and patience to court her; every day he visited the café, installed himself at a table and ostentatiously read his newspaper while sipping a cup of coffee. Although he was evidently poor, he managed to appear debonair, with his Victorian strong-man's waxed moustache and his neat clothes. He never looked up until, in frustration at his studied indifference, she slapped the paper out of his hand. They married after a brief courtship, and Renée was born in 1917.

Their first home was a two-room flat in Bloomsbury. Renée slept in the kitchen where her feet brushed the cold metal of the gas stove; a curtain separated her from the sitting room and they shared a lavatory with the other lodgers. They alternated between speaking French and English for three months at a time: French for Renée, and English so that her parents could improve their grasp of the language. Decio always spoke with a strong Italian accent, and never failed to refer to *Lie-cester* Square, but at home he cherished a library of classic French writers, including Emile Zola and Alphonse Daudet.

As a small child Renée enjoyed visiting her father's Mayfair workshop. Decio employed the prettiest workers, who arrived at 8 a.m. to begin cutting, sewing or pressing the garments with the great iron that spluttered on a gas ring. The workshop was a noisy, hectic room where the six machinists and a cutter chatted to one another or to the mice, which they named, that scurried about the floor. When Renée visited she dropped crumbs for them or collected pins with a heavy magnet. Decio regularly sent one of the staff to sketch the newest fashions as they arrived in Bond Street so that he could copy or adapt them for chic stores like Harvey Nichols. Wealthy women customers came to an annexe where they tried on coats and dresses, and Renée was allowed to buy *Vogue* if it featured her father's clothes.

As the business prospered they moved to a house in St John's Road, near Archway, and Decio sent Renée to boarding school in Bognor Regis when she was twelve, although she was convinced he could not afford the fees. Despite the term-time separations they remained close, and during the holidays they went for long walks to Parliament Hill Fields and Finsbury Park, or to greyhound racing and international athletics meetings. Decio encouraged his daughter to take up running and became her coach; he was careful not to force his political beliefs on her but was keen for her to join the Labour Party's League of Youth because of its emphasis on sport.

While his Mayfair business provided the trappings of respectability Decio never stopped worrying about the wider world. He was secretary of the Italian League of the Rights of Man, and in 1935 he distributed pamphlets attacking Italy's invasion of Abyssinia so the Italian government viewed him as a dangerous anti-Fascist. Although he longed to return to the country of his birth he knew it would lead to his immediate arrest. As she grew older, Renée and her fiancé, George, whom she met at a League of Youth meeting, helped to produce anti-Fascist leaflets from a flat above the King Bomba delicatessen in Soho's Frith Street, which was run by a family friend. Like the tailor's workshop, it was a hive of activity: helpers typed furious leaflets praising the freedom-fighters in the Spanish Civil War, while others stuffed envelopes and licked stamps.

Away from this political hothouse the Anzani home was a haven for exiled Italians. They visited most Sundays to play cards or a version of billiards, to sing songs and listen to the Italian musicians who performed for them. On these occasions Decio would send Renée to buy a bottle of Graves, Chianti or Sauternes. He also liked to drink absinthe, but as he grew older he was forced instead to consume pints of milk and cream crackers to soothe his stomach ulcer.

When Renée and her mother began to worry that they had heard nothing from Decio, they contacted his friend Sylvia Pankhurst, the prominent suffragette and a keen opponent of Mussolini, and William Gillies, head of the international section of the Labour Party, to ask for help. Pankhurst promised to raise his case with Herbert Morrison, a well-known Labour MP and minister of Supply, and wrote articles to publicise what had happened. Morrison reassured Victorine: 'You'll see your husband walking down the street any day now.' In the months that followed, Victorine and Renée clung to those words.

At the end of June Hilda, too, was waiting for news. On 22 June she wrote to Ludwig in Seaton:

> Today is Saturday, the day when we always looked forward to an afternoon and evening together. It always seemed a special day and a day when we were always exceptionally happy – at camp – walking with Pleisch in Sefton Park – shopping – bathing – dancing – reading – the many ways we have spent Saturdays. This Saturday I have been on my own all day . . . I am still without news from you – you might be anywhere, I have heard nothing for two weeks.

She had picked up rumours that some internees were being sent to Canada and wondered whether Ludwig might be among them. Three days later she wrote, 'Instinct seems to have told me that you are no longer at Seaton.' She was right.

In the spring of 1940 he had been interviewed by an official, whom he had assumed was an MI5 agent. The man had leafed through several ring-files stuffed with papers, then asked what Ludwig later described as 'silly questions' about people he either did not know or whom he had long forgotten. Among the bundle of papers he spotted application forms to join the Tailors and Garment Workers Union that he guessed had been stolen to prove his involvement in trade unionism. Later, he was taken under armed guard in a limousine to the Royal Courts of Justice for a tribunal. There, he was asked how he would react if Britain were involved in a war against the Soviet Union. He replied that he could not answer such a hypothetical question. It was nearly two months – by which time he was back in Seaton – before he heard that his case had been filed 'for further consideration'.

Although Seaton was several hundred miles from London, its highly educated and politically aware prisoners probably had a better appreciation of world affairs than most of the British public. They tuned in to 'an illegal radio receiver' and knew exactly what was happening in the rest of Europe. Germany's advance caused great excitement: around 240 of the almost seven hundred prisoners were Germans, and included the crew of the passenger ship *Adolf Woermann*, German businessmen, and diehard Nazi thugs, two of whom bragged about their part in the murder of Rosa Luxemburg – she had been a founder member of the German Communist Party and was killed in 1919 by soldiers who were later tried for murder and acquitted. The Germans lived on the west side of the camp, while the Communists, Jews and refugees kept to the east. For the Nazi PoWs, the fall of France meant freedom was a step closer; for enemy aliens, like Ludwig, the implications were catastrophic. Each day he and his fellow anti-Fascists, including men who had fought in Spain, discussed the political and military situation and the likelihood of invasion. When their guards arrived one day armed only with bayonets, no guns, they suspected that their weapons must be needed elsewhere and that the threat to Britain was now severe. Ludwig and his fellow inmates concluded that Germany would not risk a

Channel crossing while the RAF remained unbeaten but they worried that Britain might instead face a major air assault similar to the attacks on Madrid and Guernica.

Through the first half of 1940, Hilda continued to write to Ludwig regularly, telling him about life in Liverpool and the efforts being made to secure his release. She described the films she had seen – *Peter the Great, Good-bye Mr Chips* and *Over the Moon* – and how some shops had been ransacked after Italy's entry into the war. Her letters were intimate and occasionally brutally honest, as if she wanted him to be able to pick up his life without having missed a tiny detail. Although their physical contact was limited to one meeting in the spring she kept him up to date with her physique – perhaps to reassure him that she was eating well. She remained petite but, remarkably for someone surviving on rations, she gained an inch round her chest, two and a half on her waist and one and a half on her hips. Although these details may have put Ludwig's mind at rest, they must also have been galling to a man who complained of constant, gnawing hunger. She also revealed that her father was cross with her for going out with other men but she protested that she preferred 'lads' company' and that she told her 'boyfriends' she was married to Ludwig. In June she sent him a photo of herself in a bathing-costume: she had been told it made her look like one of Jacob Epstein's statues. She kept herself busy: dancing, fulfilling her ARP duties and in physical exercise classes. She found weekends without him hardest to bear: 'It is strange, sometimes, I feel almost as if I am haunted and I cannot get you off my mind,' she wrote, after one lonely spell.

By June 1940 the war cabinet thought it had found a solution to its enemy-alien problem: the Commonwealth could deal with this awkward group of foreigners. South Africa declined, but Canada and Australia were amenable to the idea and on 22 June a passenger liner, the *Duchess of York*, set sail from Liverpool with its first shipment. Ludwig and Decio were not on board – this time. The ship was painted battleship grey and carried nearly twice her peacetime capacity: 500 German PoWs, 1700 German merchant seamen, 400 civilian internees, the ship's crew, and some British troops sent to keep order during the voyage. It was a highly combustible ethnic mix with which to embark on an Atlantic crossing – especially since the prisoners thought they were going no further than the Isle of Man. On the open sea the balance of power shifted: Nazis outnumbered other prisoners and threatened to throw Jewish passengers overboard or to divert the ship to Germany. On the first evening after leaving Britain a few prisoners were enjoying a spell on deck after dinner when some guards, acutely aware that they were now in the minority and could not summon reinforcements, grew nervous at their charges' slowness to comply with a request that they should return to their bunks. Exactly what happened next is disputed but it seems that an officer ordered a soldier to level his gun at the prisoners, who were starting to move towards the stairs, then told him to prepare to fire and pointed out someone to aim at. The soldier tried to raise the muzzle of his rifle so that the shot would arc above the men, who were about fifteen yards away, but the officer pressed it down, and ordered him to shoot.

In the panic that followed the soldier fired, killing a German merchant seaman, Karl Marquart, and injuring fifteen other men. The tragedy shocked the passengers and their guards into a semblance of calm and the prisoners were hurried below decks, some with bayonets at their backs. The ship continued on its way to Canada, and the event was reported back to London as proof that the internees were indeed dangerous prisoners.

It was an ominous beginning to the government's transportation plans.

12

The Nun with the Hairy
Arm and Other Rumours

———————◆◆◆———————

In the summer of 1940 everyone watched and listened; it was a duty and a compulsion. An official pamphlet warned of the omnipresent and insidious fifth column and a poster campaign confirmed that traitors were everywhere. They lurked in the shadows, like the faces of Hitler and Goering that glared out of Fougasse's posters; they took advantage of the nation's respect for women and religion by disguising themselves as nuns, and abused the country's kindness to strangers by blending with the thousands of refugees who flocked into Britain. The new menace gave children a licence to build fantasies around strangers or loners, and adults saw a neat way to settle old scores or indulge their prejudices – all in the name of national security. Margery Allingham noted,

> If you thought anything or anyone was a bit funny or a bit queer, you could go and talk about them to your heart's content to the local bobby, who would put the magnificent machinery of the CID in motion. Anything promising meant that M.I.5 would turn up, and even though you heard no more about it you could rest assured that all had been gone into. Well, what a chance! What an opportunity! What a picnic!

Anyone who looked and listened hard enough discovered something that pointed to the existence of a fifth column. Survivors from Dunkirk assured members of the 4th Cambridgeshire Battalion Home Guard that the rash of 'curious cryptograms' that suddenly appeared scrawled on trees and walls were identical to the coded scribbles they had seen in France, Holland and Belgium immediately before the countries' fall. The markings suggested that spies were already in Britain, lurking behind trees and exchanging unfathomable messages. General Ironside reported that similar marks had been found on strategically important telegraph poles. In calmer times the disfigurations could have been explained away convincingly by any number of logical theories, from rutting deer leaving their signs on trees to small boys peeling away layers of bark with penknives. But as future generations found, in times of extreme nervousness the human eye seeks out bizarre interpretations of everyday phenomena: the face of Christ in a fried egg, or a terrorist's profile in a plume of smoke. The summer of 1940 was one of those times. The authorities felt obliged to investigate every suspicious incident – or, at least, to listen to the person who hurried into their local police station with a tale: a trail of blue string might lead to a radio transmitter, or a municipal flowerbed had been planted in such a way that the blooms would form a white arrow to guide enemy bombers to a munitions factory.

An ex-BBC employee was one of the people whose job was to investigate the unusual happenings which erupted that summer. At one time he had been the youngest theatre manager in the country. When H. R. V. Jordan joined the army it seemed his career would be limited by ill-health until he was called to an informal meeting at the War Office. From this point on his story reads like a James Bond novel – at a time when Ian Fleming was himself working in naval intelligence. After the meeting he received a sealed envelope marked 'Secret'; inside it, he found another plain envelope, which contained a letter inviting him to an appointment in Liverpool. He assumed this would be another civil-service type interview and arrived at the address in a 'dingy quarter of dockland' wearing the appropriate uniform of black coat, striped trousers, white shirt with stiff collar, and Homburg, carrying a neatly furled umbrella.

As he approached the 'forbidding, half-derelict dockside warehouse at the end of a grimy cul-de-sac', he became embarrassingly aware that his 'regalia failed utterly to merge into the background'. He found a back door and walked into a dank, bare room with rotting sacks at the window and a massive table in the middle. A middle-aged man with neat silver hair and a navy blue pin-striped suit announced, in a Whitehall accent, 'Please identify yourself,' then offered him a Craven 'A' cigarette, which Jordan declined. After a few questions the man asked him when he could start work. So began his career as a member of the Counter-intelligence Branch of General Staff at Western Command.

Jordan's brief was to recruit and run a unit to combat espionage, sabotage and enemy propaganda. The man who had interviewed him was his new boss, a veteran of the intelligence service, who spoke German, Spanish, French and Arabic, and had served in the Middle East on and off since the First World War. His inscrutability had earned him the nickname 'Buddha' – it was applied behind his back, which he never left unguarded.

Buddha believed that the biggest threat in 1940 came from people who had insinuated their way into positions of importance over several years. 'They are a greater menace to the safety of the country than a little man crawling around the barbed wire of an army camp with a box-Brownie . . . and very much harder to identify,' he told Jordan. 'It could be a university scientist . . . or that jovial Brigadier who hangs out in the Annexe . . . But that doesn't mean . . . that the man with the box-Brownie can afford to be missed.'

Jordan's 'patch' covered an area that stretched from the Scottish borders to the Bristol Channel and Wales and he worked closely with naval intelligence, the RAF, the police and Special Branch to patrol it. Although it was not as vulnerable to invasion as the east coast it contained several trouble spots.

Wales, Northern Ireland and – to a lesser extent – Scotland each harboured political factions who felt no sympathy for the British government. Jordan's territory included important cities, ports and industrial areas, each of which were ideal targets for saboteurs, and internment camps on the Isle of Man, at Huyton and a disused cotton mill in Bury, which were believed to contain dangerous aliens. Buddha reminded him of Napoleon's belief that one good spy was worth twenty thousand men and of Stalin's warning: 'It takes an army to win a battle. A single spy can lose it.'

'We dared not risk missing that single one,' Jordan wrote later in his unpublished memoirs. 'Britain faced the threat of imminent invasion. Pessimists at home forecast that there was little to prevent them [the Nazis] crossing the Channel and simultaneously taking Scotland with an invasion force launched from the Scandinavian ports.'

His sweeping duties included investigating the theft of weapons and explosives, monitoring postal censorship and following up suspicious telephone calls and illicit wireless signals. He vetted lecturers, entertainers and other staff who worked for the army, guarded codes and ciphers, organised specialist training and development for new weapons, and made soldiers aware of the need for secrecy.

Despite these wide responsibilities he lacked sophisticated surveillance equipment. Eavesdropping meant exactly that: during one investigation he and his interpreters squeezed into the narrow space between the ceiling and roof of a boarding-house, then used a stethoscope and glass tumblers to spy on the foreigners below. On another occasion one of his staff hid under floorboards. Jordan's job description had come straight from the pages of a thriller but his day-to-day work was like a scene from *'Allo, 'Allo*.

'The threat of invasion brought an outbreak of spy mania throughout Britain,' he wrote. 'We were submerged by an avalanche of reports, of extraordinary variety, from people whose suspicions were aroused by abnormal behaviour or dubious incidents . . . every report was pursued until its validity was established and potential danger contained.'

Jealousy might have been behind the many tip-offs Jordan received about suspicious women. He investigated several cases in which females were accused of trying to obtain information from susceptible men. Mostly the accusations were groundless, but on one occasion he stumbled on a woman who was a genuine Nazi sympathiser. A chief constable in mid-Wales had asked him to investigate her after a policeman turned up to interview her as a witness to a minor car accident and discovered a party in full swing at which she was drunk and highly voluble in her criticism of the war and Winston Churchill. Further investigation found that she was Irish and worked as a clerk at a military establishment where she had access to confidential files. Off duty she mixed with Irish friends, of whom one, her new boyfriend, was already under surveillance. When Jordan interviewed her he found 'a somewhat coarse blonde, [who] turned on the glamour, professed anxiety to give every assistance, and in half an hour's questioning spoke barely a word of truth'.

She denied knowing her boyfriend but when confronted with a photograph of him

> her cool and confident attitude snapped at once. Flushed with alarm and anger, she leapt from her chair, sprang rigidly to attention, and with arm outstretched in a Nazi salute screamed 'Heil Hitler.' She swung round and bolted hell for leather. After a chase and a struggle, she was brought back cursing violently. I had not moved from my chair. I motioned for her to sit down opposite me. Then followed the customary reaction. One was inured to it. Threats; indignation; then denials, next, tears and sobs etc, and finally the facts, more or less.

He concluded that probably she had not yet passed on any secrets but that her boyfriend was grooming her for the task.

Actresses were almost as suspect as the Irish. The peripatetic nature of their work gave them ample chance to scour the country for secrets, and their glamour helped them to entrap their victims. Jordan used his inside knowledge of the theatre to create a cover as an official of ENSA (Entertainments National Service Association) to investigate one actress who was performing in a small town in the Midlands and who had aroused suspicion by asking too many questions, then being caught reading papers from the brief-case of an officer in the Green Howards who was infatuated with her. Jordan was deeply suspicious, not least because all her friends were serving officers: 'She had alien connections. Certain aspects of her background were unsatisfactory from a Security point of view. She showed an unhealthy curiosity in locations, training and movements of the units of her Army boy-friends.' Her job allowed her to move on before he could take action but he passed her details to his colleagues in the south.

The budding spy did not have far to look in the summer of 1940 for a treasure trove of information or unwitting informants. Most observant Britons had a passing knowledge of troop movements and where to find RAF bases; a glance out of their window would tell anyone living near the seaside how it was defended; it was difficult to miss barrage balloons, and the state of public morale was a common topic of conversation. Those with a little insider knowledge might be able to guess at the firing capacity of the south-coast batteries, to give details of shipping movements and how they were protected by convoys. It was exactly those commonplace snippets that Duff Cooper, the minister of information, hoped to stop people bandying around. On 11 July he launched his 'Silent Column' initiative, which urged the public not to indulge in rumours and defeatist talk and to report those who did. Southampton held an anti-gossip week that vicars launched from the pulpit with sermons warning about the evils of rumour. A cat's cradle of banners crisscrossed the town, proclaiming, 'Scraps of news give Hitler clues', 'If you know don't crow', and asking, 'Did you sink that ship by gossip?' The council had cards printed with the message, 'Don't you think gossip may be dangerous?' and distributed them to responsible citizens, who were told to slip them into the palms of anyone who was a bit loose-tongued.

The Silent Column was backed up by a series of prosecutions against anyone who had 'spread alarm and despondency'. The campaign gave the public one more excuse to inform on their neighbours and was instantly unpopular. It was seen as unEnglish: gossiping, after all, was a national pastime and grumbling integral to the British character; the campaign flew against the principle of free speech, for which the country was fighting, and transformed neighbours into the enemy. Those who followed the minister's edict were nicknamed 'Cooper's Snoopers' and by 22 July Churchill assured Parliament that the Silent Column had quietly been dropped.

In the summer of 1940 Britain was a perfect breeding ground for rumour. It was difficult to determine the truth in a world that, for most people, was becoming smaller and smaller. The government

urged citizens to consider whether their journey was really necessary; telephones were to be used only for emergencies, not gossip;
letters, newspapers and radio were censored, and Parliament often
met behind closed doors – as it did to discuss the Norwegian
débâcle. But while most of the country was restricted to a smaller
paddock the boundaries for two communities shifted constantly:
the armed forces and refugees. The heady mixture of gnawing
anxiety, poor communication and groups of roving people enabled
rumours to ricochet round the country in the style of a pinball
machine. One of the most virulent centred on the nun with the
hairy hand.

The rumour stemmed from the fear that the Germans would
land in disguise. Soon Nazis in habits were popping up all over the
country, from London's St John's Wood to East Anglia, Sussex
and the Scottish islands. The sisters travelled either by bus – as in
the rumour Virginia Woolf heard on 25 May – tube or train,
sometimes alone, sometimes in twos. Usually a hairy forearm gave
them away, typically as they stretched out to pay for their ticket –
as in Woolf's account – or to retrieve an item they had dropped. In
another version the nun even had Hitler's face tattooed on 'her'
arm. At the beginning of June the story had reached Norfolk and
the *Lynn News* published a tale gleaned from the *Daily Herald*. A
woman on the London to Aylesbury train had noticed two nuns
and when one bent to pick up a dropped book, 'from the folds of
her habit emerged a hairy, muscular, indubitably masculine hand'.
She reported the incident to the police who gave her ten pounds
and confirmed that the nuns were spies. The following day the
story had acquired a French setting, and it was said that nuns were
being gunned down on the Boulogne train as a precautionary
measure. Diana Cooper, wife of Duff, the government minister,
commented wryly, 'An English uniform would have been a better
disguise for the expected invaders.'

'To judge from the alarming messages hastily brought to our
notice,' Jordan noted, 'England had also become the unwilling host
to hordes of hirsute individuals lurking in the vicinity of airfields,
apparelled in the enfolding concealment of wimples and black

gowns.' Clearly, the summer of 1940 was not a good time to be a nun. In Nancy Mitford's *The Pursuit of Love* Uncle Matthew referred to the sisters who taught at the local convent as 'those damned parachutists': 'He was absolutely convinced that whatever time they could spare from making machine-gun nests for other nuns, who would presently descend from the skies, like birds, to occupy the nests, was given to the seduction of the souls of his grandchildren and great nieces.'

Naomi Mitchison, the novelist and politician who kept a diary for Mass-Observation, recorded how an estate worker in the remote fishing village where she lived on the Mull of Kintyre in western Scotland observed that all nuns had big feet and that probably half of them – whether Nazis or not – were men. Almost a year after the Germans had invaded Holland nuns continued to symbolise German treachery. A cartoon in the *Daily Express* showed a nun perched on a bar stool, a pistol in one hairy hand and a drink in the other, cigarette smoke seeping out of each nostril; at least a day's growth of stubble is evident on her chin and she is wearing a pair of clumpy boots. A member of the Military Police confides to a worried waiter, 'Of course at the moment it's just a suspicion.'

Another common rumour focused on a similar fear that that the Nazis were already in Britain, disguised as members of the community previously felt to be above suspicion. It contained the same ingredients and preyed on the fear that Britain would be caught off guard. In it a blind man is spotted reading a newspaper, and the institution where he lives is unmasked as a nest of spies. Alternatively, a house full of blind refugees is found to be stacked with machine-guns.

The suspicion that the government was not telling the public the whole truth, and that the situation was much worse than everyone feared, contributed to the growth of rumours. There were whispers in south London that the government was preparing to drain Pen Ponds in Richmond Park to prevent German seaplanes landing on them. Official plans to prepare for the heavy casualties expected when the bombing started led to wildly exaggerated tales of supermorgues, 'corpse racks', and stockpiles of papier-mâché coffins to accommodate the dead, which some said would number as many as fifty thousand a week. The trenches in Hyde Park were said to have been dug for mass burials rather than as defensive positions for soldiers. In Edinburgh the corporation inadvertently stoked the rumours by banning anglers from its reservoirs because it felt the disguise was perfect for anyone wishing to poison the water supply.

On the distant Scottish island of Barra, Compton Mackenzie heard the shocking – and unfounded – story that the deputy leader of the Labour Party, Arthur Greenwood, had been thrown into the Tower of London for high treason. He believed it had reached the Outer Hebrides through a tortuous round of Chinese whispers, which started when a Major Armstrong from Canada was arrested as a fifth columnist. He became linked mistakenly with another Armstrong – a Welshman – who had recently been found guilty of poisoning his wife with arsenic. Mackenzie guessed that, in relaying the story, someone had said the Canadian fifth columnist had the same name as the Welsh poisoner. The confusion arose because of a second, similar case in which another Welshman, this time called Greenwood, had poisoned his wife with arsenic. By the time the story had reached Scotland the fifth columnist had become Greenwood, the well-known Labour politician.

In Cornwall soldiers practised machine-gunning by aiming at a *buoy* in the harbour. The following day news had reached a nearby village that a *boy* had been hit by machine-gun fire while he was playing on the beach. A day later sixty children had been massacred by German planes, which had strafed the sand.

Other stories focused on the Nazis' technical superiority and how they were prepared to use their expertise without mercy. Many came from the deep-seated fear that the Germans would use gas. Although this never happened, the cumbersome gas masks that Britons were urged to carry at all times were a constant reminder of the enemy's intentions. Struggling into the rubbery headgear was like entering a world after the Germans had won: inside, it was claustrophobic and distorting. For many people the smell of a gas mask still remains the most potent reminder of that summer. A nasty rumour circulated that the Nazis had devised a gas to melt the rubber in the mask so that it fused with the skin.

Just as sinister was the rumour that swept the country soon after war was declared in September 1939: that Germans had filled toy balloons with poisonous gas and transported them to the Warsaw ghetto to entice children. In the following summer the *War* magazine warned that fifth columnists in Paris had used pencils filled with poison gas, clocks that were in fact time bombs and boxes of poisoned chocolates. The magazine helpfully included a picture of a lethal pencil.

Concern about gas, and the conviction that the Germans would use it, led to a rash of false alarms. One of the problems in recognising whether or not it had been released was that no one had first-hand experience of what it smelt like and the official advice described it in such florid terms that many foodstuffs and household products were mistaken for it. At a time when the country was being told to look and listen for anything suspicious, the government added a third sense to the battery of home defence: smell.

In a glorious summer when windows were thrown open, unfamiliar odours crept in to cause alarm. Most wartime pantries and cupboards held jars whose uncorked contents could masquerade as noxious fumes: floor polish, bleaching powder, horseradish, mustard and pear-drops might all be mistaken for something less wholesome. In the country geraniums, musty hay, decaying vegetables and rotting manure made civilians reach for their gas masks. The novelist Naomi Royde Smith experienced the terror that a funny smell could produce: she caught a whiff of something when she was repainting an old chair and wondered whether the economy paint she was using was responsible. The fumes, which smelt like burning onion, sparked a panic in the Southampton area. ARP wardens paraded in gas masks, while hairdressers slammed their windows and told customers to keep their heads in the washbasins. Eventually the 'gas' was traced to a fire at the local pickle factory where onions and vinegar had mixed together to produce the stench.

Even greater than the fear of gas was the belief that the Germans were developing weapons so advanced and terrible that they were beyond human imagination. In mid-June the *Lynn News* reported that specks of soot had fallen in towns on the south-east coast and were thought to be connected with 'new Nazi fog weapons'. The smuts were said to be electrically charged and to smell of incense; a reporter even found a professor at the Royal School of Mines who appeared to lend the story credibility.

Some elements of the rumour were used on the German-based New British Broadcasting Station but its version was so outlandish that the propaganda intent shone through. The home-grown version was much more plausible, partly because it did not go into detail but allowed the reader to plug the gaps with their personal fears. NBBS told listeners that German parachutists had been issued with 'fog pills', which allowed them to hide in their own little cloud and float there, unseen, for up to ten hours. They also mentioned an 'electro-magnetic ray', which was rumoured to have been used to help the Germans capture the fortress of Eben-Emael, between Liège and Maastricht. In May the Nazis took the modern fort, which had been considered impenetrable and was vital to Belgium's defence plans, using a bold plan that entailed landing men by glider and blowing up its steel and concrete cupolas with a new type of bomb. The intricacies of the plan remained a mystery to the Allies and the source of much speculation.

The speed with which the Germans had overcome the once formidable French added fuel to the rumours that they had developed some secret – semi-magical – weapon. Royde Smith heard that they had a giant gun that could destroy London in thirty minutes. As well as reports of a device that prevented rifles firing, there were tales of German experiments with a cobweb-like material that they had tested over France in 1939. The substance, which they had released in large white balloon-like capsules, had covered several square kilometres and clung to people's hands and faces. In another version it was reported that the substance had appeared over Britain, but it turned out that this was gossamer produced by spiders mating in mid-air.

Some rumours arrived in America: anxious letter-writers were keen to unburden themselves to friends on the other side of the Atlantic. From America they boomeranged back to Britain, causing further alarm. At the end of May the *New York Times* reported a rumour – which preyed on fears about food shortages – that German scientists had reared a rapacious strain of grasshopper, which they planned to release in Britain to devastate farms and force a starving nation to surrender. Almost as alarming was the story that the Germans had destroyed Britain's entire supply of tobacco. In Washington people heard that the Germans were building a tunnel through which to invade Britain.

Lord Haw-Haw's name cropped up frequently in the trials of those accused of spreading rumours. All over the country – from Banstead in Surrey and East Ham in Greater London to Cambridge's Guildhall and Darlington town hall – Lord Haw-Haw was said to have noted that a clock's hands were slipping round the dial at the wrong speed. Most often the clock was two minutes slow – perhaps because such a minor shortfall was hard to disprove. Some newspapers repeated the rumours as fact: the *Lynn News* reported that Lord Haw-Haw had stated that the clock in Gayton, a village outside King's Lynn, had lost two minutes. The thought that hidden Nazi eyes were already gazing at the clock faces Britons passed every day was chilling enough in its confirmation of a fifth column. Still more disturbing was the rumour that Lord Haw-Haw had promised that the Germans would put the clocks right when they arrived – if they had not already flattened the villages and towns with their bombs.

Lord Haw-Haw's knowledge of Britain did not stop at clocks. He was said to have remarked that Orpington high street needed widening and that it was a job best left to the Luftwaffe. Likewise, he had apparently told residents of Commercial Road in Portsmouth not to bother taking up the old tramlines: this was another task for the German bombers. He seemed to have informers not just at factory gates but in the works' canteen: another rumour maintained that he had broadcast his regret that a munitions works had been blown up because it would disrupt the staff's pontoon circle, and that an explosion at a gasometer in Ipswich would make the girls at the nearby factory slide faster down the banister. He was said to have warned workers at another factory in the Midlands that they were about to be bombed and that there was no point in applying the final coat of paint to a shed. The rumours were all the more insidious when they contained a grain of truth: workers *did* play pontoon, the girls *did* slide down the banister, there *was* a gasometer nearby and the factory *had* a half-painted shed. Lord Haw-Haw was far from omniscient but the British newspapers he read in Berlin were a useful source of detail that gave a report the touch of authenticity.

Many did not believe the rumours, but the fact that they were freewheeling round the country suggested that a fifth column was starting and stoking them. The government decided that jamming broadcasts from Germany would merely add to their mystique, but the *Daily Mirror* took it upon itself to set up an Anti Haw-Haw League, who promised not to listen to the German traitor or to mention his name. The paper printed a handy reminder that members could stick to their wireless, which read: 'This set is Anti Haw-Haw. It hears no evil, speaks no evil.' By midsummer his power was waning and the league was wound up on 26 July. One of the most emasculating factors against him was that he was so easy to poke fun at. A cartoon in *Punch* showed two women gossiping and one saying, 'I heard a rumour that Lord Haw-Haw has given the inside story about Mrs Robinson and the Women's Institute Prize Cake Competition.'

However, Lord Haw-Haw and the outbreak of nun-worry showed how difficult it was to tell friend from foe. Haw-Haw, whose voice has been described as 'Cholmondeley-Plantagenet out of Christchurch', and nuns should have been unimpeachably British. That they were not shifted the concept of national identity and put English mores under the spotlight. As Vere Hodgson, a young woman who worked for a charity in London's Notting Hill Gate, wrote in her diary on 5 July, 'If we were one hundred per cent British we should be all right. It is the Fifth Column we fear!'

" I heard a rumour that Lord Haw Haw has given the inside story about Mrs. Robinson and the Women's Institute Prize Cake Competition."

Lord Haw-Haw was believed by many people to know even
the smallest details of their everyday lives, as in this *Punch* cartoon
from 10 July 1940.

In 1940 Britons were unused to foreign accents and any variation in speech was thought suspicious. When Ed Murrow stopped
for a drink in an Essex pub his American twang branded him a fifth
columnist. In another, almost certainly apocryphal story, British
manners exposed the spy. A clergyman's daughter had grown
suspicious of a British officer billeted with her family. Her theory
was confirmed when she discovered that he had not removed the
plug in the wash-basin after washing his hands following a trip to
the lavatory in the middle of the night. Significantly, it took a
vicar's daughter – who could be more English? – to spot such
unEnglish behaviour. Shortly afterwards the man was found to be
helping German aeroplanes by signalling to them at night. Apparently he was not alone and as bombing raids on Britain became
more common the country was beset by reports of flashing lights
that were believed to be fifth columnists guiding bombers to their
targets. An orange sky was often attributed to flames caused by

Nazis who had just landed and were hurriedly burning their parachutes.

In other cases British identity was as straightforward as an attitude of mind. In one of his *Postscripts* talks J. B. Priestley reported that a man outside his house had insisted on working through an air raid, declaring that anybody who went off to a shelter was 'no better than a Fifth Columnist – in fact, *was* a so-and-so Fifth Columnist . . .' Winston Churchill confided his views about the origin of the threat to Hugh Dalton: 'It isn't in the workshop; it's all the upper middle class.' He might have been thinking of Fascists, like Oswald Mosley and Unity Mitford. Everything offered the potential for a second and more sinister interpretation. When the wife of the Speaker of the House of Commons spotted a foreign-looking man clutching a map outside Westminster Abbey she had no hesitation in telling a policeman. Even a typically English exchange on the letters page of *The Times* worried MI5. It began when a vicar wrote to the paper pointing out that this was the first year that the spotted fly-catcher had not nested in his garden and wondering whether the war had prevented its migration. A Cambridge professor replied, and soon the exchange had spun into the kind of heated discussion for which *The Times*'s letters page is famous. Fryn Tennyson Jesse, a mystery writer and author of *A Pin to See the Peepshow*, relayed the genteel debate to a group of friends in America to whom she had been sending regular bulletins about life in wartime Britain. One of the recipients was the playwright S. N. Behrman who, on hearing that Britain's ornithologists had concluded the bird population was holding up well, sent his friend a playful cable: 'TREMENDOUSLY RELIEVED ABOUT SPOTTED FLY CATCHERS [. . .] LOVE SAM.' Before she could accept the telegraph someone – she assumed it was either the police or MI5 – phoned Tennyson Jesse to demand an explanation for the cryptic message.

Margery Allingham experienced a similar misunderstanding when her American literary agent asked her to update her short story 'Black Plumes' for *Collier's Magazine* with a wartime setting. She telephoned to cable her consent: 'Plumes realize exceptional circumstances demand alteration plan. Trust Colliers not to ruin construction.' Within twenty minutes the phone rang and an urgent voice demanded to know the names of the colliers and the construction they might attack: the caller must have decided she was involved in a miners' plot to commit an act of sabotage.

In some cases the accused had to deal with more than an abrupt phone call from a disembodied voice. Eight policemen, including one from Scotland Yard, searched the house of Jimmy Bomford, a friend of Frances Partridge, and left with papers and farm accounts. When Partridge rang the house the line was out of service. She concluded that he was a victim of village gossip and his only crimes were having foreign friends and a beard. She did not say whether a beard was innately suspicious or whether its owner was believed to be wearing a disguise. It was rumoured that in Belgium the SS had worn false beards and wigs to pose as Jewish refugees.

Fifth columnists were blamed for anything from a sharp rise in prices to a problem with a factory's production line. An RAF officer based in Norfolk reported that German aeroplanes were suddenly changing direction and that a radar station was experiencing unexplained interference. He became convinced that an electrical engineer who supported Mosley, and whose brother was found to own a map apparently showing the bearings of the radar station, was responsible. Soldiers and police raided both men's houses and found at the engineer's home a small locked box equipped with an induction coil, wire and crocodile clips. The engineer denied all knowledge of what was thought at first to be a radio transmitter. It was left to his mortified wife to explain that it was a device she had bought for the removal of facial hair.

In the Channel Islands rumours could barely keep up with the pace of events. On 17 June, boats carrying British troops evacuated from northern France arrived on Jersey. Overnight they transformed the island from a naked and unguarded extension of the United Kingdom into a khaki outcrop that rattled with the noise of soldiers digging trenches and settling their machine-guns in sandy pits. The next day the flurry of activity continued, but it was rumoured that the soldiers were only passing through and, sure enough, they disappeared as quickly as they had arrived.

The war cabinet had decided that Britain could not afford the manpower to put up a fight over a distant, strategically unimportant outpost. The islands were demilitarised and their citizens given twelve hours to decide whether they wanted to leave or stay. The deadline caused panic: islanders camped overnight at the town hall to secure their permits to leave and the curfew was extended by an hour to ten o'clock to try to calm nerves and the many drunks who were stumbling about. It was an agonising decision: whether to abandon one's home and possessions for a distant and, to many, foreign country. Was flight simply putting off the inevitable? The reaction of one person who stayed was typical: since England would be occupied anyway, 'they might as well be occupied in their own homes!'. About thirty thousand people – roughly a third of the islands' population – decided to go. Some left the decision until the very last moment, abandoning their cars near the port and scrambling on to overcrowded boats and barges; the rich chartered yachts and aeroplanes.

After the evacuation the islands slumped into a deathly calm. Thousands of cats and dogs had been hurriedly destroyed in the rush to leave and canaries and budgies that had been freed were commonly seen in the lanes and hedgerows where they scavenged for food, their flashes of colourful plumage bestowing an exotic patina. Police searched deserted houses for any forgotten food and were often surprised by stacks of provisions that had been illicitly squirrelled away. German planes circled overhead.

On 28 June, Jersey and Guernsey were rocked by explosions. The Germans, unaware that the islands had been demilitarised, were bombing them. Several civilians were killed and the artificial air of calm disintegrated. Leaflets fluttered down warning the islanders that the Germans were about to invade and ordering them to display white crosses as proof of their intention not to put up a fight. If they did not comply, the islands would face heavy bombardment.

The official occupation started on 2 July. Home Guard members burned their uniforms. The invaders ordered all guns to be handed in and instituted a curfew between 11 p.m. and 5 a.m. Islanders were told they could listen only to German radio stations and to put their watches and clocks forward an hour, in line with their occupiers' time zone. The most humiliating sight was the makeshift white flags that fluttered from every building: handkerchiefs, table napkins and pieces of clothing.

Over the next few months the Germans took away twenty Jews, who were never heard of again. On mainland Britain the occupation was viewed with resignation. The islands were physically much closer to France than to their nominal mother country, and in outlook, too, they had a streak of independence that made them something other than purely British. The occupation was less threatening to most people than the German presence in the far north of France – whence the enemy would soon be hurling missiles that landed in Dover.

PART FOUR

July, Defending Britain

13

Ludwig and Decio on Board the *Arandora Star*

At the beginning of July, after an absence of nine months, Ludwig Baruch was back in Liverpool. But there were no fond reunions: as far as Hilda was concerned, her fiancé was still several hundred miles away in Devon. For Ludwig, home was a mirage that vanished as British soldiers marched him aboard what had been a luxury liner but was now painted battleship grey, its decks and lifeboats strung with barbed-wire.

Summer in Seaton had been almost pleasant as the camp settled into the season for which it had been built. Prisoners were allowed to bathe in the sea and the swimming-pool, which, during the icy winter, had been used for skating and 'target practice' – when they hurled the tins in which margarine was then packed at its frozen surface. Ludwig and his friends sat outside in the sun making camouflage netting, dug their vegetable patch, which yielded lettuces, radishes and tomatoes, or even swam in the sea. By the middle of June it was obvious that the internment camp was about to close.

One evening about three hundred names were read out, a mixture of Nazis, non-Nazis and Jews, and the men were told they must be ready to leave the following morning. They were permitted luggage weighing no more than fifty pounds; anything above this had to be stored at the camp. Matches and cigarette lighters were banned, which made many suspect they were about to be sent on a sea voyage. Some thought the war must be over and that those leaving were being extradited to Germany. If that was so, the prospect for those left in the camp was just as grim.

Ludwig, and the others who did not leave with the first group, were ordered to clean it and move into the huts nearest the main building. A few men sent some of their possessions to relatives for safe-keeping. Speculation continued to fly round the emptying camp: some thought they were being sent to the Isle of Man. On 29 June they were told they would be leaving the next morning. As their train set off from Seaton at 6 a.m. a camp officer told them not to worry. They arrived at Liverpool in the afternoon and waited on the pier, allowing Ludwig and other internees from the city a painful moment to savour the sights of home.

The *Arandora Star* had been built for the Blue Star Line by Cammell Laird at nearby Birkenhead – a further irony – in 1927. During the 1930s she was adapted into a luxurious floating hotel, which carried rich and famous passengers, such as George Bernard Shaw and the music-hall star Max Miller on cruises to see the midnight sun in Norway, the Mediterranean and the Caribbean. Her four hundred customers relaxed in deep leather armchairs, on parquet floors amid parlour palms, and ate in the Louis XIV-style dining room or danced across the ship's vast ballroom. Her white hull and red stripe earned her the nicknames 'Wedding Cake' and 'Chocolate Box', which were appropriate to a ship built with hedonism in mind.

At the outbreak of war the *Arandora Star* was on her way across the Atlantic. She set down her passengers in peaceful New York and headed for Falmouth to begin her transformation into a warship. The Admiralty considered fitting her with experimental anti-torpedo nets but by the summer of 1940 had abandoned the idea and sent her out to pick up soldiers and refugees on the run from the Nazis: troops and airmen stranded in Norway and then, in several cross-Channel dashes during which she dodged bombs and enemy fire, hundreds of refugees, British and Polish soldiers. On 1 July she was ready for her next job.

Ludwig and the others from Seaton filed on to the *Arandora Star* where the ship's doctor peered into their eyes for signs of trachoma, a highly infectious disease that causes inflammation of the inner eyelid. A steward allotted them cabins: two men in a single room, four in a two-berth cabin, but most in an airless, dark storeroom. As in the camps, the internees quickly worked out a system that suited them better, putting more men into the cabins so that no one had to endure the storeroom. Months of incarceration had shown them which social groupings worked best and Ludwig had a cabin with three Austrian Communists. The Nazis had held one, Karl Olbrisch, for four years and only released him after he signed a declaration that he would not take part in any anti-Fascist or Communist activities. He fled to Czechoslovakia where, in an irony that he found unbearable, the Communist Party expelled him because of the undertaking he had signed.

Their cabin commanded an ideal position on a level with the main deck and close to the exit to the forward part of the ship. It was the sort of exclusive accommodation that, under normal circumstances, Ludwig would never have chosen, even if he had been able to afford it. The internees and prisoners-of-war were ordered to stay below decks where he was struck by the chaos around him. He found few guards as he wandered around the ship, collecting an armful of lifejackets to take back to his cabin. Fitted with cork for buoyancy, they were dangerous for the uninitiated since they had to be put on *after* the wearer was in the water. They were rigid and fitted the torso in such a way that the upper body was unable to absorb the jolt of hitting the sea. If you jumped in wearing one, you risked breaking your neck.

From their luxurious cell Ludwig and his room-mates discussed what to do if the overcrowded ship was attacked or hit a mine. They decided their best course was to stay close to the German seamen with whom they had built up a relationship of trust at Seaton. The eighty-six or so PoWs recognised Captain Burfend of the *Adolf Woermann* as their leader. Ludwig kept his distance from the 734 Italians on board, Decio Anzani among them. As recent entrants to the world of internment, they were disoriented by their arrival in a society where Jews and Nazis were herded around by the same guards.

It became apparent later that Decio was on the *Arandora Star* by accident, that he had been rounded up 'in error' after MI5 had put his name on a list of dangerous Italians and Fascist sympathisers, which had been sent to internment camps. Commandants had twenty-four hours to identify anyone on the list and send them to

Liverpool. Later it was confirmed officially that at least twenty-six were the wrong men. An inquiry blamed these incidences of mistaken identity on the speed with which the men had been rounded up and, rather lamely, on the confusion caused by alternative spellings of Italian names. In a few cases it was suggested that some internees had paid fellow inmates to take their place on the ship.

The Italians who boarded the *Arandora Star* reflected the pattern of immigration to Britain. Dozens came from Scotland where for decades they had been tending the nation's sweet tooth with their ice-cream parlours and confectionery shops. A large contingent from London included pastry chefs and restaurateurs; a few practised more esoteric trades such as glass-blowing and mosaic work. MI5's list hid lives of quiet industry and devotion to family, as well as the occasional rebel and professional entertainer. Enrico Muzio, a forty-eight-year-old opera singer from Naples, lived in London and had performed at the Coliseum and for the BBC. Silvestro d'Ambrosio ran a restaurant and sweet shop in Hamilton, Scotland, and had lived in Britain for forty-two years. Of his ten children one had survived Dunkirk, another was in the Gordon Highlanders, a third served in the Canadian Expeditionary Force and two were registered for active service. Silvestro had applied for naturalisation three weeks before Italy entered the war but the paperwork had not been processed in time to save him from internment.

Alfonso Paolozzi's loyalties lay elsewhere. He had settled in Scotland with his Italian-born wife but each summer they sent their young son, Eduardo, to a Fascist youth camp in Italy. There, the boy whose sculpture would sit one day outside the British Library acquired a liking for uniforms, badges and aeroplanes. When Italy entered the war the family's ice-cream and sweet shop in Leith, near Edinburgh, was looted. Eduardo's father, maternal grandfather and uncle were all on board the *Arandora Star*. The sixteen-year-old Eduardo was interned in Saughton Prison for three months, and his mother and sister were forced to move away from the coast where, as enemy aliens, they were thought to pose a security risk.

The *Arandora Star*'s mercy dashes to Norway and France had rubbed off some of her glamorous sheen: the portholes and promenade decks were boarded up and sentries guarded the cabin gangways. Traces of a heady lifestyle remained in some of the fittings and in the ship's spacious ballroom, where some Italians bedded down on palliasses. Dinner was served on china plates; the food was the best the prisoners had tasted in nine months, and there was much more of it than the usual meagre rations.

During its time as a luxury liner the *Arandora Star* had carried a total of six hundred people, including crew; as a transportation ship, she had 1673 on board, of which 174 were officers and crew and 200 were military guards. Around 479 passengers were described as German interned males. On the whole the Italians were much older than the other passengers and the German PoWs were mainly sailors who were obviously more at home than most on a ship. The seamen might have been surprised by the lack of a safety drill or worried about the battered state of the lifeboats or that lifejackets were scattered around the cabins. If they had stopped to think about it, they would have realised that the twelve lifeboats – each with capacity for sixty – would leave a thousand people to fend for themselves.

The *Arandora Star* left Liverpool at 4 a.m. on Monday, 1 July, crawling forward in absolute darkness, all outer lights extinguished, the sentries silhouetted in the dawn. The ship had no escort for protection; it was not flying a Red Cross flag or giving any other indication that it was transporting PoWs. Instead it relied for protection on zigzagging its way west in an attempt to outwit any lurking U-boats. After lunch the ship passed the Isle of Man, where the wives of some of the men were interned, and headed north into the open Atlantic. It seemed clear now that they were on their way to Canada, which caused elation in some of the younger men, eager for a clean start in a new country, but despair for those who were leaving their families on the other side of an ocean-sized gulf.

In the evening a Sunderland flying-boat wheeled overhead as they passed the northern tip of Ireland. Beneath the calm water a famous German submarine was on its way home. The *U-47* had been responsible for one of the earliest outrages of the war when, a month after hostilities had begun, it slipped unseen into Scapa Flow in the Orkneys and blasted a hole in the side of HMS *Royal Oak*, killing more than eight hundred sailors. The disaster shattered Britain's sense of inviolability and confirmed the Nazis' reputation for treachery. Now the same submarine and its captain, Günther Prien, who had been decorated by Hitler, were on their way home to Kiel with one remaining, but damaged, torpedo.

Before they went to bed that night Ludwig and his friends tried to raise Olbrisch's spirits: he was deeply depressed at his expulsion from the Communist Party to which he had given so much of his life. When they finally fell asleep Ludwig and his cabin-mates, ever conscious that the ship was a floating target in the open sea, lay down fully clothed, apart from their shoes, heads on their lifejackets. Ludwig slept well, soothed by the ship's gentle movement and the distant hum of its engine.

Just before seven the following morning, when most passengers were still asleep, a huge boom thudded through the ship, lifting Ludwig a few centimetres off the floor. Throughout the *Arandora Star* prisoners and guards flicked light switches, which failed to respond. The ship was listing slightly to starboard. In the eerie silence that followed, thoughts turned to mines and torpedoes. Then . . . panic, muffled cries, an urgent, wailing alarm and hurried steps along the corridor. Ludwig had no doubt that the ship had been torpedoed and that he must get off the *Arandora Star* quickly. He led his cabin-mates along the corridor, feeling his way in the gloom. At the end he found a soldier in a tin hat, plimsolls on his feet, a bayonet fixed to the end of his rifle. He seemed shocked and confused, and when Ludwig asked him what he was doing he replied, 'Nothing.' Ludwig warned him that the ship, now listing at the stern, was sinking and that they had probably twenty minutes before it went down. He urged the soldier to leave his rifle and helmet, grab a lifejacket and jump, but the man insisted that he could not ignore his orders. In other parts of the ship prisoners were attempting to shake their guards out of the same dogged adherence.

They arrived outside blinking in the early-morning sunshine to scenes of chaos on the boat deck. Some lifeboats were already smashed or had capsized after passengers or inexperienced soldiers had tried to lower them over the side. When Captain Burfend and sailors from the *Adolf Woermann* arrived they managed to launch a few, but Ludwig decided that he and his friends had no hope of finding a space on them. Their only chance was to jump. Ludwig, with his mastery of both German and English, climbed on to the ship's bridge where he used the public-address system to try to persuade the frightened men to leave the ship and to tell them the safest way to jump. At the last minute, he returned to the deck where he started frantically to tear up anything that would float – seats, bits of wood, planks – and hurl it over the side, urging others to follow his example. Then, with time running out, he told his friends, 'You must get into the water.' No one moved. He explained to them that he would go first, that they should hold the lifejackets and jump into the sea on the port side as the ship was now taking water on its starboard. Then they must swim as quickly and as far away as possible from the struggling vessel. This last piece of advice was perhaps the most valuable. Despite her stricken state the *Arandora Star* was still drifting fast and it was important to be clear of her – not only to avoid injury but because a sinking ship sucks down with it anything nearby. Ludwig was probably unaware of how ships behave in their last moments but his instinct was sound.

As he jumped he left behind a ship in the grip of panic. No one had prepared for such a disaster and the armed guards, out-numbered but hidebound by orders, were unsure what to do. It was later claimed that soldiers fired on internees who were making for a lifeboat reserved for troops and that the same guards used an axe to cut the boat free when it was only half-way to the water, leaving the occupants to plunge to their deaths. Other soldiers undoubtedly saved lives by guiding the internees up the darkened stairs to the decks. There, however, they found rafts tied down with wire and no tools to free them. Barbed-wire and blocked entrances hampered escape and many men were caught in a nightmarish maze.

Hysteria broke out in many parts of the ship. The explosion had shattered lightbulbs and window-panes, and left a layer of broken glass in the dark corridors, some of which were rank with fumes from the blast. Many could not find their shoes and were forced to trample over the splinters so that they arrived on deck with bleeding feet, some still in their pyjamas. One young man returned below deck to look for his two brothers and eventually found them by using the family signal of whistling an extract from Beethoven's 'Pastoral' Symphony. Even in the most uncivilised situations culture came to the aid of the internees.

For some, particularly the old and infirm who had already experienced so much terror, this latest trial was unendurable. Many could not even scramble up the listing stairs to the higher decks, and others – mainly Italians – knelt in prayer. One man hanged himself. A sixty-two-year-old Jew sat in despair on his suitcase and could not be persuaded even to put on a lifejacket. Some men, ignorant of the risks, leapt into the water in their lifejackets and landed with broken necks, or unconscious, to float among the debris and those still alive in the water. Others would not let go of their suitcases and held them grimly as they jumped. One man, bizarrely, entered the water by executing a perfect swallow dive. Only the German PoWs behaved as if they knew what they were doing.

Ludwig was a strong swimmer, familiar with the natural buoyancy of salt water and landed deftly in the sea, which he was surprised to discover was not as cold as he had expected. The water was calm with a gentle swell, a light breeze and the suggestion of drizzle. He ploughed his way through it, dappled with sunshine, and the odd patch of oil. By the time the ship had drifted a few hundred yards away he had found an upturned deck seat with two metal buoyancy tanks underneath it and handles on both sides. He struggled to lift himself on to it but failed each time. Eventually a British soldier and two sailors joined him and by pinning down a corner each they managed to hoist themselves on to the seat. From there they bobbed up and down surveying the destruction before them, like a group of holidaymakers watching a game of quoits.

They could see the *Arandora Star*, its stern almost completely awash now and men darting about the decks. Then the bow tipped skywards and two great gashes appeared in her decks out of which smoke seeped. The ship appeared to stand on its stern, as if it were taking one final look at the earth, then slipped quickly below the waves. The movement sent the passengers bouncing down the tilting decks to be sucked under with the ship. Captain Burfend was among those still aboard.

The men sat on the bench in silence, each absorbed in his own thoughts, perhaps daring to wonder about the possibility of rescue. Ludwig was hungry, but otherwise felt well. His clothes were drying in the light wind, the water was calm; it was not cold. The ocean was scattered with debris, some with people attached to it, lifeboats and dead bodies; many men had been killed by pieces of wood hurled from the ship. The wreckage was drifting further away, covering a larger area of water. Prayers and cries floated on the air in different languages. In the overcrowded lifeboats people were being sick, from the movement of the ocean, the trauma of their experiences and the oil and water they had swallowed. Although they did not know it, they were 200 miles west of Scotland, and the nearest land was 125 miles to the south-east, the Bloody Foreland of County Donegal, overlooking the Atlantic.

After about three hours, at 9.30 a.m., a dark speck appeared in the sky and the noise of engines confirmed it was an aeroplane. The lifeboats fired distress flares and raised their oars to let the pilot know they were there. The Sunderland flying-boat dropped a message, 'Keep your chins up. Help coming,' with watertight packages of biscuits, chocolate, first-aid supplies, cigarettes and matches, which the *Arandora Star*'s one motor-boat gathered up and distributed among the survivors. The plane circled the area to assess their number and to make sure everyone had spotted it, then left.

In the early afternoon another dark spot appeared on the horizon. It was the seaplane accompanied by a destroyer, *St*

Laurent. Lifeboats rowed towards it while the ship's motor-boat scoured the sea. The crew of the flying-boat helped to hoist survivors aboard; many were bulky men, barely able to stand after hours in the open sea and coated with thick black oil. The *St Laurent* sailors gave them rum, cocoa, food and clothes, and helped them to wipe off the muck. Four men had died by the time they were hauled on board. An Austrian and a German doctor worked through the night to tend those who were struggling with the shock of their ordeal and, in particular, the effects of waiting nearly twelve hours, many in their night clothes, for rescue.

The *St Laurent*'s motor-boat picked up Ludwig and took him to the destroyer. He climbed a rope-ladder to the deck, where two sailors supported him under his arms and asked if he was all right. He said he felt quite fit and went below deck for a boiled egg, a beaker of cocoa, biscuits and a slice of bread. The younger men, like Ludwig, chatted with the sailors who made them feel – some for the first time – that they were part of the struggle against Hitler. Ludwig recognised one of the sailors as a Communist Party member from Bootle. He promised to let the Party know that Ludwig was safe.

The rescue mission was completed as quickly as possible: loitering in the open ocean was highly dangerous, especially as they did not know whether the U-boat that had sunk the *Arandora Star* was still in the area. As the ship filled with bedraggled survivors Ludwig searched for his cabin-mates; everyone was safe except Olbrisch who had made no attempt to flee but instead sat on deck as the ship went down. More than a hundred men from Seaton had been drowned.

The ship finally turned its back on where the *Arandora Star* had gone down and wove its way past Ailsa Craig, a rocky island off the Scottish coast, and up the Firth of Clyde to Greenock, just outside Glasgow. On the way Ludwig spotted another familiar face among the sailors. This time it was a man from Seaton, whose house Hilda and Ludwig's mother had stayed in during visits to him at the camp; the sailor had visited him too to pass on gifts. The ship arrived on the morning of Wednesday, 3 July; the following day

Britain's newspapers told the story of the disaster in a version that many of the survivors did not recognise.

The headline in *The Times* read:

```
Arandora Star sunk by U-boat
1,500 enemy aliens on board
Germans and Italians fight for lifeboats
Ship's officers on bridge to end
```

The accompanying story described the panic that ensued as the ship went down, especially among the Germans who 'thrust aside Italians in their efforts to reach the boats first'. Survivors, the report said, had 'terrible stories' to tell of struggles between Germans ('great hulking brutes') and Italians, 'in striking contrast' to the liner's captain and many of the ship's officers who stayed with the ship as she sank. Further interviews in the next day's papers stressed how 'but for the disgraceful panic by the Germans and Italians on board many more lives could have been saved'.

Renée, who had received a letter from her father a few days earlier postmarked the Isle of Man, heard news of the sinking on the radio. Since the report had said that the prisoners were all Nazis and Fascists she gave the item little thought; she had no reason to suppose that Decio might be on board. But after several days had passed with no further news from him, doubt crept into her mind, and Victorine decided to visit the Brazilian embassy, which had assumed the duties of its Italian equivalent in London.

Hilda was also consumed with worry and visited the Blue Star Line's offices in Liverpool. Staff said they could not help because Ludwig was an internee, not a paying passenger. The Home Office suggested that he had escaped. A few days after the sinking she wrote:

My darling Ludwig

I am writing to you in complete ignorance of your whereabouts and trying to make myself believe that even if you were on the 'Arandora Star', which I think is most probable, you are now quite safely back in England quickly recovering from shock! I cannot understand the callousness with which they refuse information about you and apparently refuse you permission to wire me – the suspense is terrible and I cannot get you off my mind – I have never before had such a disturbed mind, it would only take a few kind words from someone to make me cry very hard. I only hope that you have never seen the 'Arandora Star' and are quite contented and ignorant of the tragedy.

Good night darling – all my love and many kisses. I wish you were with me.

Your 'sweetheart, wife and secretary'

A postcard with the words 'L. Baruch safe' arrived just after she had finished the letter and allowed her to add a postscript telling him she knew he was alive. The Rev. J. R. McKenzie of Greenock, ignoring army instructions to the contrary, sent out this and similar notes to families of survivors he had helped care for.

When Ludwig managed to write to Hilda, he reassured her that he had not even caught a cold but hinted at the terror he had felt: 'Dont ask me to write much more about the disaster because the sights I witnessed were not fit for human eyes to see.'

Ludwig admitted that conditions at Greenock were cold and dirty, but he praised the local people for giving the prisoners food and cigarettes. The German and Austrian survivors were sent to an army camp near Edinburgh where they slept in tents and were well fed. Some obtained newspapers that allowed them to catch up on months of war news. They read unbelievable reports about the evacuation of Dunkirk, the fall of France and how the *Arandora Star*, carrying scores of undisciplined Nazis, was sunk despite the heroism of its crew.

They were given itchy, second-hand army clothes to wear – probably from the Great War – which had a huge red cross painted on them to indicate that they were not soldiers. Later Ludwig joked, 'We looked a real sight.' His one complaint was that the Edinburgh soldiers did not seem

politically as bright as the lads of the Clydeside with whom we were able to have some really good discussions and who treated us

anti-Fascists not as prisoners but as pals. In fact when they took us
to the camp the chap next to me (Guarding me?! The experiences
of the last few days have really proved to us how idiotic our
treatment really is) said to me on the bus: 'We [would] rather go
with you fellows, we don't feel comfortable with the Nazis!' Yes!
The dirty face of working class Clydeside has given us new
courage and hope after the dreadful experience in the Atlantic.
I hope we won't stay here long because there are no books, games
or sports facilities.

A week later Ludwig was back in Liverpool but, again, just
passing through. On the landing-stage he witnessed what he described as the 'most shameful episode of the internment saga'. In a
'frenzy of looting' troops brutally robbed about a hundred internees
of what valuables and little money they had managed to hang on to
after the sinking of the *Arandora Star*. The looting continued on
board the *Dunera* where Ludwig was one of 2600 prisoners. The
soldiers pounced on the luggage of those who had avoided the
Arandora Star and therefore still had cases. When the ship set sail
the prisoners were unaware they were heading for Australia.

Victorine did not expect to gather any news at the embassy but
went to make sure. She waited in a room while an official read out a
long list of several hundred known survivors. A second list followed
and if, as seems probable, it was read out in alphabetical order
Victorine would have heard her husband's name within minutes –
nineteenth in a list that numbered nearly five hundred dead. As no
records were kept of exactly who was sent on the *Arandora Star* the
number of victims remains unclear. However, it seems probable
that of the 734 Italians on board, around 446 died. Certainly they
were more vulnerable because of their age and infirmity. All three
members of Eduardo Paolozzi's family drowned. Ludwig put down
his survival to regular dips in the sea at Seaton.

Over the next few weeks several bodies were washed up near
Compton Mackenzie's home at Barra in the Outer Hebrides. One
was that of a young soldier serving in the Lovat Scouts who had
originally come from the island of Benbecula and whose body had

'drifted almost to his home'. Children found the body of the Neapolitan tenor on a long white beach, his business card damp but still legible. Locals wrapped his body in a sheet and laid it in the dunes surrounded by a driftwood fence. The wind 'herringboned the sand around him' as they guarded the site for three days and nights while they waited for instructions from London. He was eventually laid to rest at the ancient burial ground of Eoligarry near the ruins of three ninth-century churches. When the vice-chairman of the Italian Internees' Aid Committee wrote to Mackenzie asking for a description of the grave so that she could pass it on to the victim's relatives he replied: 'It looks across the sound to South Uist and the hill where Charles Edward met Flora Macdonald at midnight, and to the white beach at Eriskay where he landed first, himself a traveller from Italy. I think it would be difficult to find any place so full of peace after the woes and troubles of this century, and the sea as blue as an Italian sea.'

Renée never gave up hope that her father – as Herbert Morrison promised – would 'come walking down the street'. She fantasised about happy endings in which he had been washed ashore on some distant part of Ireland, made his way to Canada or was suffering from amnesia from which he would suddenly awake. In idle moments she sat on the settee she had positioned to give her a clear view of the street so that she would be the first to spot him when he came home.

14

Leonard Marsland Gander –
Family Life on the South Coast

Just before Chamberlain signed his fateful agreement with Hitler at Munich in September 1938, *Daily Telegraph* journalist Leonard Marsland Gander decided to move his wife and two children from their home in London to what appeared at the time to be one of the safest spots in Britain. Angmering-on-Sea, on the Sussex coast, possessed an intense quiet that he believed would protect his family from the fearful Blitzkrieg that was expected to hit London. By July 1940 it was plain that Gander had chosen exactly the wrong place for his safe haven. 'The nearer danger comes the less terrifying it seems,' he wrote in his diary, on 2 July 1940. 'At least that is how I feel after spending a few days on holiday in Britain's front line of defence . . .'

Gander was an old-school journalist. Sometimes he seemed bumbling and often opened a question disarmingly with 'This all seems crystal clear to everyone except me . . .' then went on to display an incisive knowledge of his subject. He was tall and gangly, and what little hair he had was fair. Before the war his job was to listen to German broadcasts and report anything newsworthy. Since he understood only limited German he asked two Poles and his secretary, Miss Henman, who had once worked in Berlin, to translate for him. As the war progressed Gander developed into a general reporter.

That summer he used the extra petrol allowed him as a journalist to commute between his offices in stifling, drab London to his family's second home, a bungalow between Littlehampton and Worthing. He watched as barbed-wire and Bren-gun emplacements sprang up to overshadow the tamarisks, planted to protect the coast from nothing more sinister than gales, and carefully nurtured palm trees, which gave the area a whiff of the Riviera. Angmering-on-Sea's residents gazed out over the Channel, a watery no man's land and the only barrier between the two warring sides.

The villagers adapted quickly to their new position on the front line and went about their business while studiedly ignoring their new neighbours, the Coldstream Guards, many of whom had recently returned from the other side of no man's land via Dunkirk. An elderly neighbour who lived twenty yards from the seafront with her terrier for company chatted to Gander over the garden gate about this and that, telling him about her family whom she described as 'pukka sahib'. She repeatedly asked him whether she should retreat inland. ' "I'd like to stay and see the Germans thrown out," ' she told him, 'as if she were talking about some shabby drunks at the village pub'.

The Defence Zone had been extended and now stretched as far as Selsey. Civilians were allowed to visit the shore but not between 5 p.m. and 5 a.m. and then found it transformed by the paraphernalia of war. When they went for a swim Gander's wife, Hilda, casually enquired whether he would prefer 'the machine-gun beach' or the 'anti-tank-gun beach'. The couple watched soldiers cavort in the waves until someone opened fire, forcing them to duck behind a breakwater. They emerged only when they saw the men dragging themselves out of the waves and realised that the burst of machine-gun fire was the equivalent of a dinner gong. Eventually they lost their fear and took a dip as machine-guns 'chattered away to right and left' and shells whined overhead. It was their last swim for some time: the next day the beach was put permanently out of bounds.

In a flurry of activity the soldiers burrowed their way into the coastline, knocking a hole in someone's front wall and popping up in numerous gardens. Some thirty soldiers perched on the roof of a large house that offered an ideal look-out post, and when Gander stumbled upon an anti-tank-gun emplacement he described the troops as looking 'for all the world like some new animal species hidden in their neat little nest. Even the entrance had been covered with branches to conceal these human rabbits from the mechanical hawks.' An encounter with a sergeant in battledress, who said he had had only three hours' sleep the previous night and had not removed his boots for three days, reinforced the image of the soldiers as hunted creatures. At the end of his walk Gander came across a camouflaged van with a vertical aerial sticking out of it; inside, a radio operator said good morning politely, then returned to his headphones and barked into his mouthpiece, 'Number one Charlie troop, fire.' There was a long pause, followed by a bang and a high-pitched whistle. Out to sea a column of black smoke rose against the horizon before a dull thud reached the shore. Two soldiers scanned the waves through an instrument mounted on a tripod and flying-boats swooped down on a floating target. Occasionally the scream of missiles pierced the air, and white puffs hung above the water.

The army moved locust-like through the area, tearing up anything that might obscure their view of oncoming tanks. When Gander went for a walk with his young sons, Julian and Nigel, he was shocked to see guards sawing down ornamental shrubs. The general in charge explained that he wanted a clear line of fire for his Bren gun. His troops complained that Angmering was deserted – meaning there were no girls to entertain them. Gander noticed that 'Since their experience of France and Belgium [they] are terribly "Fifth Column" conscious, needlessly so I think, for I am sure there aren't any here.' A few weeks later Gander was arrested for walking in what had become a prohibited area.

At about the same time the diplomat Sir Alexander Cadogan got lost near Benenden in Kent because there were no signposts to guide him; he was later arrested for straying on to the sands at Camber. Further east in Sissinghurst, Vita Sackville-West had noted, 'The only nice thing that comes out of the war is that we now have a guard on top of the tower. In a steel helmet and rifle he looks most picturesque in the moonlight over the parapet.' His ghostly silhouette would go some way to make up for the damage to her woods inflicted by tank exercises.

All along the south coast people peered at the sea through

barbed-wire, while soldiers disguised local pillboxes as chalets and tea stalls, and beach huts were torn up or filled with stones ready to block roads, or were used as ammunition dumps. Piers were mined, and locals and holidaymakers banned from sitting close to them; in some places it was no longer possible to saunter along the promenade. Ed Murrow noticed that unusual objects were cluttering the nation's seafronts. The buses, rusting cars and trucks, 'as though left by drunken drivers', were there to prevent the Germans using the wide, smooth esplanades as landing strips for aircraft.

As Gander returned from the coast to his London office his second-hand fourteen-horsepower Rover zigzagged its way round logs of wood, derelict cars filled with rubble and old railway sleepers, which reduced the traffic in places to single file. All over the south of England roads were turned into scrapyards as steam-rollers, tar barrels, tree-trunks and any other large debris was hauled into place, to stop German planes landing or to hamper foreign troops as they marched towards the capital.

In London General Raymond E. Lee, United States Military Attaché, described the crowds as drabber than ever: 'There is no colour of any sort. No bands. No flags and people seem to have let appearances go completely. The only exception is the doorman.' Even fashion was defensive, as those who could afford it took their helmets to the hatters to have a comfortable lining fitted; White's of Jermyn Street did the job for Lee. He complained that no one 'dressed' any more – meaning it was rare for anyone to wear evening dress. Uniforms were ubiquitous among both sexes. Lee noticed more women in jobs traditionally filled by men – they replaced waiters in clubs, drove cars and ambulances, worked as bus conductors, in factories and on the land.

Lee was forced to carry with him a large selection of documents: a National Registration Identity Card; an Alien's Certificate of Registration; an Official Pass and Identity Card, which marked him out as a foreign official; a permit to take photographs (aliens had been forced to hand over cameras and telescopes) and his ration card. As a diplomat he was allowed three times the amount of food as a British citizen, although no restaurant or club ever asked to see his ration book. Diners were expected to get by on just one lump of sugar and a thin shaving of butter; there were no iced cakes and fewer types of cheese. Several theatres had closed and hotels were short of guests.

On 15 July Lee wrote in his diary, 'I believe Hitler will attack this island with everything he has at any moment from now on. I also believe that if he is not successful by the fifteenth of September, he will never be.'

Many of Angmering-on-Sea's residents held similar views, as Gander recorded in his diary:

> I spend much time trying to persuade windy neighbours that the Jerries will not land here for the following reasons (a) the beach . . . with machine guns will be a death trap, (b) the roads don't lead anywhere in particular and are narrow and winding, (c) the Downs behind should be a barrier easily defended.

One morning, though, he feared he might be proved wrong:

> We were awakened just before dawn by a savage fusillade of machine gun and rifle fire. Was it invasion? Only a hundred yards away Brens were banging away. The bullets whipping the sea. Hilda nudged me urgently and asked me what we should do. I couldn't think of anything useful to do except to lie where we were and await developments. There was no artillery fire & no sound of aeroplanes so I concluded that it might after all be practice in the grey light. The fire grew desultory and rippled away along the coast, finally ceasing with a few cracks.

He was one of countless people who, confronted with the prospect of imminent invasion, decided to stay in bed.

Gander joined the local branch of the Home Guard as a 'weekender'; 150 volunteers shared fifteen uniforms and twenty ancient Lee Enfield rifles. A decade previously, he had spent his spare moments while working for *The Times of India* serving with the Bombay Light Horse Regiment. His Home Guard unit suggested he joined its mounted section; local riding schools would provide the horses, and guards would patrol the downs at night, trying not to stumble into rabbit holes.

The mounted section was unarmed and Gander decided that bluff might offer some protection. Miss Henman helped him to draw up a list of German phrases, each one designed to give the impression that the British held the upper hand: 'You are surrounded by a superior force. Surrender or you will be wiped out'; 'You are my prisoner'; 'I have you covered, surrender.' Gander confided to his diary that he could not work out whether the locals thought this crib sheet 'really useful or whether they thought I was mad'. Some Home Guard units and ARP stations kept a list of words designed to trip up a disguised German. The pronunciation test included: 'North Sea', 'clothes', 'tough', 'through', 'trough', 'buckle', 'throat', 'soothe', 'wrong', 'wretch', 'rats' and 'those'. Within a week the mounted section was disbanded due to problems with the supply of horses.

The regular Home Guard helped man roadblocks and Gander and Hilda were stopped four times in one night on their way home from the cinema in Worthing. But it was only at the final roadblock, controlled by a burly guardsman who had served at Dunkirk, that anyone thought to demand their identity papers.

In London fifty or sixty Americans who had ignored their government's advice to leave formed their own branch of the Home Guard, the First American Squadron. Where available, members wore the uniform of the British Home Guard with a red eagle shoulder-flash. The new squadron caused disquiet at the Foreign Office where civil servants felt its creation set a precedent that might allow other foreigners – such as the Japanese – whose home countries were 'neutral' to set up similar armed bands. Joseph Kennedy was said to have told a member of the squadron that their unofficial status would leave them liable to execution when the Nazis occupied the capital.

By the third week of July Gander had decided to take his wife and two boys back to London. Perhaps the south coast felt too much like a battleground. Bombs had fallen close to their bungalow and there seemed little sense in staying where they were just as vulnerable to aerial attack as they were at their principal home. Hilda referred euphemistically to the bombs as 'pennies from heaven' but they were both acutely aware of the danger that they and their children faced. They loaded the car with forty pounds of potatoes, beetroot, lettuces and turnips, and gave away their pet rabbit, Willie. 'The children are a turbulent and excitable couple,' Gander wrote. 'They look in much better health than when they went down to the bungalow a year ago. A pity that they have to be uprooted again.'

Most parents were consumed with fear for their children: how they were coping with the disruption of moving house or losing their father to the armed forces 'for the duration', how they would react to an air raid and what would happen to them if they suddenly became orphans – or Germans. 'They [the Germans] are carrying off little girls hardly older than Ellen and Claire to German brothels,' the novelist Margaret Kennedy wrote in anguish. At times parents' fears turned to fury that their children should plunge them into a pit of anxiety: 'Always before, in any trouble or anxiety, they have been an unfailing source of consolation,' Kennedy wrote. 'Now I can hardly bear to look at them. They are a sword in my heart.'

Mothers tortured themselves with what-ifs. What if they could not fit their baby's gas 'mask' – an all-encompassing sack with a manual pump that supplied air, and a window for the infant to peer through – in time? What if their husband was on fire-watch and they couldn't manage the pump? What if they never saw their evacuated child again or they were billeted with abusive strangers? Official advice placed the onus for children's safety firmly on mothers. A government poster showed an anxious woman sitting under a tree while her two happy children played with a toy plane; a city skyline is on the distant horizon while the ghostly figure of Hitler whispers in her ear, 'Take them back!' In case she has any doubt about the right course of action, the poster urges: 'Don't do it, mother – leave the children where they are.'

Mothers faced the agonising decision of whether to send their
children away to the apparent safety of the countryside. In this
poster the ghstly figure of Hitler tries to persuade the woman
to take her family back to the city.

While parents mouthed their fears above the children's heads or talked in a code that they believed only grown-ups could decipher, the stuff of adult nightmares became fodder for childish fantasies. Now that adults believed in spies, hunting one was great fun; stalking an old woman who in peacetime might simply have been seen as a witch assumed national importance, and gangs spent hours in their dens working out detailed plans of what to do when they captured a German parachutist. Following trails or identifying marks on trees was more satisfying because grown-ups had joined in with the game. Playing at soldiers meant shadowing the troops who drilled in the square, and the piece of wood you held against your shoulder in place of a rifle was curiously similar to the weapon Granddad took to his Home Guard meetings.

The fine weather made spotting aeroplanes easy and gave boys something to collect beyond scrap metal: shrapnel, still smouldering, if possible, and if they were really lucky, pieces of wrecked aeroplane. A Penguin book of aircraft silhouettes allowed spotters to become experts at recognising planes and judging their height above the ground. *Boy's Own* pandered to its readers' obsession by printing a list of slang words supposedly used by German airmen: an *Emil* was a young pilot; a *Friedensemil,* a peaceful *Emil* or old pilot; a young airman was a *Häschen* (literally 'young hare'); an ace was a *Kanone* (cannon); bombs were *Eier* (eggs) or *Zigarren* (cigars); a single-seater plane was a *Püppchen* (dolly). Now boys could gaze up at the sky and imagine what one *Emil* was saying to another as they dropped their *Eier*. Children filled their scrapbooks with cuttings such as 'Get your Nazi! We teach you how to use a rifle!' which suggested four firing positions, told readers how to load a magazine and warned against pulling, rather than squeezing, the trigger.

Children had no memory of the Great War or expectations of the horror that a new conflict would bring. To most, in 1940, war meant new games: fumbling in the blackout, sudden dashes to the air-raid shelters or gas-mask drill, in which they took care of their dolls in the same way that their parents and teachers protected them. It gave them new points of reference. An old vegetable could now be transformed into more than a potato man: a piece of paper and spent matchsticks would turn it into a paratrooper to launch from windows and the tops of stairs. They learnt the Morse code for vital acronyms such as RAF, ARP, AA (anti-aircraft) and ATS.

War brought disadvantages too: there were few sweets, and new toys were rare, but also kites were banned, in case they were used to signal to the enemy, and fireworks had to be handed in. But its paraphernalia and rituals presented children with endless possibilities for new amusements. If a mine washed up at the seaside it lent that beach kudos. The metal drum, which was so large that the member of the naval mine disposal unit sent to make it safe could only just straddle it, offered a wandering climbing frame that was relocated with each tide. They practised air-raid procedure in groups: one child emitted a high-pitched scream to mimic a bomb while the others threw themselves on to the ground in the recommended ARP position. An eight-year-old girl gave names to the sounds she heard from inside the comparative safety of her air-raid shelter: 'Powder Puff', 'Cracking Ronnie' and 'Humpty Dumpty' – the last representing the sound she imagined the nursery-rhyme figure would make as he slid off his perch. The war was a game with increasingly realistic special effects.

To children, Hitler was not so much a bogeyman as a swear word. When one young boy was scolded he retaliated by marching down the street giving the Nazi salute and shouting, 'Heil Hitler! I shall do all the wairst things in the wairld. Heil Hitler!' rather as children now attempt to break taboos by using forbidden words. Hitler was a cartoon villain to rival the Joker, the 'Jee-stay-po' (Gestapo) his evil gang. When Britain attacked French battleships at Oran, on the Algerian coast, to stop them falling into German hands most adults were shocked by the loss of nearly 1300 lives. Children, though, reduced the tragedy to a simple minus score for the enemy. Margaret Kennedy overheard two of her children acting out a scene in which Goebbels tells Hitler about the disaster:

'Bring me my carpet that I may bite it.'

'Which flavour, *mein Führer?*'

'Lemon, Joe. And I'll have a nibble at the raspberry rug.'

As Gander and his family returned to London they seemed to be journeying deeper into the battlefield rather than leaving it behind. A lorry carried an RAF plane; the fuselage and its wings, which were folded back like a wounded bird's, were riddled with bulletholes. At the Kingston bypass they noticed peculiar objects 'like galvanised iron chimney pots'. 'Are they making a sort of Siegfried line as London's last defence?' Gander wondered. 'An ancient Morris car filled with earth seems a feeble, inefficient means of defence . . . incredibly crude and messy by comparison with a battleship or a Spitfire.'

When he paid a brief visit to Angmering-on-Sea he found it 'practically deserted'. 'It is a curious state of affairs for the height of the holiday season. All the shopkeepers are in despair and wondering how they can possibly pay their rates.'

East Anglian seaside towns were in equally desperate straits. On 28 July a curfew was introduced between one hour after sunset and one hour before sunrise in a five-mile-wide coastal strip, excluding major towns and villages. In peacetime, workers from boot factories in the Midlands flocked to west Norfolk for their annual break and it was difficult for a chance traveller to find a spare bed; now the resorts were deserted. One hotelier cheekily promoted Hunstanton, which looks out on to the Wash, as a 'west coast' resort to fool visitors into thinking it was less exposed than other East Anglian towns. By mid-July half the population of East Anglia's coastal towns and two-fifths of Kent's had left, shrinking away from the Defence Zone as the sea and sand had attracted holidaymakers during peacetime. The evacuation was disastrous for the local economy and transformed buzzing resorts into ghost towns; the population of Folkestone shrank from 46,000 to 6000 in just a few weeks. Councils had fewer residents from whom to collect rates, and those who remained were slow to pay. In desperation, Hunstanton's asked its bank for a two-thousand-pound overdraft. Railway stations, which usually transported carriages full of trippers, reminded passengers that the seaside had lost its monopoly on summer fun. Notices warned that more than seven hundred destinations were out of bounds for 'holiday, recreation or pleasure'.

J. B. Priestley captured the sadness of the abandoned seaside resort when he visited Margate and broadcast his impressions in a *Postscript* on Sunday, 14 July:

> Everything was there: bathing pools, bandstands, gardens blazing with flowers, lido, theatres, and the like; and miles of firm golden sands all spread out beneath the July sun. But no people – not a soul. Of all those hundreds of thousands of holidaymakers, of entertainers and hawkers and boatmen – not one. And no sound – not the very ghost of an echo of all that cheerful hullabaloo – children shouting and laughing, bands playing, concert parties singing, men selling ice-cream, whelks and peppermint rock, which I'd remembered hearing along this shore. No, not even an echo. Silence. It was as if an evil magician had whisked everybody away. There were the rows and rows of boarding-houses, the 'Sea Views' and 'Bryn Mawrs' and 'Craig-y-dons' and 'Sans Soucis' and the rest, which ought to have been bursting with life, with red faces, piano and gramophone music, and the smell of roast beef and Yorkshire pudding, but all empty, shuttered, forlorn.

An anonymous poem in *Punch*, which appeared on 7 August, gives a less sentimental description of the transformation:

> At England's many beaches, from Tweed to Lulworth Cove,
> Among the chines at Bournemouth and the stately streets of
>   Hove,
> On the sunny strands of Margate and beneath the Palace Pier
> We have made our preparations for the guest who'll soon be here.
> For we'll give the Hun a holiday,
> A bumper summer holiday
> At England-by-the Sea.

There'll be lots of deep-sea bathing
(how we hope they all can swim!)
With a paddling-pool for Goering if we catch a glimpse of him;
There'll be donkey-rides for Goebbels, and a restful pleasure-trip
For Admiral Raeder's navy in a British battleship.

There'll be shies and shooting galleries, with prizes to be won,
Each bullet-head a bull's eye, every coconut a Hun,
And the Grand Illuminations will delight each Nazi eye
As the Heinkels fall like Catherine-wheels and light the English
    sky.

There are boarding-houses waiting for the few who care to stay,
With barbed-wire mottoes round the door and bayonets all the
    way;
While for those the fun has wearied,
Who have spent their early zest,
We have six feet of British earth for their eternal rest.
Oh, we'll give the Hun his holiday,
An unexpected holiday,
A short but crowded holiday
At England-by-the-Sea.

Exactly when Hitler would launch his 'holiday' in Britain was a
key talking point; most people had a set day in mind. Alan Brooke,
one of Churchill's most experienced generals who on 19 July
would replace Ironside as commander-in-chief, Home Forces,
had already started to tour the south of England to ascertain
the country's readiness. He was horrified by what he found and
on 2 July wrote in his diary:

The more I see the nakedness of our defences the more appalled I
am! Untrained men, no arms, no transport, and no equipment.
And yet there are masses of men in uniform in this country but
they are mostly untrained, why I cannot think after 10 months of
war. The ghastly part of it is that I feel certain that we can only
have a few more weeks left before the Boche attacks!

Harold Nicolson's fears of an invasion became most acute after the second weekend in July. His unease was based on several factors but the fine weather, so necessary for a sea crossing, the alignment of the stars (Hitler was a keen follower of astrology) and a 'goodish gibbous moon', which would guide the Nazi bombers and navy, were the most important. On 20 July he reported: 'How strange it all is! We know that we are faced with a terrific invasion. We half-know that the odds are heavily against us. Yet there is a sort of exhilaration in the air.'

Joseph Kennedy was vociferous in his belief that Britain would be beaten by the end of July; when this deadline passed, he revised his estimate to the middle of August. On 26 July Virginia Woolf recorded: 'Invasion may be tonight: or not at all . . .' Newspapers and magazines wrote wistfully about the 'land we are fighting for' and revisited previous moments when the country had been threatened with invasion, making repeated allusions to Julius Caesar, the Spanish Armada, which God had dispersed by sending bad weather just as He had kept the sea calm for the evacuation of Dunkirk, and Napoleon. *Punch* depicted Hitler dressed as a Roman emperor looking greedily across the Channel at England, and editorial writers scoured history books for heroes who had saved Britain in the past, from Nelson to Hereward the Wake, who had taken on the most recent successful invader, William the Conqueror.

Cinema-goers relived their victorious past in films such as *Mary Queen of Scots*, while the short propaganda film produced by the GPO Film Unit, *Britain at Bay*, opened with sweeping shots of haymaking and waves lapping at beaches that had remained inviolate for more than a thousand years. These traditional scenes were now under threat, as J. B. Priestley's familiar voice told audiences: 'The future of the civilised world rests on the defence of Britain.' A country that had seen off Napoleon could do it again and, to drive home the message, a tin-hatted soldier waits defiantly by the coast, his bared bayonet glistening in the sun.

Churchill, too, was using Elizabethan rhetoric to inspire the country to rise to an historic challenge:

Should the invader come to Britain, there will be no placid lying down of the people in submission before him, as we have seen, alas, in other countries. We shall defend every village, every town, and every city. The vast mass of London itself, fought street by street, could easily devour an entire hostile army; and we would rather see London laid in ruins and ashes than that it should be tamely and abjectly enslaved. I am bound to state these facts, because it is necessary to inform our people of our intentions, and thus to reassure them.

At around the same time Hitler was drawing up a secret memo, Directive No. 16, 'Operation Seelöwe [Operation Sealion]' in which he put forward plans for an amphibious attack on Britain. In this early draft he envisaged a surprise assault on a broad front stretching from Ramsgate to just west of the Isle of Wight. He recognised that the assault could only go ahead if a number of factors were in place. One of the most important was that the RAF had been 'neutralised' – both numerically and in terms of morale – so that it offered no resistance to an invasion. Sea lanes had to be cleared of mines and the Royal Navy pinned down in the North Sea and – with the help of the Italians – in the Mediterranean. He ordered that preparations for invasion should be completed by mid-August.

15

The Defence of Southern England –
Jenny, Muriel and Frank

One of the sights that soldiers trapped on the coast of northern France remembered most vividly was the great palls of black smoke. At Dunkirk it belched out of the burning oil refineries and at Boulogne oil from a stricken tanker seeped into the water to produce a lake of fire that sent up a curtain of thick smoke. For those lucky enough to return to Britain, the results of this elemental clash remained seared in their minds.

In July 1940 Geoffrey Lloyd, secretary for Petroleum, told one of his staff, Donald Banks, that if the Germans invaded, the destruction of Britain's petrol stocks must be a priority. He added that the act of wiping out the country's fuel reserves might also provide a way to eliminate some of the invaders or, to use a popular phrase of the time, they might be able to 'take a few Germans with them'. The job of the Petroleum Warfare Department, set up on 9 July 1940, was to create ingenious ways of using Britain's fuel stocks as a fearsome new weapon to repulse the invader. Its scientists dreamt of encircling Britain in a protective fiery ring of biblical proportions. Failing that, they hoped at least to cause the Germans some discomfort as they fought their way inland from Britain's beaches. 'The whole thing according to the normal rules was a "foul",' Banks wrote later.

But the normal rules no longer applied. At the end of June Churchill requested a report on the possibility of using poisonous gas and other chemical weapons if the Germans invaded. He wanted to know whether any could be dropped as bombs or fired from guns, and what stocks Britain held. Alan Brooke had also decided that he was prepared to use mustard gas to defend Britain's beaches.

While the reality of gassing or burning the enemy was gruesome, Banks and his department preferred to cast themselves in a more romantic light. Like many people in the summer of 1940, he and his department instinctively fell back on the Elizabethan era for inspiration. Sir Francis Drake's ploy of 'singeing the King of Spain's beard' by setting fire to the Spanish fleet in Cadiz harbour made him the perfect role model; Britain was cornered once more and instinctively she waved a flame in the face of her enemy.

Over the next few months grown men were encouraged to play with fire. In the tranquil setting of a Scottish loch scientists set a small boat burning in a bid to create a wall of flame but quickly discovered how hard it was to control the blaze while it was alight and then to stop it going out. In other experiments they primed revolving lawn sprayers with petrol to scatter their surroundings with flames and, in a deadly form of Pooh Sticks, sent lighted fuel floating down a river at Moody's Down, in Hampshire, in an attempt to reach pontoon bridges further downstream. They were forced to abandon their tests because of the effect on fish stocks.

The department considered how best to bother enemy aircraft as they landed on British airfields and decided that sending flaming, unmanned cars hurtling towards them would be most offputting. They tried out this idea at Hendon airfield by filling twenty specially adapted vehicles, their front doors removed and steering-wheels locked into position, with just enough fuel to carry them half-way across the airfield. The test run quickly turned into a farce and nearly ended in tragedy. Once the cars were on their way they veered to the right and some rolled over; one almost hit an aeroplane donated to the war effort by the people of Jamaica. The scientists were forced to continue their experiments on a remote farm in Hampshire where they tried out an anti-aircraft device that could throw flames 300 feet into the air.

Another device, the 'Flame Trap', aimed to give the invader a warm welcome as he arrived on Britain's beaches. It was the Home Guard's job to ignite the trap by hurling a Molotov cocktail at a hidden petrol tank, which would send fiery fuel down a series of perforated pipes concealed on either side of a sunken road, narrow bridge or gorge and on to the Germans. Scientists experimented with the trap at Dumpton Gap, in Broadstairs, Kent, at a spot between Dover and Canterbury, in Devon and in Cornwall.

All of these experiments were highly dangerous. Sappers were blown up by beach mines during trials and there must have been other casualties who eluded public scrutiny because the press was censored. Often scientists allowed their enthusiasm to blind them to potential dangers. A Dr Bourdillon took the precaution of donning asbestos waders to paddle through fuel that had been set alight only to discover that the massive heat caused his trousers underneath to burst into flames; frantic colleagues debagged him to save his life. Apart from the danger to the participants, the unexplained fires and lights in the sky must have terrified local people and led to many false alarms, which had nothing to do with the enemy.

Among the outlandish Heath Robinson devices dreamt up by the Petroleum Warfare Department, one stood out as a weapon that might just cause the invaders a few problems. Tens of thousands of metal drums were camouflaged and, in groups of four, dug into banks and hedgerows along the south coast. The Royal Engineers and members of the Home Guard who installed the 'flame fougasses' chose points where traffic slowed – on hills, at roadblocks or sharp bends – so that, once detonated, the drums would discharge their deadly cargo of forty or fifty gallons of petrol, oil and rubber on to a German tank as it laboured along. The flame fougasse only became useful – and highly dangerous – when the Home Guard fitted a charge, which would take place when strictly necessary so that children and animals could not set it off by accident. Until then the barrel sentries waited, concealed and rusting, deep in the undergrowth.

The Petroleum Warfare Department's ultimate dream of setting the sea alight was fulfilled only briefly. But although the feat went no further than the experimental stage, news of the spectacular blaze, perhaps glimpsed by German aeroplanes on sorties to the south coast, ignited rumours that sped round the rest of Europe. It was a major propaganda coup and one of the few occasions on which the British were believed to have devised a devastating new weapon. Soon Germans were rumoured to be placing large orders for asbestos suits to wear when they crossed the Channel.

While generals saw flame and flood as part of their armoury of defence, ordinary Britons became preoccupied with nature and the hidden messages it seemed to offer. The summer of 1940 is remembered as endless days of perfect sunshine and cloudless skies but this is not entirely true. Perhaps people perceived it to have been so because their senses were heightened – or because the country, which the glorious weather showed to its best advantage, was at risk.

Like so much else in 1940, meteorology was subject to government scrutiny to prevent the Germans using it to their advantage when planning bombing raids. People who had lived through unusual weather conditions waited a fortnight to read of their experiences in the newspapers; another British staple – discussing the climate – joined the list of rationed goods. A radio reporter was not allowed to say that his view of the Oxford and Cambridge Boat Race had been obscured by strong sunshine and a newspaper could not reveal that a football match had been postponed due to frost – it was simply 'off'. The wind never blew down trees: they fell of their own accord. Cyclists skidded – but never on wet roads. Ice-skating was mentioned weeks after it had taken place.

The blackout brought the night sky closer, allowing many people – especially those in cities – to appreciate its beauty for the first time. The moon, anonymous to most since childhood, once again assumed a personality. Newspaper readers, deprived of weather forecasts, became preoccupied with its phases. Mollie Panter-Downes reported, 'Everyone echoes Bottom in *A Midsummer Night's Dream*: "A calendar, a calendar! look in the almanac; find out moonshine, find out moonshine".' At first the moon was seen as a boon: it helped stumbling pedestrians in the blackout. Then it became sinister: a 'bomber's moon' which guided the Luftwaffe to their target, or helped the invasion force find their way to Britain. The actor Anthony Quayle, who served as a gunner on the south coast, was caught up in a false alarm in which a soldier mistook the rising moon for a fire presaging the start of the invasion.

General Lee noted in his diary, 'I wonder if Churchill, too, watches the almanac and suspects the moment of the waxing moon and the high tide.' The American reporter Ben Robertson detected a direct link between the phases of the moon and the level of nervousness: 'As the moon got full, the tension increased throughout the island – the Germans had bombed Boulogne during the full moon of June; during the full moon of July they would bomb London. Gradually the July moon swelled – big and yellow, it was like a full moon in America, yellow like the moon over Miami.' His chambermaid at the Waldorf, conscious of Hitler's belief in the stars, had bought an astrological chart and was consumed by anxiety when someone at Covent Garden's fruit and vegetable market told her that Venus would soon be in conjunction with the moon and Hitler's star sign.

For those who lived by the sea the tides became as ominous as the moon that governed them; just as moonlight might guide German aircraft to Britain so the waves threatened to sweep a fleet of troop-bearing ships on to the beaches. In Snettisham, after a week of nightly air-raid warnings, Muriel recorded on 1 July that yesterday had been the day the schoolmaster knew the invasion would take place because it was the highest tide of the year. 'I thought about it several times yesterday but it didn't come off,' she added.

Life had reverted to a waiting game but Britons knew now what they were waiting for. The boredom of the Phoney War reappeared – but this time the tedium was tinged with fear. There was no doubt of what Hitler planned: in overrunning six countries in three months he had shown his hand. Britain's priority was defence, which meant converting as many men as possible into soldiers. 1940 was a peak year for recruitment: in June and July the call-up age rose to thirty-four so that by 1 July half of all males between the ages of twenty and twenty-five, and a fifth of the male population between sixteen and forty were in the armed forces. Everyone knew someone who had been called up or volunteered, and bombing was now a reality, not a vague possibility. The novelist Margaret Kennedy watched the soldiers drilling in

Housewifes manned the 'Kitchen Front' and were told to recycle waste to help the war effort. Most household metal, though, was not good enough to use in aircraft production.

Cornwall: 'I realise that I have never before seen soldiers on ground where they expect to have to fight. I have only seen them training, on leave, on parade, never on a potential battle-field.'

Jenny and Muriel spent more and more time with their schoolmaster friend, who had been called up. He had become a more interesting companion since they had discovered he was not engaged to be married. He took them both to see *The Wizard of Oz*, telling them – a little ungallantly – that it was cheaper to take them together since he would only have to pay for his ticket once. In wet weather he taught them to play bridge and they went often to the shore but found it less fun now that, like Hunstanton, it was deserted. At their 'beach house' they sorted through oddments of aluminium and scrap metal, anything from pots and pans to old bathroom taps and coat-hangers, for Lord Beaverbrook's 'Saucepans for Spitfires' appeal. 'Send your pans flying', his posters read, and assured housewives that five thousand could be converted into a fighter plane, while twenty-five thousand made a bomber. In reality none of the nation's cooking utensils got into the air: such a low-grade metal would hardly have kept a tin soldier airborne, let alone a fighter plane. The sisters were more sceptical of the government's other posters, particularly the 'Go to it!' campaign, which was meant to inspire the population to 'do their bit'. Although the simple slogan was generally well received, some people found it meaningless and 'What is *it?*' was scrawled on a few posters.

Matthew had virtually given up work and spent his whole morning cleaning, then showing off, his 'parashot gun'. 'Everyone else about here seems bored to death with their enforced leisure too,' Jenny wrote. Even long cycle rides failed to take their minds off the war. At Sandringham they noticed that a three-mile common on the king's estate had been given over to wheat and when Muriel sheltered in a church with the schoolmaster they were shocked to find the name of the village clearly visible, 'so any Nazi landing by parachute could have found out'.

They sensed that a stage in their lives was ending. They discussed moving but decided that, although some places might feel less vulnerable to invasion, most areas risked being bombed. They resolved to leave Snettisham if their *ennui* had not lifted by the autumn and wondered about going to a big town, somewhere like Shrewsbury. In the meantime, they decided to attend a week-long Workers' Educational Association (WEA) summer school at King's College, Cambridge. Their mother protested that she was too frightened to be left alone but they insisted on snatching what they thought might be their last chance to go. As a result, relations between Susan and her daughters became 'very strained'. Some of their older neighbours were convinced the Germans were poised to attack and suffered from acute 'nerves'. 'Mr B. says invasion is certain tomorrow. Several people think so. He brought a *Daily Mail* to show us and is quite scared,' Jenny wrote on 18 July.

'Nerves' were a common problem in the summer of 1940 and people felt 'windy' at the thought of 'it' – the invasion. After the fall of France many Britons complained of acute stomach pains; one person likened the sensation to having their organs removed. Tempers were short and people spoke in euphemisms or tiptoed round certain subjects in case an unguarded comment caused a friend or colleague to crumble. The BBC's Home Service tried to soothe nerves with advice on how to avoid 'overstrain' at a time of long working hours and cancelled holidays. It gave tips on ways to relax even if you could only fit in a break of fifteen or twenty minutes. In another broadcast a medical psychologist discussed how to deal with 'faintness of heart', which meant cowardice.

Insomnia was rife but asking a doctor to prescribe sleeping pills presented a dilemma. Should you risk reliance on medicines that might soon be in short supply? Or did it make sense to take the pills while they lasted and stockpile sleep – like the tins of sardines hidden at the back of the pantry – 'before the balloon went up'? Sleep frequently brought torment. Margaret Kennedy suffered from a recurring nightmare in which her home was hit by a gas attack but she was unable to find the nozzles for her children's gas masks. She was surprised that no one she knew dreamt of Hitler and speculated that this might be because their fears were no longer suppressed. Once the bombing intensified, going to bed became a source of dread, rather than a refuge.

Some people found solace in religion. As a poster outside an Oxford church put it, 'If your knees knock, kneel on them.' The BBC started its early-morning broadcast with what Vera Brittain described as 'lugubrious prayers for courage and a little hortative sermon in a Scottish accent . . .'. Vicars found themselves impaled on a moral cleft stick. Parts of their congregation felt uncomfortable praying for victory since they knew that Germans were making the same request and they did not want to 'put the Lord into an awkward position'; instead they preferred something vaguer, such as asking that both countries be delivered from Nazism. Other believers wanted nothing less than the annihilation of the enemy.

The confusion over how to refer to the Germans showed itself most sharply in the controversy over a radio report broadcast on Sunday, 14 July (see pp. 215–16). In it Charles Gardner described a dogfight over the Channel with all the breathlessness of a sports reporter giving a blow-by-blow account of a boxing contest. Listeners were divided over this new approach to war reporting, which made them feel like ringside observers. Some, like Vere Hodgson, declared it 'jolly good', and added that she only wished she could hear the Italian fleet being sunk. She did not think it fair to castigate Gardner: 'It is a game to these Boys – a deadly game – but if it were not, it could not be borne.' The *Lynn News* called it a 'revolting broadcast' and deplored Gardner's 'whoops of joy'. Perhaps the intrusion of the reporter's personality was responsible for the shock many listeners felt. Following the evacuation of Dunkirk, BBC announcers, who had previously maintained a stiff-upper-lipped anonymity, had started to introduce themselves by name so that their audience could identify them and would know if an impostor had hijacked the airwaves.

The two National Days of Prayer – the first during the evacuation from Dunkirk, the second to take place in the first week of September – had helped to fill churches. The BBC published *Each Returning Day*, which offered prayers 'relevant to present issues'

and included some 'for a quiet mind'. George Beardmore, the
BBC engineer, took comfort from a church in Baker Street that
kept a Bible open at a passage from the Psalms: 'I will lift up mine
eyes unto the hills from whence cometh my help', although he
wondered which hills the Psalmist meant and 'whether he had a
German blitzkrieg followed by an invasion in mind'.

Others turned to less traditional forms of help. The Canadian
diplomat Charles Ritchie described how an otherwise 'shrewd
woman' had consulted a fortune-teller before deciding whether or
not to send her children across the Atlantic. The government
employed an astrologist to analyse the birthdates and -places of
top German officers in case he could detect a day that Hitler –
who believed in horoscopes – might consider propitious for
invasion.

Jenny and Muriel did not refer to religion in their diaries, but
preparation for their summer school in Cambridge provided them
with a useful distraction. Before they went they had to write an
essay on 'Hitler aims at conquest; Stalin at security. Do you agree?'
Jenny became so caught up in the historical background that she
forgot to mention the war she was living through. When they
packed they took more clothes than were strictly necessary in case
the invasion started. Muriel was particularly pleased that the
schoolmaster had decided to go with them.

They had stopped getting up for night air raids but instead tried
to sleep through them. Their mother, however, remained desperate to know where each bomb had dropped. Towards the middle
of June, East Anglia and the Midlands experienced frequent
bombing raids but as the summer wore on their range and intensity
spread throughout the country and by the end of August the joke
that people went to London for a good night's sleep had lost its
currency.

The attacks had been anticipated for so long that when the
bombs started to fall they relieved the tension, although widespread bombing was believed to herald an invasion, as it had in
France. One elderly woman was supposed to have said that the
raids helped to take one's mind off the war. Although the remark

was almost certainly apocryphal, the sentiment was accurate: every all-clear that sounded brought a rush of relief. Home Intelligence reports for the Ministry of Information found that morale was highest in areas that had been bombed, that the mood was one of 'growing exhilaration'. The RAF, whose reputation had been dented by their apparent lack of involvement in the evacuation of Dunkirk, were transformed into dashing heroes whose exploits were clearly visible in the battlefield above the nation's heads. Their dogfights became a deadly game: 'Biggest raid ever. Score 78 to 26. England still batting,' read one newspaper vendor's board, the style similar to Gardner's unorthodox broadcast.

When Britons were not hiding in the ground, their heads swivelled skywards to watch the antics above them. The best way to follow the dogfights – and the one officially frowned on – was to lie on your back in the grass whence the planes looked like 'little white lice'. 'The world,' Margery Allingham wrote, 'hummed with planes all day like bees in a lime tree.' George Beardmore compared this period to the plague years when death had also arrived in the air, and one woman felt so vulnerable in her house that she did her ironing outside wearing a tin hat. The bomber was far from an impersonal assassin: as he waited for the attack Beardmore imagined a German pilot high above Southampton, his world illuminated only by the stars and his instrument panel.

Ears became attuned to the difference in engine noise between German and British aeroplanes. According to Vera Brittain, the enemy bomber had a 'heavy, massive hum, quite different from the lighter, more casual-sounding British machines'; it reflected the gulf between the Teutonic and Anglo-Saxon temperaments. Others were more specific: the Hun engine, a Mass-Observation diarist insisted, repeated one stressed note followed by an unstressed one – 'Pumph-er, Pumph-er.' Margaret Kennedy was adamant that a German bomber made a 'zoomzazoomzazoomzazoomza' noise, while the British equivalent said, 'zoomzoomzoom'.

While Jenny and Muriel had become blasé about their safety, they were susceptible to the rollercoaster of emotions that rocked their village as tragic – often unreliable – news reached them about the local young men who had joined the armed forces. Muriel was 'very sorry' to spot a photograph in the newspaper of one of her earliest 'flames', who was now reported missing. 'I have hardly seen him for two years but I remember today sentimental moments of when I was fifteen. He was sweet then and such a boy to be dead. I hope he is not.' Three weeks later she discovered that he was a prisoner-of-war.

Two days later, the holiday-camp proprietor, a family friend, arrived with tears in his eyes to tell her that his son, Norman, who had been with the BEF, was dead. He was one of two brothers; the other was a merchant sailor. 'It seems terrible to be born a man,' Muriel wrote in her diary. She found it difficult to push Norman out of her mind. 'It is only a month since he rushed in the garage calling "Where's my girls?" and hugged us both and told us about his French "tart". He boasted he wouldn't mind going back fighting although he hadn't slept properly for a month . . .' The next day later she was dragged out of her maudlin reverie when Norman's father 'rushed in so happy' to tell them they had received a letter from him saying he was quite safe and had been reported missing, presumed dead, 'after a narrow escape'. 'I am glad and could have cried for joy when his father told us,' she wrote.

The armed forces provided a constant backdrop to their lives. Jenny knitted a frock for the baby of a friend whose husband had been killed in the RAF in November and, less charitably, the sisters moved their chickens from the beach because they suspected soldiers were stealing their eggs. Fresh eggs, rather than the powdered substitute, were becoming rare: 'We are depending on these chickens to save us from starvation,' Jenny wrote melodramatically.

While new recruits, often far from home or a decent-sized town, were desperate for a diversion from barrack-room routine, their commander-in-chief, Home Forces, Alan Brooke, was still scuttling round the country checking Britain's defences and wringing his hands at the lack of preparedness. Even high-ranking soldiers were unsure how to deal with an invasion: it did not appear in their manuals and the British Army had no recent experience of it. On 10 July Alan Brooke was in the south-west where he was 'not at all impressed' by the man in charge of Exeter. Two days later he was writing to request that the man in command of the south-western area should be removed from his post. 'He is too old and lacking in drive ever to make a job of the defence of Devon and Cornwall,' he confided to his diary. Then he was off to Lulworth Cove, Swanage, Studland Bay, Sandbanks, Bournemouth and the Solent, where he concluded, 'All work going well, but beaches very lightly held.'

Eventually he turned his attention to the defence of London. He visited the Cabinet War Rooms, hidden deep beneath the streets of Whitehall, where he knew he would be based with Churchill, should the Germans invade. Afterwards he dined with the prime minister, who wondered whether Britain had been in such dire straits since the Armada. On 22 July Brooke reported, 'I must say that it is very hard to see where we are heading for, but I have implicit faith in God that whatever happens it is for the good of mankind in the long (and perhaps distant) run.' The next day he flew to the north-east where he was impressed by the defences; later he took the night mail to Edinburgh, where he discovered the 46th Division in a 'lamentably backward state of training'. He finished July by inspecting East Anglia's beach defences from the Wash to Yarmouth.

While Brooke was zigzagging round Britain, Gunner Frank O'Brien was still languishing in Hampshire. At the beginning of July he had told Mary that he guessed the battery might move off within a week but had no idea where to.

> Things are still the same here. I am on guard every day of the week its pretty miserable. I don't even get to the pictures I think I'll go crazy if I stay here any longer. I have very little time to myself. My leisure hours are spent cleaning my kit. Sometimes I wish I was back in France. I had a better time over there. Although the battery was in great danger, you have no idea what like the life [*sic*] in England is. Its PAR BON.

With time on his hands Frank subjected his relationship with Mary to intense scrutiny: 'I often wonder what will happen to

Harry and I after this war is over,' he wrote to her. 'I suppose both of us will get married and settle down. How would you like to marry a crazy guy like me Mary?' In the same letter, he picked away at the gnawing jealousies experienced by couples all over the country who had been suddenly separated:

> Remember Mary if there is anyone else in your mind don't forget to tell me. I was thinking about that other chap [Johnny] in your work. Your mother had a lot to do in breaking it up with him. I had no idea it was your mother that made you give him up. Tell me the truth Mary; I want to know what happened between you and him. I know how you were feeling towards him at the time. Don't be angry with me darling its only right that I should know, and if you feel the same about him Mary it's alright with me as long as I know you are happy.

Mary appears to have placated him as he apologised in his next letter for mentioning Johnny. Instead, he reassured her about childbirth: she had seen *Birth of a Baby,* a film about a couple anxiously awaiting the arrival of their child. The movie is tame by modern standards but was controversial in 1940 because the producers spliced documentary footage of an actual birth into the last reel. In some American cities cinemas showed it to single-sex audiences. 'Don't be afraid of anything you saw, after all millions of women all over the world go through the same. I'll see you alright darling,' Frank reassured her.

Mary's fears centred on the pain of childbirth but as bombing raids became more frequent mothers-to-be were haunted by the worry that labour would coincide with an air attack. One woman gave birth to a son in Glasgow's maternity hospital on 1 August half an hour before the sirens sounded, then watched nurses scramble round the ward snatching up babies, four at a time. Women who were still recovering from delivery were required to walk down several flights of stairs while the lifts were reserved for those who were still giving birth. Once they had reached the shelter they were forced to sit in the gloom for two hours, and when the all-clear sounded, they returned to bed to wonder whether the nurse had handed them their own baby or someone else's.

Women who were pregnant when their country was threatened by invasion worried about the world into which their babies would be born, but on the whole the prospect of a new life provided hope. An expectant woman from Orpington, Kent, wrote to her friend in America: 'I'd be the first to agree that this is a most unsuitable time to offer another hostage to fortune, fortune being in such a nasty mood; but so far I've no regrets about it, and still hope we may bring up our children in a world not entirely populated by little Nazis.'

It is hard to know whether or not Britain's dire situation put couples off having children because increasing numbers of men had joined up and were away from home for long periods. The number of legitimate births per thousand married women aged between fifteen and forty-four fell from 107 in 1939 to 99 in 1940. This pattern continued while invasion seemed most likely: in 1941 there were 94 legitimate births per thousand married women in the same age group.

Swelling bellies represented optimism for the future and were treated with added respect. In Mollie Panter-Downes's short story 'As the Fruitful Vine', which appeared at the end of the summer, the heroine finally feels accepted by her family and society when she becomes pregnant. That summer Winston Churchill's nineteen-year-old daughter-in-law Pamela, who was married to his only son, Randolph, was heavily pregnant – which gave pregnancy an official seal of approval.

Frank was less concerned with childbirth than he was with making sure that Mary's affections did not waver on a trip she took to the west coast of Scotland: 'Mary darling I'm giving you some advice, there is plenty of soldiers down near Prestwick keep away from their camp and don't speak to them. I know too much about soldiers to let you go near them; they don't care what they do or say to girls.' He probably did not realise that earlier in the summer, while he was in France, Glasgow had been overrun with French sailors who had found it easy to acquire a local girl on each arm. In other parts of Britain husbands and boyfriends were uneasy about the doubly attractive Canadian soldiers: they were foreigners *and* they spoke English.

In the third week of July Frank was on guard duty nearly every day of the week and thoroughly fed up. 'The only thing that makes me happy is to think of you darling and that's all I want to do, you are everything to me Mary,' he wrote. When his guard duty was cut to twice a week his spirits rose: 'We can go to the dancing or pictures anytime we feel like it. I go to Southampton every second night. I was dancing in the Y.M.C.A. on Saturday night, it was swell darling. I wish you were here with me. I would show you some life . . . I'm longing to see you darling I can't get my leave quick enough I'm just dying to hold you in my arms and tell you how much I love you Mary.' He was tenth on the list for leave and hoped he might be back in Scotland within three weeks. 'If Hitler doesn't start anything I'll get my leave okay,' he told her. 'If he does it's goodbye to leave, so pray darling he doesn't and I will also pray.'

★ ★ ★

Extract from 'Description of a German Attack on a British Convoy' by Charles Gardner (Staff)

14th July 1940. 9.15 p.m. (Home Service Programme)

Now we're looking up to the anti-aircraft guns; there's another – there's a Messerschmitt, I don't know whether he's down or whether he's trying to get out of the anti-aircraft which are giving him a very hot time. There's a Spitfire; there are about four fighters up there and I don't know what they're doing: one, two, three, four, five fighters, fighting right over our heads; now there's one coming right down on the tail of what I think is a Messerschmitt and I think a Spitfire behind him – oh darn, they've turned away, I can't see, I can't see. One crashing down there. Where's one crashing? No, I think he's pulled out. You can't watch these fights very coherently for long; you just see about four twirling machines and you hear little bursts of machine-gun fire and by the time you've picked up the machine, they've gone; there are one, two, three – oh, there's a dogfight going on up there; there are four, five, six machines wheeling and turning round; hark at the machine guns going; hark, one, two, three, four, five, six; now there's something coming right down on the tail of another; here they go – yes, they're being chased home and how *they're being chased home; there are three Spitfires chasing three Messerschmitts now. Oh boy, look at them going and look how the Messerschmitts – oh, that is really grand! And there's a Spitfire just behind the first two – he'll get them! Oh yes – Oh boy – I've never seen anything so good as this; the R.A.F. fighters have really got these boys taped.*

Our machine is catching up the Messerschmitt now; it's catching it up – it's got the legs off it, you know – they're right in the fight – no, go on . . . (?) – no, the distance is a bit deceptive from here – you can't tell, but I think something's definitely going to happen to that Messerschmitt. Just a moment. I wouldn't like to be in that first Messerschmitt; I think it's got him – yes; the machine-guns are going like anything. Oh, it's another fight – I'm afraid . . . (?) – no, they've chased them right out to sea and I can't see now but the odds were certainly on that first Messerschmitt catching it – There he goes. Look. Where? – I can't see them at all. Oh, yes, I see, yes, yes. Have they got him down? – I can't see. Yes, he's pulled away from him; yes, I think that first Messerschmitt has been crashed on the coast of France all right.

Source: BBC Written Archives

PART FIVE

August,
Hitler's 'Last Appeal to Reason'

16

Peter Fleming – Training Britain's Underground Resistance

At the height of his success, Hitler could not resist a peep at the destruction his bombers were inflicting and hitched a ride in an aircraft heading for England. As the aeroplane was nearing its destination a time bomb exploded in a flask of coffee, sending the Führer cascading through the clouds to a safe, if bumpy, parachute landing in a pond in Oxfordshire. 'He cleaned his plump backside by scraping along on the turf like a dog with worms,' then headed off into the woods.

> His padded flying boots suggested gout rather than glory. His breeches, made of buckskin and lined with fleece, were cut in lamentable taste. His raincoat, belted round the waist, bulged and rucked like a home-made frock at a dull Hunt Ball. He still wore on his head, despite the vagaries of his parachute descent, the military cap on whose visor the arc-lights had glinted in the hangar . . . headgear of a similar design is frequently worn by chauffeurs in the employment of the wives of Latin American millionaires. The Führer's general appearance, largely owing to his unlucky experience with the horsepond, was dirty.

He knocked at the door of a woman who was reading *Face to Face with Hitler* but she harangued him, and her dog, Flossie, bit him. The Führer, who 'could not face a war on two fronts', limped off. In his confusion he stumbled into a village hall and through some curtains on to a stage. As his arm movements grew wilder and wilder, the audience responded to the perfect caricature with delighted cheers. When Hitler glanced at the strangely attired people around him – an Ancient Briton, two Victorian cyclists and an Apache – he realised he had just won first prize in a fancy-dress competition in which he was believed to be impersonating Germany's tyrant. The pound of butter in his hands confirmed the suspicion.

Capturing Hitler turned out to be a false victory. The British government was sure Germany would have replaced him with an impersonator and that their claim to hold the Führer would not have been believed. Their only option was to send him home. A plane dropped him over Germany where he landed in a bog.

Peter Fleming, a successful travel writer, had dreamt up this fantasy of Hitler's trip to Britain during a period of enforced bedrest while he was recovering – appropriately enough – from German measles. A few readers objected to *The Flying Visit*'s satirical tone at a time when Britain was fighting a desperate battle but most found a huge release in Fleming's depiction of the Nazis as bumbling buffoons rather than slick automatons. Jonathan Cape published the book in July 1940 and it raced through six reprints. Rudolf Hess's unexpected arrival in Scotland the following year made it seem astonishingly prescient.

It had been an eventful year for Fleming. By the start of the summer he had been declared dead once and had twice put himself in an ideal position to face the enemy. In April 1940, while serving in the Grenadier Guards, he had volunteered to lead an expedition to Namsos in Norway to discover whether the Germans had taken the port. He handpicked a team and asked the Bank of England for a suitcase of Norwegian notes. They flew in a seaplane to Namsos where he was eventually joined by the Allied commander Adrian Carton de Wiart, who had 'only one eye, only one arm, and – rather more surprisingly – only one Victoria Cross'. De Wiart hoped to use Namsos as a base from which to recapture Trondheim but his troops were woefully equipped for the Scandinavian winter and he sent Fleming back to England to find out what the government wanted him to do. While he was away the *Daily Sketch* picked up a snippet broadcast by a Swedish radio station; the story turned out to be erroneous but by then the newspaper had run a report under the headline 'Author Killed In Norway'.

On his way back to London Fleming missed a train in Scotland due to bad weather. 'Hitler had missed the bus in Norway, I had missed the train at Inverness, but it didn't seem to have made much difference to Hitler, and I determined that it should make as little to me,' he said later. He persuaded the station-master to lay on a special service, which he assured him the War Office would pay for; he ate dinner while he waited and offered some friends at the hotel a lift.

His second experience of waiting for Hitler was in the Essex seaside town of Southend. MI5 had received an anonymous letter from someone claiming to be a German agent. He was posing as a refugee but had been treated with such kindness that he felt compelled to warn the government about the blow that would fall on the Essex town at 0100 hours on Whitsunday. His letter was convincing in every detail. Using the sort of grammatical and spelling mistakes that would trip up a German speaker, he outlined the strategy of a battalion of parachute troops. He was *au fait* with the tides that weekend and named correctly the streets along which the invaders would carry out a pincer movement against the post office.

Fleming felt confident that the warning would enable the British to repulse the invader but his experience as a journalist told him that it was not enough to beat the Hun: they must also beat him to the front page. If news of Southend's epic struggle was allowed to leak out, the story would be too late for the Sunday papers and Dr Goebbels, Hitler's propaganda minister, would turn the battle into a coup for the Nazis. To avoid this, Fleming and his brother Ian, who was personal assistant to the director of Naval Intelligence, were sent there as official witnesses to the coming battle.

They had expected to find strategically placed tanks, barbed-wire and a tense atmosphere. Instead, Southend was buzzing with evacuees and weekenders, bands played in palm-court lounges, couples strolled along the promenade and holidaymakers queued outside the cinemas. He wrote later, 'Phlegm, we felt, was being carried a bit too far.' They visited gunners at nearby Shoeburyness who did not have any guns and soldiers from the Pioneer Corps, who dug themselves into the sand as night fell without knowing what their officer looked like. The two brothers joined naval officers on an observation post at the top of a large hotel and to the strains of 'South of the Border' and 'The Lambeth Walk', which wafted up from the blacked-out ballroom, 'waited for history to be made'. As one o'clock came and went there were no signs of unusual air activity and the two official witnesses returned to their car where they put their drunk and dozing driver on the back seat and headed for London. It was their first and only visit to Southend.

Peter Fleming's exploits have led to the theory that he might have inspired his brother's James Bond. He was handsome enough, and a master of understatement, but his tastes were unsophisticated: he preferred camping to cocktails and haversacks to helicopters. He had no sense of smell and such underdeveloped tastebuds that at Oxford, where he read English and kept a pet lizard called Perkin Warbeck, he lived off marmalade and sausages. The books he wrote in the 1930s were hugely popular: *Brazilian Adventure, One's Company: a Journey to China* and *News from Tartary* each evoked a *Boy's Own* panache that Fleming made his own. His fact-finding mission to Norway left him wondering what part he could usefully play in a war that seemed to be nearing a climax. His other brother, Michael, had been captured in France and, like many, Peter believed the next episode of the war might be played out on British soil.

August was a month of omens. Alan Brooke was among many who noted in their diary that on 4 August 1914 Britain had declared war on Germany. Perhaps Hitler, who liked where possible to make history symmetrical, would choose this date to seek revenge in the same way that he had forced General Charles Huntziger, leader of the French delegation, to sign the armistice agreement in the railway carriage that had witnessed Germany's defeat in 1918. As if to confirm this hunch, the Führer wrote to Britons trying to persuade them to surrender. The Luftwaffe delivered his message on the night of 1/2 August in leaflets headed 'A Last Appeal to Reason', which fluttered down, mainly in Hampshire and Somerset, to be scooped up and auctioned in aid of the Red Cross. Newspapers pictured groups of stolid housewives chortling over the misguided invitation, which included the translation of a speech Hitler had made to the Reichstag on 19 July in which he seemed to hint at a peace offer. Although the leaflets were easy to laugh off as yet another example of Hitler's megalomania, and his inability to understand the British psyche, they were still unsettling. It was illogical and out of character to use the Luftwaffe for leafletting when they could have been dropping bombs – especially at a time when raids were intensifying.

The ominous behaviour continued when, on the night of 13/14 August, German aeroplanes scattered a selection of curious objects over the Midlands and the Scottish Lowlands. It gave every indication that a group of Germans had parachuted into Britain to prepare the ground for invasion. It also suggested an intimate knowledge of the country and how it worked. Among the objects the police found were parachutes, wireless transmitters, high explosives, maps of key installations, photographs, lists of prominent people and where they lived, and instructions to German agents, outlining their role in the forthcoming invasion. Everything seemed to point to an attack on the east coast. Then BBC monitors heard the New British Broadcasting Station (NBBS) announce that German parachutists – in civilian clothes and British uniforms – had landed near Birmingham, Manchester and Glasgow: 'One thing is clear – that this stage of the offensive cannot last many more days. It will be followed by large-scale invasion. It is to be presumed that the enemy has details of all the important harbours, armament factories and railways, and within a short time the country will be in the enemy's hands. Churchill will then be earning his lecture fee in America, whilst our own people are starving in the streets.' The NBBS repeated the announcement the next day with a few more details. By then *The Times* had picked up the story. The parachutes might have had more impact if some had not landed in cornfields: as no tracks led away from them, and because so much valuable material had been abandoned, it became obvious that the escapade was a hoax. But by the time the Ministry of Information had explained this, the NBBS was reporting that the parachutists were safely ensconced with fifth columnists. It embellished the tale throughout the last ten days of August, marvelling at the accuracy of the plans, the lists of names and maps that the parachutists had brought with them, and claimed that three policemen had been shot dead during the search for the intruders. The main German stations, it added, were beaming coded instructions to the parachutists and their protectors.

The elaborate charade was as unsettling as the leaflets. For a time, many people who lived in the areas where the parachutists were said to have landed were afraid to answer their door in case they encountered one. A *Daily Telegraph* reader suggested that the point of the exercise had been to find out how long it would take the British authorities to discover the parachutes – and thus how long a real parachutist might go undetected. The incident probably fanned a rumour that several thousand Germans had landed in Gloucestershire but, within hours, had been killed and buried in a mass grave by British soldiers. It was a typical wartime concoction that was both shocking and comforting: Britain could deal with invaders – no matter how great their numbers.

Publications as diverse as *Picture Post* and the *Tatler* discussed how the invasion might take place, but people remained determined to cling to normality in an increasingly topsy-turvy world. Many landowners ignored the government's attempt to move the 'Glorious Twelfth' – the start of the grouse-shooting season – to the fifth: ministers wanted to avoid the extravagance of farmers hand-rearing their birds. Gamekeepers argued – with some justification – that by early August the grouse had already been hand-reared. When the August bank holiday was cancelled, crowds flocked to parks anyway for the traditional day of fun.

In London the streets were thick with bravura. Thursday, 15 August, was believed to be the day on which Hitler had promised to march through London, and many were convinced he would keep his word – just as he had arrived in Paris on time. The Over-Seas League marked the date with a special tea dance and Sir Alexander Cadogan observed gleefully in his diary, 'Can't find him . . .' But while Hitler failed to make a personal appearance German planes took to the skies over Britain in savage air battles and daylight raids that included an attack on Croydon. The following day fourteen people died in a raid on Wimbledon, and sightseers arrived to view the aftermath of what was still a novelty. Londoners, who were used to reading about regional bombings, were shedding the complacency of the past few weeks and instead felt a growing sense of excitement. On 18 August Vera Brittain heard a siren for the first time in two months; less than a week later the first bombs fell on Central London.

In Kent Peter Fleming was leading General Andrew 'Bulgy' Thorne and his aide-de-camp, Ralph Arnold, deeper into thick woodland on a hillside not too far from what Arnold described as the most 'invasion prone' strip of coastline on the British Isles. It was the worst kind of fairy-tale wood in which the dense foliage made it all too easy to imagine you were being watched and in which every snapped twig resounded in the silence. Perhaps the knowledge that they *were* being watched made them all the more uncomfortable. While Fleming strode confidently forward the other two stumbled in the half-light until they reached a small clearing where he challenged them to find the entrance to a hide-away that housed a group of specially trained men. As Arnold wrote later:

> We poked about unsuccessfully for a few minutes, and then our guide casually kicked a tree stump. It fell back on a hinge to reveal a hole with a rope ladder dangling into a cavern that had been enlarged from a badger's sett. In this cave, sitting on kegs of explosive and surrounded by weapons, booby-traps, a wireless set and tins of emergency rations, were some Lovat Scouts and half a dozen Home Guards – game-keepers and farm labourers chosen for their toughness and for their knowledge of the countryside. Their role was to go to ground when and if the Germans landed, to allow the first enemy wave to pass over their heads, and then to emerge at night to wreak general havoc on the invaders' lines of communication. It was pure *Boy's Own* . . . stuff, and the Corps

commander . . . simply loved it. In my experience very senior officers were always inclined to cherish clandestine forces. They made such a nice change.

These men formed the first 'auxiliary units' to be set up in the summer of 1940. The term was chosen deliberately to convey the dullest kind of bureaucracy and to hide an organisation that many of its surviving members are still reluctant to talk about. The idea of a 'stay-behind' force grew out of concern over the ease with which Hitler's army had breezed into France, apparently with little or no resistance. General Thorne, who had controlled a division in France and was now commanding officer of XII Corps, with responsibility for defending Sussex, Kent and parts of Surrey, was particularly keen to find a way to slow the Germans' advance once they had landed. He believed that a bit of 'scallywagging' – a term generals used to describe guerrilla warfare behind enemy lines – would buy him valuable extra time.

Fleming seemed the obvious person to set up the first unit. He had lived off his wits while travelling across some of the world's most remote areas but his love of the typical Englishman's country pursuits had turned him into an equally adept backwoodsman. As a guardsman he understood how the army worked but he was also a maverick who enjoyed using his own initiative and bending the rules, as he had done in his mission to Norway. He believed that Britain's defeat in France had created the ideal conditions for the 'unorthodox warrior'. He likened Britain's current dilemma to a game of cricket: when the play turned against your side, you should call up an unconventional player – someone like T. E. Lawrence, who had used panache and cunning to outwit the Turks in the desert. According to Fleming, the unorthodox warrior needed 'tact, and patience, and friends at court . . . In manner and appearance he should be conventional rather than farouche. Let him, if he likes, carry a sjambok or an ice-axe or a knobkerrie when he is training his private army; but let him leave the gimmick behind in his jeep when he comes to GHQ to try and scrounge a supernumerary typewriter.'

MOST SECRET.

IST OF ARMS, AMMUNITION, STORES and EQUIPMENT required for
ne Patrol, Auxunits.

1.   ARMS.

    7 Revolvers .38 American
    2 Rifles .300
    7 knives fighting
    3 knobkerries
    48 Grenades, 36 M. 4 sec.
    3 Cases S.T. Grenades
    2 Cases A.W. bottles
    1 Rifle .22 with Silencer
    1 Thompson Sub Machine Gun

2.   EXPLOSIVES

    4 Auxunits (boxes containing explosives and
       concomitants)

3.   AMMUNITION

    40 rds .38 American
    200 rds .300
    1000 rds .45 for S.M.G.
    200 rds .22

4.   EQUIPMENT

    7 Holsters (Leather American)
    7 Groundsheets
    7 Blankets
    7 Pairs Rubber boots (Agricultural workers type)
    7 Water bottles, carriers and slings
    1 set of equipment Thompson Sub Machine Gun
    1 pair of wire cutters
    1 Monocular and case

5.   The provision of one Elephant Shelter for construction
    work. The necessary equipment for furnishing the
    base, i.e. one Tilley Lamp, Two Primus Stoves,
    Elsan chemical closet.

                              P.T.O.

This list shows some of the rations and equipment stored
in hideouts to keep resistance fighters going once the Germans
arrived. The rum often proved too much of a temptation during
training on a cold night.

While Fleming carried neither a sjambok, a long whip made from rhino hide, nor a knobkerrie, a short stick with a rounded head used by the indigenous people of South Africa, he experimented with all sorts of unusual weapons such as flaming arrows fired into thatched roofs. Officers and VIPs trekked to his headquarters at a ramshackle cottage called The Garth, at Bilting, near the South Downs, where they sat on boxes of explosives and dined off tables that were crates of gelignite while they discussed how to make life difficult for the enemy.

The location was ideal: it was secluded, but close to London, and directly on the route that Hitler's marching army was expected to take. It was also surrounded by the sort of thick woodland that Fleming needed to train his men and to build hideouts or OBs (operational bases). He instructed his team in a range of unlikely skills. They built booby-traps with milk churns and sewage pipes, and crept unseen round the grounds of country houses to plan where best to position a sniper when a German general took up residence there. He taught them the importance of knowing the enemy's eating habits so that they could exploit the distractions of mealtimes, and made them train wearing special goggles to simulate night-time. He instructed them on how to blend seamlessly into the landscape and tested their ability to remain motionless. His ingenious hideouts were legendary to those who knew of them: the trapdoors, hidden behind a curtain of trees or undergrowth, closed silently on a dark, dank world of tangled roots and hidden stores. Most made use of existing features: a slight dip in the ground, a fallen tree stump, an abandoned chalk-pit or the cellar of a derelict house. They also reflected a region's history – disused Welsh and Cornish mines, for coal and tin respectively, were pressed into service. One OB reclaimed a hiding-place from the last war: a great pit on the edge of a deer park that had housed a secret airship.

As the threat from Germany became more pressing the units spread from the south-east to cover the most vulnerable parts of Britain under the ultimate leadership of Colonel Colin McVean

Gubbins who, at Military Intelligence (Research), had been re-cruiting likely candidates for subversive work since before the outbreak of war. Each unit found men who could effortlessly 'go to ground' at a moment's notice and who brought their own skills. At times this meant poacher and gamekeeper sharing the same musty burrow, forced to confide their secrets to a man they had pre-viously thought of as the opposition.

Anthony Quayle, who became famous as an actor after the war, was in charge of a unit in Northumberland. 'If the Germans had landed in the North-East hell would have erupted beneath them and I mean *beneath*,' he said later. 'The idea was to have under-ground hide-outs and allow the Germans to sweep over us. We would then have popped up behind them to give them a touch of the jitters. We had no official motto – we didn't even wear official uniform – but unofficially the motto was "Terror by night".' A man in his unit was a one-armed molecatcher whose family could trace their involvement in the trade further back than their employ-er, the Duke of Northumberland, his ancestors. He was an ex-cellent shot despite his disability but – much more importantly – he knew the moors intimately.

Scotland eventually had around a hundred auxiliary units under the control of Captain Eustace Maxwell of the Argyll and Suther-land Highlanders. His brother Gavin, the naturalist who wrote *Ring of Bright Water*, ran a training camp in the north. As their hideouts the units used ancient domed stone huts known only to shepherds, long-forgotten ice-houses and ruined castles sur-rounded by the sort of velvet moss that springs back instantly to obliterate tell-tale footprints. In Berwickshire one unit set up camp in a cave that could only be reached by scaling a cliff, then jumping through a waterfall. On one occasion its men entertained important military visitors with salmon poached from a nearby river where the king's brother-in-law owned fishing rights.

In England many patrol leaders were ordered to spend a week-end in the grounds of Coleshill, a grand seventeenth-century house near Swindon, in Wiltshire. The recruits were told to report to 'GHQ Auxiliary Units, c/o GPO, Highworth'. When each man arrived, the postmistress, a Mrs Stranks, would ring the big house and announce, 'I've got one of your lot down here,' and a car would appear to whisk them off to start their training.

Mary and Katherine Pleydell-Bouverie owned the house; their brother had been killed in the First World War. They stayed at Coleshill from Monday to Thursday while training was relatively quiet – camouflage, map reading, night movements and silent killing – but abandoned it at weekends. Then it shook with the blasts of the new plastic explosive, nicknamed 'marzipan', which was more stable and easier to use than gelignite, and sent their dogs into a frenzy. The park became littered with targets – mock tanks, aircraft and lorries, with a few genuine ones that had been damaged beyond repair – and practice hideouts. Would-be saboteurs and members of the recognised intelligence services practised blowing up objects with the latest gadgets such as the new 'time pencils', a chemically activated delayed-action fuse. They learnt how to use Thompson sub-machine guns, sticky bombs, and mines made to look like lumps of coal or horse manure that could be attached to tyres.

Only men who could engineer a weekend away from home without arousing suspicion, and who lived close enough, could visit Coleshill. Most had to make do with clandestine training sessions at their own hideout. But whatever the level of instruction they received, they all knew that once the invader arrived they were on their own.

It was hoped that wires would stop German aeroplanes landing on roads; machinery was dragged into the middle of fields for the same reason.

Sandbags and roadblocks transformed even the most suburban street.

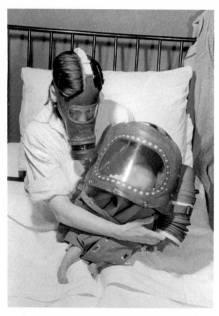

A mother who has just given birth demonstrates how to pump air into the baby's gas 'helmet'.

A sergeant in the Dorking Home Guard gives his rifle a final polish before turning out for parade; his wife does her bit by knitting.

One farmer painted his cows with luminous white lines to avoid them being hit by cars in the blackout.

This pill box in Edinburgh was painted to resemble a florist's shop; another was made to look like part of a church.

A mock beach hut draws the eye away from the pill box nestling below it on the seafront near Folkestone.

A pillbox on the south coast was given a covering of hay – the deception would have been even more effective from the air.

Winston Churchill watches soldiers hurling Molotov cocktails in an exercise at Wareham in Dorset.

Local authorities practise what to do if the Germans used gas. 'Plenty of soap and water' was thought to be helpful.

Scientists tried to set the sea on fire as a way of repelling the Germans; rumours about the experiment were later linked to tales of a failed invasion.

Women appear to be hurling beanbags in an exercise to teach them the correct way to throw a hand grenade.

Some enemy aliens were held in a council estate at Huyton, near Liverpool. The buildings were not finished and many inmates slept in waterlogged tents.

Decio Anzani, who was always a dapper dresser, with his daughter, Renée. The photo was taken when she was at boarding school.

Soldiers round up enemy aliens in a northern town in May 1940; one man hides his face from the camera.

Many of the prisoners on board the *Arandora Star* slept in cabins which retained some of their former glory, although the ship was badly overcrowded.

In the 1930s the *Arandora Star* was known as the 'wedding cake' or the 'chocolate box' because of the luxury liner's white hull and red stripe.

'A mad, mad world' painted at Huyton internment camp by the Austrian-born Jew, Hugo Dachinger on a page torn from the *Manchester Guardian*. Dachinger is thought to have used his own hair as a brush.

The Blitz exposed private houses to public view and left the air thick with dust and grit.

Frank Hurd, a member of the Auxiliary Fire Service, half-hoped for 'something to happen' and then felt ashamed when it did.

A pall of smoke hangs over London's docklands after the first mass daylight bombing of London on Saturday, 7 September 1940.

17

Charlie Mason – The Resistance Fighter

At first glance it is difficult to believe that Charlie Mason is a trained assassin. Now in his nineties, he is still tall, wiry and has the gaunt features of someone who has spent most of his life outdoors. His natural charm and humour only evaporate when he talks about his time as a member of an auxiliary unit near Hull. For Charlie this was no *Dad's Army* lark but a deadly serious business, whose consequences had been carefully thought through: 'We had agreed that no one was left behind injured after an operation. If you couldn't take him with you you killed him or you booby-trapped him. You never left him to be interrogated because they would kill him anyway – so you killed him.'

In 1940 Charlie was twenty-six. He had five brothers and four sisters, all of whom lived with their parents at South Cave railway station, in the countryside west of Hull. Their father was the assistant station-master, and they were a well-known family of poachers. 'We didn't have to do it, we did it for the hell of it.' At ten he learnt to shoot and roamed the countryside at night, getting to know its rhythms and workings as well as he did the comings and goings of the freight trains that rattled past his home. For Charlie, the countryside was full of signs you had to learn to read. If a field of sheep stopped grazing to look in one direction it usually meant that someone, or something, was lurking there; a flock of birds only made a noise when they had been disturbed. He could obtain a 'compass fix' from a tree's shape because the branches were usually healthier on its south side; he knew that the becks, or streams, around his home flowed south towards the river Humber. He discovered the best places to lay animal traps and became such an excellent shot that engine-drivers and stokers would toss him money with a request for fresh game that they would collect on the return journey.

When war was declared Charlie was working as an engineer for the nearby flying school at Blackburn aerodrome. He serviced the Tiger Moths in which RAF recruits learnt to fly, a role that assumed such vital importance as Britain raced to catch up with the Luftwaffe's abundant supply of aeroplanes and trained pilots that he was not allowed to join one of the armed forces. But Charlie longed to be in the air rather than tending aircraft on the ground. One of his closest friends, Stanley Andrew, had left the aerodrome in 1937 to train as a pilot and had already seen the sort of excitement Charlie yearned for. His squadron had sailed to Norway where he flew Hurricanes until the campaign looked hopeless and he was ordered to land his plane on HMS *Glorious* – the first time an aircraft had successfully alighted on a ship. The following day the Germans sank her and Stanley was one of only two pilots from his squadron to survive. He was evacuated home and, with the indecent haste of that urgent summer, returned to the skies and the Battle of Britain.

But Charlie was based at home: 'Unless you actually lived through that time you can't understand. I would rather have been up in the air but I couldn't. There was a feeling that you wanted to do something. You didn't think about life, because life didn't matter. People were being killed in towns and what you wanted to do was to kill some Germans.'

And Charlie had no doubt that the Germans were coming – the flying instructors he met every day told him so. They had recently returned from tours of duty during which they had seen the build-up of boats and barges on the other side of the Channel. 'Rest assured, they're coming,' they told him.

Strange things happened at the aerodrome. The man who came to cover the hangars, factory buildings and runway with camouflage paint asked endless questions about the work Charlie and his friends were doing until they became suspicious. They were on the point of reporting him when he disappeared. To this day Charlie remains convinced that the painter was a fifth columnist.

Copy

Copy Number: 2.

S E C R E T.

AUXILIARY UNITS, HOME FORCES

A. Organization etc.

Object:

1. The object of Auxiliary Units, Home Forces, on the fighting side, is to build up, within the general body of the Home Guards, a series of small local units whose role is to act offensively on the flanks and in the rear of any German troops who may obtain a temporary foothold in this country.

The other role is Intelligence.

Method of Employment:

2. These Auxiliary Units are equipped with special Molotov bombs, delay action fuzes and plastic H.E., incendiary bombs and devices of various kinds from non-military stocks, as well as the rifle and grenade. Their task is to harry and embarrass the enemy by all means in their power from the first day he lands, their particular targets being tanks and lorries in lager, ammunition dumps, H.Q.s, small straggling parties and posts etc. Their object is, in co-operation with the regular forces, to prevent the invader establishing a secure foothold, and thus to facilitate his defeat.

3. These units must operate mainly by night and therefore are constituted entirely from local men who know their countryside intimately, i.e. farmers, game-keepers, hunt servants etc. under a selected local leader. In certain areas where woodlands or heath are of considerable extent, particular units have the special role of occupying prepared 'hide-outs' as a base for operations. These hide-outs are being prepared and provided with

The job of the resistance fighter was to 'harry and embarrass' the enemy.

Charlie was in the right frame of mind and had the right credentials to join an auxiliary unit. One day he was walking along a street when a friend, with whom he played football, approached him. Charlie assumed Jack Cross wanted advice about his car but instead he took him to a bench near the village stream. Here, in oblique terms, he told Charlie about the stay-behind force. Charlie wanted time to think before he committed himself, but Jack said there was no time: their first meeting was scheduled for that night. Charlie agreed, the seventh and last man to join the unit. The others were members of the Home Guard and all worked at the Blackburn aerodrome. When he asked why they wanted him Jack lifted an imaginary rifle to his shoulder and said simply, 'Out in the woods at night – bang-bang!'

At the meeting, Charlie and the other men were told: ' "You must understand that this is very serious. There's a very great possibility that you will not survive. You can back out now before you sign but you must know this is a suicide squad." I replied, "That suits me," because I really wanted to have a go.' He signed the Official Secrets Act and was handed his equipment, which didn't amount to much but it was 'the special stuff': a dagger, a revolver and 'ammo'.

The men learnt how to lay explosives, how to handle detonators and fuses. Their mission was to blow up anything that might help the Germans, such as petrol stations and railways. They believed that Hull would be an early target and that it was vital to disrupt communications between the city, in the extreme east of the country, and the industrial heartland of the Midlands and Liverpool. Over the next few months Charlie planned in minute detail the destruction of the railway that had been the economic lifeblood of his family and whose workers he knew by name. As well as mining the bridges they would drop explosives down air vents to coincide with a train's approach. 'We could have made ourselves quite a nuisance.'

Their leader, Bob Williams, never told them beforehand what they were going to do in each training session. They sauntered to their meeting-place casually in dribs and drabs, never showing any sign of urgency. One night Bob took them to a track in the woods near a road and ordered them to find a bunker hidden there. They walked back and forth searching but could see no sign of it until he pulled away some briars and branches that hid a small door. Perversely, the bunker had been built near a track so that if they were spotted they could pretend they were following the path on some spurious errand. Beneath a few feet of earth they discovered a cell about eight feet square, with corrugated steel sheets for sides and a concrete floor. Charlie thought it didn't look very big for seven men to live in.

The unit used this base for two months, then moved to a new one near the Barnsley–Hull railway line. It was much deeper and Charlie had to crawl through a little arched opening and down a ten-foot shaft into a sort of Nissen hut with a small table, bunks and lights. One side was stacked with explosives, detonators, fuses and ammunition, but Charlie never had any problem sleeping there: 'If you're tired you just go to sleep.' The smell of paraffin, especially when they were cooking, was almost overpowering. The hide contained two weeks' supply of food, which they were forbidden to touch, and a jar of rum that they dipped into if it was particularly cold. They brought sandwiches from home and ate rather more chocolate than they would have been allowed in the outside world.

This hideout was fairly sophisticated in that it had an escape tunnel, which would give the unit a chance to flee if their front door was uncovered: one of the men's greatest fears was that the Nazis would hunt them down with dogs, then hurl in grenades. That hideout also featured ventilator pipes, which allowed air to circulate; others had 'chimneys' hidden in trees or their roots to allow smoke to mingle with the early-morning mist or late-night fog. 'That was going to be our home for the rest of our lives. That was it. When the Germans came we never had to appear again in the village or be seen by anyone – ever. You couldn't go for food, you couldn't go to the doctor, you couldn't do anything.'

The unit trained at night, usually after a hard day's work. Sometimes they took part in exercises with other nearby units,

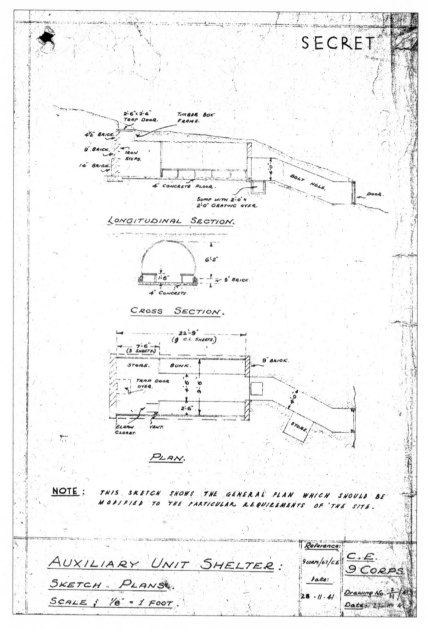

Teams of saboteurs, or 'auxiliary units', built elaborate hideouts in which to wait for the invader.

occasionally glimpsing familiar faces but knowing their nocturnal exploits would never be a subject for daytime chit-chat. They practised attacking disused chalk-pits that the Germans might use to store equipment, or they put the regular army to the test by creeping into their camps and leaving chalk marks to prove they had been there, unseen and unchallenged. Charlie's secret life of crawling through the undergrowth gave him scratches that were difficult to explain until he invented a dense area in his garden and told work colleagues he was clearing it to plant vegetables in his bid to 'dig for victory'. He stopped washing the heavy denim he wore at night so that with every outing it became more caked with dirt and grease, helping him to blend into the nocturnal countryside.

Charlie's forte was shooting and he practised firing in pitch darkness. At special training camps members of the regular army taught him how to kill a sentry using a cheese wire or knife. He learnt how to creep up behind a man, knee him in the legs and pull one arm backwards as he slit his throat. Killing a sentry was a last resort since it would alert other soldiers to the presence of an assassin and probably lead to reprisals.

At some point the local gamekeeper became aware of their hideout and told Charlie, 'You lot think I don't know what's going on, but I know everything.' Charlie reported the conversation to his superior: 'We decided that when the Germans came the first thing we'd do would be to kill him.' They calculated their life expectancy at about two weeks once they had gone to ground and did not want it cut even shorter by a nosy gamekeeper.

Charlie told his family that he could not explain what he did on his nightly outings, but secrecy was second nature among poachers and it went unchallenged. When he married, his wife knew he could not reveal where he went at night and that she was safer in not knowing. She was a tough farmer's daughter, from a generation that had no qualms about obeying husbands. Other wives were not so trusting and became convinced that their husbands were having affairs. Charlie's wife knew that when the Germans arrived she had to lock up their home and set the chickens free to scavenge for food rather than starving. Then she must cycle to her parents in Beverley, because when Charlie went he would not come back.

The threat of reprisals lingered in the back of his mind: 'It didn't matter how many they killed because we weren't fighting for a group of people in a village. This was for the country, the whole country. It didn't matter if they burnt the village down. We couldn't have stopped.'

What worried Charlie was *when* they would have to go to ground. If it happened when the leaves began to fall or, worse, when the snow came, the chance of detection was high. Not only would the naked trees rip back a protective curtain but the snow would highlight their every move.

Peter Fleming, too, knew that low-flying reconnaissance aircraft, by then backed up with local knowledge, would have raised the hideouts from sunken anonymity to become areas for investigation. Late summer was the most effective season in which to be a saboteur.

18

Leonard Marsland Gander and
the Best Spy Story Never Told

Towards the end of the summer Leonard Marsland Gander was, by his own admission, on the 'verge of a nervous breakdown'. There was simply too much news around – most of which he was not allowed to print – and too few pages. His editor had put him on the 'Dover patrol', which meant covering a part of Britain that was under almost constant attack by the Germans and permanently besieged by journalists – many of whom, he was convinced, had formed a 'ring' against the *Daily Telegraph*. As well as the British press, American reporters, representing news media ranging from the *Chicago Daily News* to the Hearst news agency and United Press, gathered at Shakespeare Cliff, near Dover, to watch the dogfights playing out over the Channel. Several had reported on Italy's invasion of Abyssinia and were curious to see if events would unfold similarly for Britain.

Dover rarely disappointed its audience. It provided a ringside view of the war, and the reporters nicknamed it 'Hellfire Corner'. The American journalist Ben Robertson, who had bought some tannic acid jelly to rub on to his hands to exclude air from a burn in the event of a mustard-gas attack, was mesmerised by the vapour trails the sparring planes etched on the sky, like skaters on an ice rink. Churchill realised he had the perfect opportunity to show America what Britain faced, and how resolutely she was dealing with the onslaught: on 28 August he took a delegation of American diplomats to Dover and answered questions about a possible invasion. He dismissed the idea of a Channel crossing, claiming that the Germans could not navigate. When he was asked if the mists would help to conceal the invaders, he concluded, 'Yes, but with mists come storms and rough seas.' During the visit they watched a German plane 'take its death dive, whirring down almost vertically with a whining note, finally ending in a dull "whoomph" as it hit the ground'. The pilot bailed out, as 'delicate-looking as a bubble'. At the same time a German bomber splashed into the sea and a British motor-boat raced to capture any survivors.

At Dover Castle the observers squinted through a telescope at Calais and the German shipping chugging to and fro. 'It seemed queer,' General Lee, who was among the Americans taken to the port, recorded in his diary, 'to observe the long stretch of French coast and think that along it are strung the hordes of Hitler, crowding up against the Channel for a pounce upon England, just as Napoleon camped along the same coast with the same intention nearly a hundred and fifty years ago.' Ben Robertson's overwhelming impression was of a shrinking world: the stretch of water had become a 'three-minute channel' and the people of Dover now referred to the French coast as 'the Fatherland'.

Outside his long working hours Gander found little release from the tension and described the atmosphere in London as 'unbelievable'. 'The sirens make such a hideous bloodcurdling row that they always come as a bit of a shock,' he observed, on 16 August, in one of his last diary entries before he became too busy to keep a record of his daily life. He took part in firewatching, perched on the roof ready to raise the alarm if he spotted a blaze, but his wife, Hilda, remained unconvinced that this 'skygazing' was really necessary. On his way home one day, he was caught in a raid and found his sons, in a state of high excitement, hiding in the cupboard under the stairs. When he visited some Jewish friends in Hampstead he discovered that they had abandoned their home, with its underground concrete air-raid shelter, to flee to America. They had left behind a mansion with six bathrooms, a ballroom, a Wild West bar and a garden equipped with a wendy house, an electrically powered toy car, tennis and squash courts. For some, loitering in Britain was just not worth the risk.

For Gander, the best story of 1940 – possibly of his life –

cropped up at the beginning of September but he was forbidden to report it – as, fortunately were his rivals.

Just after midnight on Tuesday, 3 September, two men in their twenties, one of whom was exceptionally tall, landed in a small dinghy on a desolate beach between Dungeness lighthouse and Lydd coastguard station. The sea was dead calm and it was high tide. The pair struggled up the shingle beach, crawled through the barbed-wire entanglements, then across the steel spikes and tram rails embedded in the ground until they reached an upturned lifeboat that had drifted ashore after the evacuation of Dunkirk. They took with them into their hidey-hole bread, corned beef, sardines, chocolate, tinned beans, 'concentrated iron', possibly a dietary supplement, and brandy. One still had his revolver; the other had lost his overboard in an early mishap that might have been the leitmotif for their mission. They also had with them fifty pounds in pound notes, small change and two black leather boxes, about the size of gas-mask containers, which contained radio transmitters.

When they had rested they crawled out and headed inland, stopping to sleep for an hour or two in a holiday bungalow that had been evacuated when the south coast became part of the Defence Zone. Then they scuttled across sparsely covered ground to a clump of trees.

Later that morning, but still very early, Somerset Light Infantry soldiers were patrolling Romney Marsh, an area of extreme sensitivity that shared with Dover an uncomfortable proximity to the enemy. Private Sidney Tollervey caught a flicker of movement in the grass opposite the beach and then the shadow of a man running across the road to fling himself against the sea wall. The soldier gave chase until the man turned and blurted out, ' I do not know your code word.' Private Tollervey asked if he had any form of identification but the stranger claimed not to understand. The soldier asked him to step forward so that he could see him better. It was immediately obvious that this was no master of disguise. He was dripping wet but he had a spare pair of shoes and, more sinisterly, a set of binoculars slung over his shoulders. He spoke with a thick, guttural accent, had high cheekbones and looked Asian – one of the unpublished newspaper reports said he had 'slit eyes' and 'smooth, coloured skin'. He claimed he was a Dutch refugee who had arrived from Brest.

When Tollervey marched him into the Somersets' headquarters the man produced a Dutch passport and, on being asked if he was armed, handed over a pistol with a set of cartridges. His name was Charles van den Kieboom and the passport had expired five months earlier. Soldiers searching the area near where he had been picked up found a small rowing-boat floating close to the shore, a sack on the steps leading from the beach and a black case dumped in a ditch and covered with rushes in Romney Marsh. Kieboom claimed he had been carrying the sack and case single-handed. Later that day a lance-corporal in the Royal Engineers spotted a man in a field wearing trousers and a coat that were both wet. When challenged he replied, 'I am a Dutchman.' Sjoerd Pons claimed he had come from Brest in a fishing-boat.

At midday on 3 September the Lydd coastguard was walking along the shore when he spotted a boat drifting close to the beach. He waded through the shallow water and rowed it back to the coastguard station. It was a Boulogne fisherman's boat, with black hull and yellow and white bands. There was ballast in the stern to weigh it down – possibly so that it could be towed easily. The oars appeared to be brand new and a continental seven was painted on the boat's side. Later that day he found a sack of provisions hidden in a wrecked boat on the shore.

The landlady at the Rising Sun pub in Lydd was busying herself with preparations for opening when a tall man in his mid-twenties appeared at around 9 a.m. and asked for a drink. He spoke with a Canadian accent and used American slang. The woman explained that she could not legally sell him one and told him to come back at 10.30 a.m. He compounded his mistake by asking if he could use her bath. She told him that she did not offer such facilities and suggested he went to look at the church until the pub opened. On his return, he ordered champagne cider, but was persuaded eventually to settle for a pint of mild and bitter. The landlady, by now convinced that this was no regular customer, launched into a conversation about how the Germans were facing starvation. 'How do you know they are?' he snapped.

She slipped into the neighbouring bar where Horace Mansfield, an aircraft examiner from Esher who was recuperating after being injured in a blast at a factory near Rochester, was playing darts and asked him to take a look at the stranger. As soon as he entered the foreigner rose to leave, slamming half a crown on the counter, which he said he hoped would be sufficient. He was surprised to find that his drink cost only fourpence ha'penny. As he left the pub he bumped his head on an electric lightbulb and set it swinging wildly. Mansfield watched him buy groceries at the local shop, then tapped him on the shoulder. He showed the man his own Air Ministry pass and demanded to see his identification. The stranger seemed unfazed but surprised that he might need his papers in a restricted area; he claimed he was a Dutch refugee who had arrived from Brest and, without being asked, offered Mansfield fifty pounds. Mansfield took the man to the police station, where Carl Maier (or Meier) handed round cigarettes and brandy. He soon dropped the refugee story and said he had been intimidated into crossing the Channel and that he was one of a party of four men whom the Nazis had sent ahead of the invasion.

As Maier continued to chain-smoke, even sending Mansfield out to buy more cigarettes, police and soldiers hunted for the final member of what became known as the 'Four Men and a Boat' case. Troops finally discovered him hiding in a hole. Jose Waldberg was the only German in the gang and had rigged up aerials in a tree from which he had managed to send a few inconsequential messages across the Channel, such as: 'MAIER ARRESTED. POLICE SEARCHING FOR ME. CAN HOLD OUT TILL SATURDAY. LONG LIVE GERMANY.'

All four men were charged under the Treachery Act, which was introduced in 1940 because treachery was easier to prove than treason. The trial, which was held *in camera*, allowed the intelligence service to piece together how the spies had been recruited and something of their mission to Britain. Waldberg was clearly the leader, and the only one driven by patriotism rather than money or threats. He held his fellow conspirators in contempt and believed he was the single properly trained spy among them. Maier was half German and half Dutch and had studied medicine at Freiburg University. He had become so desperate to earn extra money and join his fiancée in America that he had accepted a part-time job in translating and decoding. The Gestapo discovered he had been smuggling money and jewellery and threatened him with the death penalty unless he agreed to take part in the mission. Kieboom was born in Japan of a Javanese mother and Dutch father – hence his inability to blend into wartime Kent – and was married with children. Pons was a commercial traveller; both he and Kieboom had been caught smuggling and threatened with death or a concentration camp unless they agreed to go to Britain.

The night before they set off from France they had one last meal together in a private villa near Le Touquet. The evening sounds as if it was full of false bravado: someone took a photo of them and they probably drank too much – perhaps Maier had developed such a raging thirst that he had been forced to stroll into the pub. Surely even they must have realised how conspicuous and ill-suited they were to their task – they did not even have a tin- or bottle-opener among their provisions. Motorised cutters had brought them from Boulogne to within a mile of the Kent coast where they had split into pairs and rowed ashore. Their orders were to gather as much information as possible about the south coast and its defensive capabilities and to send back regular coded radio messages to France. They were convinced the Nazis would land in Britain within days and their supplies were calculated to last for no more than ten.

No matter how ill-planned the operation, the war cabinet could not afford to ignore the implications of the 'Four Men in a Boat' case and William Kerr Bliss of the *Evening Standard* and the *Sunday Express* was ordered to hand over his notes from interviews with those who had encountered the men. The story he wrote was marked 'Hold till after war'.

PHOTOGRAPHS OF SOME OF THE CAPTURED AGENTS.

Reading from left to right -

1st row: PAZOS DIAZ (No.28): MARTINEZ (No.26):
MEIER (No.2): KRAG (No.23).
2nd row: JEZEQUEL (No.25): KIEBOOM (No.4):
WALDBERG (No.3): PONS (No.5).
3rd row: COLL (No.7): ERIKSON (No.14):
HECHEVARRIA (No.29): Van DAM (No.24).
4th row: WALTI (No.15): De DEEKER (No.13):
ROBLES (No.27): EVERTSEN (No.22).

The 'Four Men and a Boat' spies (Meier in the first row, Kieboom, Waldberg and Pons in the line below) pictured with other agents caught later in the war.

Novels about spies were popular and Jack Train made the most
of their comedy potential by creating Funf, an incompetent spy,
for *ITMA*. A Ministry of Information film offered advice on how to
deal with the real thing and the *Lynn News* posed the question that
was on everyone's mind:

> What sort of people are spies? We can usually spot them on the
> screen, but can we recognise them in real life? We assume there
> aren't such people in our little world, but I wonder? . . . On the
> screen we see the spy in all sorts of sinister attitudes that give him
> away to us, but he generally manages to fool the rest of the cast.
> Presumably, in real life, the well-trained and successful spy never
> gives himself away.

Alastair Sim and a fifteen-year-old George Cole starred in the
West End thriller *Cottage to Let*, which became a box-office hit and
eventually a film with John Mills in the cast. The action takes place
in a Scottish stately home where a brilliant scientist is working on a
secret military invention, which a German spy ring is desperate to
capture; the house is also an RAF hospital and home to evacuees.
No one is quite what they seem and the play exploits audiences'
fears of being unable to detect spies and the effect of careless talk.

As the summer ended, the knowledge that the Germans were
just across the Channel led to renewed suspicion of strangers, or
any sort of unusual activity – including, as the artist Keith
Vaughan discovered in September, setting up an easel on a
country verge. Although he had taken care to ask permission of
the officer in charge before he began to paint a tank trap at
Guildford, a policeman arrested him, ignoring his protests. When
his status as a conscientious objector came to light, his mother's
London flat was raided at two in the morning. He spent eight days
in jail before his trial, at which his half-finished picture was
produced as evidence. It was, he commented, 'the first picture
of mine ever to be publicly exhibited'. He was fined twenty-five
pounds and his painting confiscated.

Suspicious behaviour took many forms. So H. R. V. Jordan
discovered as he doggedly followed up endless tip-offs he received

in his work in counter-intelligence. Anyone gazing out to sea through a pair of binoculars or waving their arms in what might be interpreted as semaphore risked investigation. Picnicking near an airfield, taking a snapshot of a factory, holding a meeting in a church crypt, keeping pigeons – which could be used to exchange messages with the enemy – or expressing anti-war views were all likely to attract attention. One of the most common reports from the vigilant public was that they had spotted someone guiding German bombers to their target. Torchbeams that strayed into the night sky or even clothes strung along a washing line in an unusual formation – which implies that there was a 'regulation' way to hang them – might lead to accusations.

Anxiety that German airmen were being helped on the ground produced a phenomenon similar to the corn circles that appeared in Britain in the summer of 1990. Jordan dealt with several reports from RAF pilots: one had spotted what appeared to be a sign in the middle of a field of wheat that pointed to a nearby Royal Ordnance factory. It was about 150 feet long and seemed to grow more vivid each day. Jordan discovered that the farmer had sown wheat, then found some seed barley and, not wanting to waste it, drilled it down the middle of the field. As the two crops grew the barley appeared to point to the factory. Another pilot noticed that a field had been ploughed in such a way that the outline of a hammer and sickle was clearly visible. The farmer confessed that, far from harbouring Soviet sympathies, he had wanted to make his wife laugh. A third pilot became convinced that he could see a white arrow glinting in the sun. It grew longer each day, and seemed to point to ICI's chemical factory, an important target for the Luftwaffe. A close investigation on the ground found that the 'arrow' was a granite path under construction in the grounds of a sanatorium.

Often tip-offs coincided with a sudden increase in the ferocity of air attacks. A man in Bolton became convinced that someone was flashing Morse code messages from a hillside but closer investigation found nothing more sinister than courting couples carrying torches. A scientist living near an RAF airbase in Cheshire was equally sure that he had discovered the site of a heliograph – a signalling device that reflects sunlight using a movable mirror – which was flashing out the words 'Hier ist' ['Here it is'] in Morse code. He even replied to the message, until investigators discovered that the lights were sunbeams bouncing off the windscreens of cars as they trundled along a bumpy road.

Many rumours of that late summer showed a subtle shift in emphasis. Rather than relating to the horrors the Nazis were about to inflict, they stressed how a certain place would be saved. Perhaps as the bombing became more widespread people wanted to feel they had exclusive information that reinforced rather than undermined their sense of security. In September the novelist Naomi Royde Smith heard a rumour that the Luftwaffe would spare Winchester because Hitler wanted its cathedral to survive undamaged so that he could be 'crowned' there. A variation on this story suggested it would remain inviolate because it was such a useful landmark for bombers, although Royde Smith later heard that British pilots found it difficult to spot from the air. These stories were imbued with one-upmanship, which suggested that only the run-of-the-mill might be obliterated. In another variation, Vera Brittain heard that Oxford was safe because Hitler wanted to maintain the glittering spires as a suitable background for when he collected his honorary degree.

19

Better Dead than Nazi?

The early afternoon of Friday, 16 August, was warm; a slight haze hung over the Channel. Twenty-three-year-old Flight Lieutenant James Nicolson was waiting with the newly formed 249 Squadron at Boscombe Down, in Wiltshire, for his first taste of aerial combat. By the standards of the time, he was a relatively experienced flyer, having trained as a pilot four years earlier. His fellow officers called him Nick and recognised him as a dogged, 'press-on' airman. His wife was at home in Yorkshire, waiting to give birth to their child.

Just before one o'clock the always uneasy calm of an RAF base was shattered by the order for pilots to 'scramble'. Nick sprinted to his Hawker Hurricane and raced up into the cloudless sky with Squadron Leader Eric King and Pilot Officer Martyn King (no relation). They were heading for Southampton where bombers were battering the city.

Nick spotted three German Junkers 88s ahead, but as he and his comrades prepared to attack, a band of Spitfires beat them to it. They climbed to 18,000 feet and were poised to return to base when a lurking Messerschmitt bore down on them from above. The squadron leader's aircraft was the least badly damaged and he limped home. Pilot Officer King's plane was enveloped in flames and he was forced to bail out. Then four cannon shells ripped into Nick's Hurricane. The first tore through the cockpit canopy and sent a jagged shard of plastic through his left eyelid, which brought down an iodine red curtain to obliterate the sky. A second shell hit the reserve petrol tank, which burst into flames, and a third plunged into his left foot. The fourth caused relatively little damage.

Soon he was sitting in a blazing cockpit. The instrument panel in front of him was melting into distorted, crazy shapes, the glass fronts cracking and popping in the heat, which also caused his hands to swell and blister. His trousers were on fire. As he undid his safety-belt and prepared to bail out a German aeroplane appeared in front of him. He struggled back towards his controls to drive the Hurricane forward in one last attack, shouting, 'I'll teach you some manners, you Hun.'

The enemy plane went whining into the sea, and Nick fell head-first out of his Hurricane. According to one account, he plummeted several thousand feet before he remembered to pull his parachute's ripcord. Freed from his burning plane, though, he became an easy target, his torn face, scarified hands and smashed foot melding into a streamlined exclamation mark of pain. When a Messerschmitt appeared to be closing in on him he slumped forward in the limp posture of a corpse. As soon as it disappeared, he steered the parachute away from the sea, dodging electricity cables, towards the safety of British soil. As he was nearing the ground a member of the Home Guard, assuming he was a Nazi, opened fire with a twelve-bore shotgun, hitting him in the buttock – one of the few parts of his body that had been unscathed. He was taken to hospital, barely alive. Martyn King was not so lucky: his parachute was ripped to pieces by friendly fire and he fell to his death.

Nick's actions that day were to win him the Victoria Cross, making him the sole fighter pilot among thirty-two airmen of the Second World War to receive the honour. But he was not the only one who escaped from a burning cockpit to find himself floating through a hail of bullets. Sometimes the ordeal started when the parachutist touched down. Czech and Polish airmen who bailed out often faced vigorous interrogation by armed men on the ground who wanted to know why they spoke with an accent that sounded suspiciously close to German. So great was the fear that overeager Home Guard members might inadvertently reduce 'the few' to the even fewer that at least one commanding officer offered a five-pound reward for every German parachutist who was captured alive, in the hope of saving British airmen. Sir Jocelyn

Lucas, MP, suggested that the Air Ministry should provide a similar incentive.

The British people had watched from the sidelines as German armies marched through Europe and wondered how they would react to invasion. Just occasionally – as when the Home Guard took aim at a supposed Nazi – they caught a glimpse of how it might unfold. In an article for the 8 June issue of *Time and Tide* Rebecca West summed up the horror:

> If the worst comes to the worst, and the Germans invade England, many of us will be hurt and some of us will be killed. We will see other people, possibly those whom we love, being hurt and being killed. Our homes may be destroyed, and towns which are dear to us, and woods and fields which are the fond background of our lives, may be horribly annulled. We may know fire as a pursuing enemy and hunger and thirst as our companions, so well that sudden death becomes a friend.

Margery Allingham, too, put into words what many people were thinking:

> Would you rather die, perhaps horribly, than be controlled by a force of which you do not approve? . . . Would you personally rather go out here and now, leave off living with all that entails or doesn't according to your private beliefs, leave your home and your friends and your family (and see *them* die) or settle down to make the best of a life in which your country's soil, your own soul and your children's children's souls are not yours or their own? You could cheat, couldn't you? You could think one thing and do another.

Sir Alexander Cadogan was unequivocal on the subject: 'I should count it a privilege to be dead if Hitler rules England,' he confided to his diary.

If you were Jewish, of course, the prospects of Nazi control were unremittingly bleak. A few tried to hide their ancestry by changing their names, although the Jewish stockbroker who swapped 'Cecil Isaacs' for 'Cecil Cecil' was hardly courting anonymity. Many

Jewish servicemen and -women were advised to claim the Church of England as their religion, to ensure better treatment if they were captured, but many chose not to deny their faith. In some forces, such as the Commandos and the Special Operations Executive, members were ordered to take English names.

When the Jewish Free School was evacuated from the East End of London to Ely, Cambridgeshire, the families who took in the children were acutely aware of what an invasion would mean to them. One mother told her daughter and a young Jewish evacuee living with them that if the Germans came they must say they were sisters. Since both were blonde the subterfuge might have worked. For the well-known, such as the left-wing publisher Victor Gollancz – twice damned in Nazi eyes as a Jew and an opponent of Hitler's Germany – there was no hope of blending into the background and Gollancz preferred the certainty of suicide. When the invasion risk seemed highest he carried a lethal pill with him because he could not bear the thought of torture. He also made arrangements for his younger children to be enrolled under false names in schools outside London.

That winter Virginia Woolf and her husband, Leonard, who was Jewish, kept their car filled with petrol so that they could use exhaust fumes as an exit route. On 9 June Virginia wrote in her diary, '. . . I reflect: capitulation will mean all Jews to be given up. Concentration camps. So to our garage.'

Leonard Woolf was one of a group of prominent intellectuals who believed they would be among the first arrested when the Nazis landed. The novelist Rose Macaulay told her sister, 'I am sorry that so many of my friends are on the Nazi blacklist, either as Left-Wing, anti-Nazi journalists, writers, publishers, public speakers, or what not. [David] Low [the cartoonist], is, for one, I hear. And, of course, the Jews such as Victor Gollancz and Leonard Woolf, and Philip Guedalla [the historian], who are anti-Nazi also.' She had heard that some of those who believed they were on the list planned to steal identity cards from corpses after air raids and assume a new name once the invasion had started. 'But I fear the Gestapo will be up to that . . .' she concluded. Her concerns about her friends were well founded: everyone she mentioned was indeed on the Nazis' Black List – with the exception of Philip Guedalla, although a 'Herbert Guedalla' is there. Her own name appears as 'Macaullay'. Several other writers featured, including Aldous Huxley, although he had emigrated to America in 1936, Vera Brittain, H. G. Wells, E. M. Forster, C. P. Snow, J. B. Priestley, Lytton Strachey, who had died in 1932, Stefan Zweig, who was in America, and Rebecca West. Paul Robeson and Sybil Thorndike headed the performers, and the best-known artist was Jacob Epstein. There were also prominent politicians, peers, diplomats, refugees and exiled representatives of countries now under Nazi domination, like Jan Paderewski, the Polish president, although he, too, was in America.

Rumours about the list were spreading long before mid-August when the Germans dropped empty parachutes with a supposed kit for would-be spies that included a list of prominent Britons. The Gestapo had started to compile it at around the time of the fall of France and *Die Sonderfahndungsliste GB* (literally 'The Special Wanted List') gave the names of 2820 British subjects and foreigners living in the UK who would be rounded up soon after an invasion. It was included in a booklet, *Informationsheft GB*, which was a Nazi cribsheet about how Britain operated. As well as providing school-textbook facts and figures on climate, population, transport and local government, it attempted to explain the influence of institutions ranging from the Boy Scouts, public schools and universities to freemasonry and the Jewish community.

Although the publication contains much accurate information, the Black List is riddled with eccentric spellings – Churchill's son-in-law, a politician in his own right, appears as 'Dunkan [Duncan] Sandys', with 'Beaverbrock', 'Betrand Russel' and 'Steffan' Spender. It conjures up a curious picture of the Gestapo's perception of Britain's 'most wanted' citizens. Under C, for example, Noël Coward appears next to Nancy Cunard, the heiress who scandalised London society by living with a black jazz musician and wrote anti-Fascist pamphlets, and more traditional politicians such as Violet 'Carter-Bonham' (Bonham-Carter), 'Sir Cadogan', wrongly described as head of the British Intelligence Service, and Neville Chamberlain.

Details of the list became widely known after the war and inclusion carried a certain cachet: people boasted that they had been 'at the top' of the Nazis' list – although it was laid out in strictly alphabetical order. When a newspaper told David Low that the Gestapo had singled him out for special treatment, he replied, 'That is all right. I had them on my list too.' As soon as Rebecca West discovered that both she and Noël Coward's names were there, she sent him a telegram that read, 'My dear – the people we should have been seen dead with.' I find it difficult to conceal a frisson of pride at the name 'William Gillies', even though I can hardly claim the Labour politician as more than a far distant relative.

MI5 and Special Branch, too, were gathering the names of people they planned to arrest when the Germans arrived. Immediately after an invasion the British government hoped to divide the country into regions run by commissioners who would round up known Nazi sympathisers before they could offer the invaders any help. MI5's list eventually stretched to more than four hundred and included the Marquess of Tavistock, who became the 12th Duke of Bedford, and Admiral Sir Barry Domville, a former head of Naval Intelligence who had attended the 1937 Nuremberg rally. Lord Tavistock had travelled to Dublin to try to start peace negotiations with the German legation there and had been vociferous in his pro-Nazi views. MI5's report on him stated that in the event of an invasion he was likely to 'cause alarm and despondency by public utterances and to weaken the will of his countrymen to resist the invader'. They were also worried that the Germans might set him up as the head of a puppet British government. At least five people on the list were friends of Anna Wolkoff, the Russian-born dressmaker who was arrested for trying to pass secrets to the Germans, but it included more humble citizens, too – such as a coal miner from Kent – because they had expressed pro-German views or were sympathetic to Irish, Scottish or Welsh independence.

Like so many aspects of life in 1940, death was marked by class distinction. The well-connected and well-off were likely to know a sympathetic family doctor who would procure suicide pills as a clean, foolproof escape from Nazi Britain. In *The Pursuit of Love* Lord Merlin has the wrong sort of pills – the kind you give to dogs – while the hypochondriac journalist Davey, who is worried that the Germans will torture him, keeps his supply in a jewelled box and knows the correct order in which to swallow the deadly black and white tablets. Frances Partridge and her friends talked openly of taking their own lives, rather than risking incarceration in a concentration camp. They had heard of a man who had been desperate to persuade his wife to sign a suicide pact. When she declined he shot her at her writing desk, then turned the gun on himself. A friend of Partridge said he knew a French doctor who had been asked by nearly all of his patients for a reliable poison. Physicians were not always accommodating, and when Partridge asked a doctor in Canada for some lethal pills, she refused and instead urged her to leave Britain.

She and her husband shared the torment of deciding whether or not to gas themselves and their five-year-old son, but in many couples it was the woman who planned the unthinkable. A mother of a well-to-do family who lived in West Sussex, barely seven miles from the coast, obtained enough poison to kill her three teenage daughters, their younger brother – if he happened to be home from boarding-school – herself and her husband, a member of the Home Guard. Margaret Kennedy had not yet taken such drastic measures, but as she sat on a Cornish beach with other mothers, knitting and watching her children paddle, she felt powerless to save them from 'a most hideous fate'. Although she kept her fears to herself she wrote in her journal: 'I can imagine circumstances in which I could almost think it better to kill mine.'

Vita Sackville-West and Harold Nicolson turned to a soliloquy from *Hamlet* for inspiration. Shakespeare's 'bare bodkin' refers to a dagger or a stiletto-pointed hairpin, but Nicolson had a medical application in mind when he wrote to his wife, 'What I dread is being tortured and humiliated. But how can we find a bodkin which will give us our quietus quickly and which is easily portable? I shall ask my doctor friends.' Sackville-West's mother was French, and she must have found the collapse of France particularly painful. She wrote to Nicolson in despair about a future she saw as 'scarlet and black' but took heart from their plans: 'And there is always the bare bodkin.' When he confided that he had procured what they needed he reassured her that 'It all looks very simple.'

Death was even simpler for the lower and middle classes, who had no access to fancy pills. Female weavers in Huddersfield swore they would gas themselves – presumably at home in their kitchens – if Hitler arrived, and at least one threatened to inflict the same fate on her two children. George Beardmore recorded how typists whom he worked with at the BBC said they would shoot themselves rather than give in. In Snettisham several women claimed they would poison themselves; they did not explain how but poison was easy to come by in rural areas. It was used to keep vermin in check – although rat bait promised an agonising death – and the countryside was stocked with natural poisons, such as deadly nightshade. Farmers, gamekeepers and men like Matthew, who liked to bag the occasional pigeon or rabbit, had the option of shooting until they had one cartridge left for their own dispatch.

A minority did not bother waiting for Hitler but committed suicide when life became unbearable. The fear of internment – and all it entailed – forced some enemy aliens to take their lives rather than wait to be locked up. The restrictions of internment caused many to lose their jobs, either because they were forced to quit the Defence Zone where they worked or because their employers felt they were a security risk or an embarrassment. A couple in their fifties from Richmond took poison because they feared they would be separated. A German-born Jewish teacher drowned himself in the Thames after he had been ordered out of a protected area. He left behind a heart-wrenching note in which he thanked Britain for her kindness and ended, 'May England be victorious.' The wife of an Austrian Jew interned on the Isle of Man took an overdose of sleeping tablets because she found the separation unbearable. A professor of chemistry, who had been tortured in a concentration camp then fled Germany, poisoned himself when the British police arrived to arrest him.

Those who were not prepared to kill themselves made elaborate plans for how to survive Nazi rule, and speculated, often matter-of-factly, about life under Hitler. Uncle Matthew in *The Pursuit of Love* horrified his family by ordering them to blow up their bulging larder, or 'Aladdin', as it was known, so that the Germans could not share in it. Rose Macaulay was most worried about her home: 'I shall slightly regret having to leave London if we are to be invaded, as who knows what will happen to people, or to my flat? I must have someone to look after it and keep my books and things from the Germans. Perhaps I had better lend it to someone who will take care of it and keep Mrs Browne on . . .'

Her implication that Germans were too savage and uncultured to be trusted with servants, never mind books, was one of the more polite comments about the enemy. In Snettisham, Matthew referred to German troops collectively as 'old Nasti' – which sounded as malicious as a schoolyard taunt – but the novelist Fryn Tennyson Jesse's comment to an American friend was laced with venom: 'It is a pity that the German race look like human beings. It is as dangerous a resemblance as that of the wolf to the dog or the tiger to the cat. We might just as well go and open the cages of the tigers and wolves in the zoo and say "good day" and "pretty pussy" as admit Germans to any human contact.'

There was an underlying sexual tension in some women's anxieties. Many feared that they would be made to marry Germans so that the two nationalities would become entwined as quickly as possible. Lytton Strachey's niece, Julia, who was thirty-nine, told her friend Frances Partridge that if the Germans landed she intended to make herself look as old and ugly as possible to avoid being raped.

Hitler, as leader of the faceless hordes of Nazis, became the focus of vilification. He soon lost the title 'Herr' and became a figure of fun with disrespectful nicknames, such as 'Little Tich', after the clowning music-hall star, or 'Old Nasty'. As his power and menace grew, his name shrank to the point at which he was anonymous – or at most an acronym: 'that man' or, in Tommy Handley's hugely popular radio show, *ITMA*, simply 'He'.

Handley reduced the Führer and his generals to an effete group of Boy Scouts in his song 'That Very Little Nazi':

> Does Adolf wear pyjamas or a night shirt?
> Does he take his teeth out when he goes to bed?
> Is that unruly lock of hair
> A detachable affair
> Which he hangs up on the bedpost overhead?
> He looks so big and fierce in all his warpaint
> But when once he's hung his raincoat on the door,
> And removed that awful tunic,
> Which cost fifty bob in Munich,
> There's a very little Nazi in the raw.
>
> His moustache I wonder if it's really pukka,
> Or neatly made to clip on to the face?. . .
> As the Fuehrer nears the climax of his strip tease
> Does each S.S. man avert his blushing head
> Till he lies there, gently smiling,
> And they exit backwards, heiling
> For a very little Nazi safe in bed?

Watching the newsreel, it was easy to imagine that Hitler's Blitzkrieg would transform Britain into a landscape of rubble and smoking ruins, of displaced people and handcarts loaded with worldly goods. Margery Allingham envisaged her village as a battleground and that they would have to retreat underground to listen to the fighting above. She forced herself to be practical and to consider how she could let her husband know where she was if they became separated. Her first thought was to leave a note under the sundial in her garden, as if she had just popped out to a friend's for tea, until she realised that sundials are not known for withstanding fierce bombardment. Finally, she decided that her publisher's office in America was 'the only safe address in the world' and that they would make contact through it 'somehow, if we had to swim the Atlantic or wait ten years'.

Vernon Bartlett, a journalist, broadcaster and MP, who won his seat on an anti-appeasement ticket, anticipated fleeing to the hills when the Germans arrived. In one of those pathetic details that reveal someone clinging to normality when their life has descended into chaos, he asked his wife to make him a chamois leather bag in which he could carry fifty-pound notes round his waist to help him pay his way in his new life as a fugitive.

Even before the war the BBC had been planning for a 'grave emergency', the catch-all term it used to cover any event that might disrupt the imperturbable newsreaders, from a bomb hitting Broadcasting House, which was a brash landmark on the London skyline, to the arrival of storm-troopers in the studio. Memos flew back and forth in the effort to ensure that every possibility was covered. Radio was recognised as so powerful a weapon in the hands of the enemy that security around the BBC's studios and transmitters was intensified to such an extent that, by the end of the summer, Broadcasting House felt as impregnable and claustrophobic as a bunker. Soldiers guarded transmitting stations at Daventry, Droitwich and Brookmans Park but, while they could probably stop a ground attack by 'a civil mob or by parachutists', the BBC knew it could do nothing to protect them from aerial bombardment. Broadcasting House's imposing main entrance was partially bricked up, leaving a narrow entrance through which its staff filed, and the central control room, the news studio and the emergency news room were moved to the sub-basement. The Home Guard and soldiers prowled the labyrinthine corridors and a door close to the defence room, from where the building's security was overseen, bore the unambiguous warning that anyone who failed to show their pass would be shot.

The senior announcer began his day by ringing the senior control-room engineer before 7 a.m. and stating, 'This is Howland [announcer's name] speaking. Today's Home Service code word is "Thunderbolt".' It was used to prefix all subsequent messages, handed from announcer to announcer as the day progressed; if anyone tried to communicate without it the engineer was to phone for help. Switches were installed under the desk at the main entrances and receptionists were told to push them in an emergency. But they were easily knocked, causing frequent false alarms. When Gilbert Harding worked as an Information Bureau supervisor at Broadcasting House he once inadvertently kicked the switch when he stretched his legs. Throughout the cavernous building, steel doors slammed shut, bells rang and the Home Guard pounded down the corridor.

It was the senior engineer's task to ring Reception to ask why the buzzer had gone off. If he heard 'Everything is all right, Bill', he knew it had been a false alarm or that the panic was over. However, if the reply did not include 'Bill' the engineer had to ring Scotland Yard immediately to report that the building was under attack. Scotland Yard, a memo had said reassuringly, would 'render assistance'. Only a repetition of 'Bill' would open the doors. The next day a note changed the name to 'John' – perhaps because it had been agreed that the name should change regularly.

If Broadcasting House was attacked, the engineers would do their best to interrupt programmes for just three minutes, after which Wood Norton would assume technical control while Bristol would take charge of programme content. The two centres had to maintain the illusion that all was well even if the invasion had started, and both drew up schedules to plug any gap in transmission, due to bombing or an attack by German troops. Wood Norton in particular was confident of finding performers prepared to step in: 'There are practically always two or three artists, and sometimes many more, staying in Evesham,' a memo pointed out. The two regional centres would only pass control back to the capital when they had received a secret code word that they would also use when speaking to one another. It was kept in a sealed envelope that had to be replaced immediately if it was opened inadvertently by the wrong person or if it showed signs of tampering.

Apart from the physical threat to the BBC's buildings the corporation feared that the Nazis would sneak a bogus announcement on to the airwaves by phoning in false reports. On 13 May this happened twice in one day. The first item told all RAF Volunteer Reserves who were on leave or engaged in civilian work to report to their bases; the second warned children to stay away from RAF buildings in certain parts of the country. In future the Ministry of Information checked news items before they were broadcast. A censor kept a close watch over scripts as they were read; if the announcer deviated in any way from the prepared text he could fade out the broadcast. The senior control-room engineer might take similar action if he spotted a change from the advertised programme or an 'unauthorised interpolation' from outside the building, unless it was accompanied by a specific code word. In this world of passwords and suspicion the BBC became even more choosy about whom it employed. It took on few foreigners – usually only for its overseas and monitoring services – and no registered conscientious objectors, active political extremists, anyone who expressed defeatist views or who was related to or a close associate of an internee, or – in a final sweeping generalisation – anyone 'known to be undesirable'.

The talks, plays and short stories for use in an emergency were chosen to be uplifting. The selection for the week beginning 1 September included *Hi Gang!*, *Napoleon Couldn't Do It*, *They're Off*, *Love Passes By* and *Our Empire*. In theory, an announcer was expected to shuffle through a pile of records until he found one that the BBC had permission to play while German storm-troopers battered on the steel doors outside his studio. At the beginning of September a defence regulation was put in place that allowed the BBC, if circumstances dictated, to use any recordings in an emergency, even if it did not have the express permission of the artist, composer or author. But the memo that outlined the new regulation stressed that only the minister of information could judge whether or not the BBC might play a certain record without the express permission of the artist and that the circumstances must be 'very grave'.

Imagine this in Cambridge

Imagine this

in your market place

H·M·S LOYAL & HER GALLANT MEN
HELP TO SAVE YOU FROM THIS
SAVE FOR H·M·S LOYAL!

Reports from occupied Europe fuelled fears of what the Nazis would do in Britain. These drawings, taken from a leaflet promoting war bonds, show a swastika draped over King's College, Cambridge.

PART SIX

September, 'He is Coming . . .'

20

Muriel, Jenny and Frank – Summer's End

'Awful feeling this morning about the end of a perfect week, everyone looked miserable, myself could have cried,' Jenny wrote as the Cambridge summer school she, Muriel and the schoolmaster had attended drew to a close. 'S [the schoolmaster?] had notice of medical exam for next Friday, which depressed us.'

Even education was rationed in 1940, and their time away represented a university experience compressed into a week; it was idyllic, intense, far removed from reality and crammed with opportunity. Jenny walked round Cambridge with the schoolmaster until nearly 11 p.m. as they traded intimacies and discussed the concept of marriage. The horrors of the wider world appeared theoretical next to the luxuries they had enjoyed. She wrote an essay on 'The Jewish Problem', and punted down the river to Grantchester, where Rupert Brooke had swum until a previous war had ended his life. On the way home she took a short-cut across a field and wondered whether this might be viewed as suspicious.

Jenny and Muriel discussed 'class and national loyalty' with students far removed from daily life in Snettisham: one was from India and another was a sixty-five-year-old blind man. In the evenings they took part in community singing and saw *The Invisible Man Returns* at the pictures. Both sisters attracted attention from the male students in a climate where personal loyalties were becoming blurred. Jenny received a letter from someone who had once been her 'best young man'; she had not heard from him since March and had assumed he was 'gone for good'. He was with the army in Scotland but expected to come home soon on leave. She was forced to admit that her friendship with the schoolmaster had grown much closer over the summer. 'This is going to be awkward as S is trying to get rid of some mysterious girl aged 17 in Manchester. He also had a letter this morning, asking what he was doing!'

As they took the train north across the Fens to King's Lynn Jenny sank into a despondent reverie. 'The war had seemed a long way off at Cambridge, I never heard any news all the week and only once looked in a local paper for the cinema list,' she wrote. 'It did not seem possible that there was a war on, but as soon as we got home there were the planes, gun practice and searchlights at night and it seemed as if we had come into a fighting area.'

Muriel expressed similar feelings: 'One feels v. flat on the train home after a week like that, especially when we realised the war was still on, and we were coming back into a restricted area.'

They returned to a tense atmosphere. During a violent night of bombardment they sat hugging each other on the sofa in the front room with big cushions balanced on their heads to protect themselves from the three large windows, which, if shattered, would have sprayed them with shards of glass. They had forsaken the bathroom for this more hazardous refuge because the light in the confined space dazzled them and they needed respite from Susan, who complained constantly about the Germans' bombing tactics: 'Mother kept saying they were throwing them overboard with no more regard than if they were baskets of eggs.'

The sisters had returned to a world of worries about house-keeping and the cost of living, where harvest was no longer a celebration of rural plenty but a race to extract all that could be had from the ground before winter set in. Once the farmers and gardeners had done their bit, housewives like Susan marched into battle on the kitchen front, where they strove to produce nutritious and economical meals. Home-grown produce freed space on ships bringing essentials to a beleaguered nation. Housewives were also urged to use as little fuel as possible. In the absence of military victories it was important that Britain was seen at least to be eating better than the enemy. *Punch* claimed that Germany had resorted to boiling strawberry leaves as a substitute for tea and Lord Haw-Haw – whose rantings were increasingly furious in the late summer

– hit back with accusations that wealthy Britons were gorging themselves in hotels while the lower classes starved. The *Kitchen Front* radio programme advised on food preparation, and newspapers deluged readers with tips. The *Lynn News* called for a return to ancient herbal remedies and traditional foodstuffs. The paper claimed that lad's love, an aromatic bitter herb used in absinthe, cured thinning hair and dandruff; knapweed was efficient in clearing up piles and catarrh, and Roman wood, which grew on the foreshore, kept moths and mice at bay. East Anglians, it argued, should rediscover the joys of eels, which were more nutritious than trout.

The onset of autumn brought renewed worries about whether food supplies would hold up or whether Britain would be reduced to the type of poverty that cinema-goers had glimpsed in the recently released *The Grapes of Wrath*. Housewives tried endlessly to trick the tastebuds of their families into accepting *ersatz* meals but compromise had to be learnt. When a valet told General Lee that he had run out of tea, the general suggested coffee as an alternative. The valet, who seems to have been unused to an energetic employer, was horrified: 'But that would never do, sir. Coffee keeps you awake all day.'

During the summer months it had been possible to avoid the blackout by going to bed when it got dark. As the daylight hours dwindled, though, the depressing ritual that marked the earlier onset of night returned, bringing with it the grim anniversary of the start of the war.

In August, Frank O'Brien moved to another army camp, this time at Ringwood, to the west of Southampton, in Hampshire. He was not impressed with his new home, which he described to Mary as 'this terrible place, no dancing or pictures it's Pa Bon darling'. He concentrated on trying to secure a week's leave in Glasgow and poured all his suppressed emotions into his letters home. 'I think the world of you darling,' he wrote. 'I want to do everything to please you. I don't want to lose you, I'll make you happy darling. I have a surprise for you when I come home, a thing every girl looks forward to. You might have a good idea what it is.' Perhaps he had bought a ring and planned to propose to her, or maybe the surprise was something that a good Catholic girl would have found harder to accept. Whatever it was, Mary's response failed to match Frank's excitement and his next letter was full of remorse and self-recrimination.

> God knows when I will see you again it might be after the new year, it doesn't matter how long it may be I'll always love you darling. But remember to enjoy yourself don't stay in the house, go out with Sadie and have a swell time when you get the chance. And if any boy should ask you out, go with him, I can't expect you to stay in and wait for me, it's too much to ask any girl to do. Don't be angry with me darling I want to see you having a good time the same as any other girl. I'm awfully sorry I did such bad things when I was home, I went too far. Please forgive me darling, it will never happen again and don't blame yourself, it was me who was to blame for everything. You are very sweet Mary and never said a word to me for doing such terrible things and I love you for it.

Back in 'this horrible place', he described his leave as 'seven days of heaven'. Part of Frank's unease may have stemmed from the uncomfortable proximity of his army base to airfields that the Luftwaffe had bombed recently with increased ferocity. *Adlertag* (Day of the Eagles) marked the start of the Nazis' drive to overpower the RAF in preparation for invasion, and after several delays, partly due to the weather, the aerial campaign had begun on 13 August. On 24 August over a hundred people were killed in a raid on Portsmouth, and later that night 170 German bombers attacked targets ranging from Northumberland and Lancashire to Kent and Plymouth. Although the pilots had not intended to strike at London, their bombs went so far adrift that its financial heartland was hit, for the first time since 1918, and other areas suffered, including Islington, Tottenham and East Ham. In retaliation, British bombers carried out their first raid on Berlin. On 29 August Sir Alexander Cadogan confided to his diary: 'Winston thinks German scheme is to hammer Kent flat and then attempt invasion.' Aerial photographs of the German coast showed an unusual build-up of shipping: around fifty merchant ships had gathered at Kiel and – more worryingly – 350 large motor launches, which might be used to attempt a Channel crossing, were positioned at Emden, close to the Dutch border. The Invasion Warning sub-committee took note but convinced themselves that there must be some other reason for the ships' appearance: perhaps they had been forced to wait there by mines.

Soon more and more of the country had experienced the terror of bombing. In Liverpool, Ludwig Baruch's Hilda waited to hear where he had been taken, unaware that he was now on the other side of the world. On the night of 28 August German bombers turned their attention to the city and continued the bombardment for three more; a nightly average of 157 bombers were sent to Liverpool and Birkenhead. The attacks were de-signed to disrupt the area's factories and the important west-coast ports to which vital supplies were delivered from Canada and the United States. Virginia Woolf recorded, '. . . the air raids are now at their prelude. Invasion, if it comes, must come within three weeks.'

The British Army was in better shape than it had been after the evacuation from Dunkirk. Soldiers like Frank were well trained now and had patched up the nakedness of their retreat from France. They had more field guns – only about half were new, the rest converted – and many more light tanks, armed with machine-guns. But Britain's defences were still a poor match for an enemy equipped with armoured tanks and practised in the art of Blitzkrieg. Roughly half of the soldiers guarding Britain lacked collective training, and most were precariously short of transport. The RAF, still racing to catch up in numbers with the Luftwaffe, had had little chance to practise a strategic defence, co-ordinated with the army.

Suddenly, on 3 September, reconnaissance planes flying over occupied Europe noticed an alarming build-up of barges in Dutch and Belgian ports, their long, thin bodies clinging to harbour sides like the oars of Roman men-of-war. The Invasion Warning sub-committee comforted itself that the barges might be massing to head south and gather vital supplies of iron, steel, textiles and oil, or even that the network of canals had been freed of some obstacle and they were queuing to be on their way. But the RAF pilots who had glimpsed them drew an unequivocal conclusion, as they told Charlie Mason, the resistance fighter, and others on their return to England: the Germans were preparing to invade.

On Wednesday, 4 September, *The Times* reported comments by Anthony Eden, secretary of state for War, that the threat of invasion was so acute that Britain must show special vigilance over the next few weeks. The next day, under the headline 'Hitler's New Bluster', the paper reported the Führer's speech at the Berlin Sportpalast in which he fulminated against the British bombers, the 'night pirates', who had attacked the German capital. In a voice heavy with sarcasm he told an adoring crowd, 'When people are very curious in Great Britain and ask, "Yes, why don't you come?" we reply, "Calm yourselves, we shall come." ' That day the Invasion Warning sub-committee learnt that all leave was due to be cancelled in the German Army on 8 September, and in a speech to the House of Commons, Winston Churchill reiterated Eden's warning while General Lee surmised, 'On a cold-blooded appraisal, one might say that the betting on Britain's beating off an invasion this fall is now about three to one.' Bomber Command turned its attention to the ships and supply dumps on the quays at French ports.

On Friday, 6 September, another spy with a wireless was captured soon after he landed by parachute near Denton in Northamptonshire. After MI5 interviewed him he was 'turned' – persuaded to change sides – and told the authorities that another agent with whom he had lodged in Hamburg was due to arrive later that month.

The latest edition of the *War* ran an article under the headline, 'Hitler May Still Try to Invade Us This Year', warning readers not to believe those parts of the German press that suggested he might have changed his mind: these comments were intended to 'lull the defenders of Britain'. It reminded readers that other articles had told of how German troops on the French coast had been practising rowing and climbing high cliffs. Most ominously, their training now included learning how to attack strongly fortified shore positions and studying maps of England.

21

Invasion Weekend, Saturday, 7 September 1940

The first week in September was unusually warm and on Wednesday, 4 September, temperatures as high as 87° Fahrenheit were recorded in parts of London, including Camden Square, East Ham and Kensington. August had been the driest since records began in 1815. London had experienced only one rainy day in three months, and the grass in the capital's parks was brown and parched; the leaves were yellow and shrivelled.

The American journalist Ben Robertson described Saturday, 7 September, as 'a perfect day', and RAF reports confirmed the weather as 'fair with some haze'.

After a summer of gazing at vapour trails, Robertson recognised the sort of clear blue sky that would entice German aeroplanes to venture across the Channel and he set off with two other American reporter friends, Vincent Sheean and Ed Murrow, to find the best vantage-point from which to observe the combat. If they stayed in London their view would be hampered by its low-lying position and scarcity of open spaces – watching the skirmishes at Dover had taught them that much. Instead, they followed the Thames past the docks, where the ships were carrying out their dangerous work of supplying the country with food and other necessities. As they left the city behind, the river widened into a broad estuary where convoys of armed ships escorted the merchant vessels towards the port. They paused to buy apples from a farmer, each man filling his tin hat with them before climbing on to a haystack by the edge of a turnip field to eat some. They were on the outskirts of a built-up area and needed to be sure that they had a ditch to dive into if the siren sounded – a stretch of road with no cover was considered too exposed to linger on. Then they dozed and glanced up at the sky.

The day had started quietly for the RAF pilots, whom Robertson described as 'crusaders': their German counterparts, like the American reporters, seemed to be snoozing in the warm autumn sunshine. Nothing much happened until mid-morning when around thirty aeroplanes crossed the Channel near Lympne and attacked Dover and Hawkinge, north of Folkestone, but failed to penetrate far inland. Over East Anglian skies an RAF plane chased a returning bomber across the Wash to Lincoln but failed to catch him; another pilot spotted a German over Norfolk and shot him down off the Dutch coast.

At around 4.35 p.m., as daylight was just starting to seep away, the siren sent up its shrill, unearthly wail. The three Americans hurled themselves into the nearest ditch where they were soon joined by a boy and girl, who had flung their bikes on to the ground, and a bus-driver with his passengers, who had abandoned their vehicle by the roadside. Overhead they heard British fighters firing at German bombers and the rattle of shrapnel hitting the road. As the battle raged the bus-driver started to talk about a newspaper cartoon that showed two monkeys in the jungle watching an air-raid warden approach them in full 'battledress'. One turned to the other and said, 'Let's beat it. The bloody fool is coming to civilise us.' The busybody air-raid warden was always useful as a focus for defusing tension and the driver might have developed his patter to cope with the stress of imminent danger and the awkwardness of finding himself trapped with a group of strangers, wondering whether they would be killed or spared. Most people developed tics and gave in to superstitions when they heard the crump of a bomb hitting its target. Some chattered incessantly, while the American journalist Eric Sevareid noticed that others did exactly the opposite of what they had been doing before: if they had been walking, they stopped; if they were motionless, the noise freed them to move – however they had been sitting or standing they changed position, all of which was contrary to the official advice to lie flat on the ground.

As the driver talked relentlessly about the cartoon, the British fighter planes returned to their base to refuel and a second wave of twenty-four German bombers flew over, then a third of thirty-six. 'These ships flew at a very great height, glistening like beautiful steel birds in the afternoon sunshine,' Robertson wrote. 'They flew in perfect formation and soon we heard the terrific detonation of bombs being dropped on London.' When the fourth wave passed just over their heads, awe turned to terror: they were close to an RAF aerodrome and might attract a direct hit. Murrow had wandered back to the haystack, fear suspended while his journalistic instincts took over. Then terror regained the upper hand and he shouted that his vantage-point was shrinking at such a rate that he was starting to feel 'as big as an elephant cowering behind a peanut'. Watching the sky darken with wave upon wave of aeroplanes took Sheean back to his days of reporting the Spanish Civil War and the horrors of aerial bombardment, especially at Guernica. 'This is just like Spain,' he intoned, in a dazed mantra. They were observing what would come to be known as the start of the Blitz, the first mass daylight attack on London. Goering had travelled to the French coast to bestow his blessing on the three hundred or so bombers, protected by over six hundred fighter planes, who streamed across southern England to the Thames.

The three reporters watched as great clouds of smoke rose above the capital. Then they heard the German bombers making for home, chased by RAF planes. They stood, mesmerised by the smoke, then headed for the nearest pub, where the landlady talked about the battle and her fears for the women, children and animals caught in its crossfire. When night came the journalists returned to the field to watch the 'most appalling and depressing sight any of us had ever seen . . . It almost made us physically ill to see the enormity of the flames that lit the entire western sky. The London that we knew was burning – the London which had taken thirty generations of men a thousand years to build – and the Nazis had done that in thirty seconds.' The spectacle bewitched as well as horrified them. Robertson was unaware, until Murrow told him later, that he had repeated over and over, in his slow South Carolina drawl, 'London is burning, London is burning,' while Sheean cursed in five different languages.

Further south, at Bexhill-on-Sea, Spike Milligan had been to the Playhouse cinema. As he emerged the night was filled with what sounded like relays of German bombers heading inland; cloud was low and the ack-ack guns made only a feeble effort to intimidate them. The soldiers went on to the pub for a drink, then walked home, the bombers still droning overhead. 'Someone's copping it,' the sentry said, as they entered the barracks. Milligan lay in bed smoking until someone called, 'Cor, it looks like the sky's on fire over there.' Then he pulled on his trousers and climbed up to the roof. The blacked-out country, with no welcoming street-lamps or cosy house lights, provided the ideal backdrop to the distant red glow. Someone fetched a compass that confirmed the blaze was centred on London. One man tried to phone his family but was told there was 'disruption' on the line and that all calls to London were blocked. 'We all looked at the blaze and it seemed to be getting bigger,' Milligan wrote later. 'I think we all knew it was London. My mother, father and brother were there. I'm not sure how I felt. Helpless, I suppose.'

The BBC's midnight news made no mention of the raid but many of the soldiers were Londoners and found it difficult to sleep. Their mates called out reassurances in the dark.

'They've all got Anderson shelters, they're dead safe.'

'Yer, dead safe.'

'. . . and there's all that anti-aircraft fire . . . That keeps 'em up 'igh.'

'And there's the Underground, nuffink could break them.'

Milligan's father was a fire warden and, although his son did not know it at the time, watched the start of the Blitz from the Associated Press building in Fleet Street. 'The window near my bed faced north,' Milligan wrote. 'As I lay there, I could see the glow of the fires. The bombers were still going. Some must have been on their way back as we heard cannon fire as night fighters got on to them. What a bloody mess. Men in bombers raining death on defenceless civilians.'

In Hauxton, just south of Cambridge, the Home Guard had also spotted the fires of London, as this extract from their logbook shows:

> Sept. 7th 1940 Visited by Col. Yates at 11.05 p.m. and ordered to man action stations in readiness for the anticipated invasion. Runner to be permanently posted at Police Station. Personnel to proceed to work armed and in uniform. All defences at focal points with blocks out, bombs etc. in position. Men turned out . . . Huge fires observed at 192° presumably at Bethnal Green. . .

With no guidance from the BBC Home Service, or instant access to television news, it must have been terrifying to watch the spectacle from afar and wonder whether the crimson sky was the start of Armageddon.

German radio did its best to stoke the flames of anxiety: 'Hitler may at any hour give orders for the invasion to begin,' it predicted. Monitors at Wood Norton listened in to radio broadcasts that conveyed a picture of panic in Britain. One aimed at a South African audience announced, 'London scared stiff and drunk', and added, 'The number of drunk people in the London bars and streets is increasing continuously. People drink in the big hotel bars as well as in the dives of Whitechapel. London life can be compared to that in Paris before the great offensive . . .' Another report said that destroyers were waiting in ports on the west coast of Scotland to whisk the royal family to Canada and, once the bombing of London started in earnest, 'The whole Parliament headed by War Criminal No. 1 Churchill, fled to the cellar. Only after two hours could the session be resumed in a voice which seemed to come from the cellar. Churchill then made his desperate attempt to comfort the British.'

Hauxton was one of several Home Guard units responding to the code word 'Cromwell', which they were convinced was an order to prepare for invasion. The word echoed across the country, causing confusion, and often panic, wherever it went.

The decision to release 'Cromwell' on a country already twitching with nerves was taken in Whitehall when the Joint Intelligence Committee told the chiefs of staff that invasion *might* be imminent.

The chiefs of staff met to discuss the possibility at twenty past five that Saturday afternoon; General Alan Brooke's, Lieutenant General B. C. T. Paget, attended and listened to the arguments for and against raising the alarm.

Everything seemed to point to invasion. Reconnaissance flights brought back a clear picture of German shipping massing on the other side of the Channel. Hitler's aircraft had also moved into position: aeroplanes from two squadrons had left Norway and Denmark to head south to Holland and Belgium, and other dive-bombers were clustered close to the Strait of Dover. By the morning of 7 September, around six hundred bombers and dive-bombers, and seven hundred fighters, as well as reconnaissance and mine-laying aircraft, were ready either to continue the air battle against Britain or to support an attempt to land German troops. The 'Four Men in a Boat' who had been caught in Kent appeared to be part of a wider strategy to feed back information about troop movements, particularly the formation of reserves in the Oxford, Ipswich, London and Reading areas. The tides in the south-east would be suitable for a landing between 8 and 10 September, when the moon was not yet full and the invader could hide in the shadows.

The navy was already in a state of high alert and the RAF was poised to expect a landing within three days. Twenty-four medium bombers were ready to join up with Home Forces at thirty minutes' notice, and specific tasks had been earmarked for half of the remaining medium bombers if the invasion began. The army 'stood to' each day at the most vulnerable times of dawn and dusk but otherwise were at eight hours' notice. There was no half-way house between that and immediate action.

That evening, at seven minutes past eight, the signal 'Cromwell' was issued from GHQ Home Forces to Eastern and Southern Commands, which covered the whole of East Anglia and the south-west of England, all formations in the London area and IV Corps, troops stationed on the border between the Home Counties and East Anglia, and VII Corps, soldiers, including a Canadian division and tank brigade in Surrey, in GHQ Reserve.

It was also conveyed to parts of the defence network for information only – a decision that had far-reaching implications. It is still not clear exactly who gave the signal. According to some accounts, Paget's deputy, Brigadier (later Sir John) Swayne, who was in charge at that moment gave the order without waiting for the result of the chiefs of staff's meeting. Swayne believed that the odds were stacked against Britain – many of her troops were poorly trained and their camps were linked by feeble, unreliable communications – and that it would have been wrong to delay the warning until the risk of invasion had become a certainty. Churchill wrote later that neither he nor the chiefs of staff were aware that the 'decisive code-word "Cromwell" ' had been used.

Alan Brooke stated in his diary that he had taken the decision before settling down to dinner with a friend and that the meaning of 'Cromwell' was clear: those who received it must propel themselves into a state of the highest *readiness*. Troops should take up their battle stations and assume control of certain civilian telephone and telegraph lines. What it did not mean was that the invasion had started. However, as Chinese whispers set off round the country, the confusion multiplied. In some parts the code word arrived at dead of night and the junior officer who took the call was at best baffled by the unfamiliar word, at worst convinced the Nazis were on their way.

An English woman described her family's experience of the panic that followed in a letter to an American friend: 'Please, censor, don't cut all this out; it is quite harmless and will be useless information to the enemy by the time it arrives,' she pleaded. She and 'Phil' had been at the cinema watching *The Thin Man*, the screen adaptation of Dashiell Hammett's stylish thriller, when a message flashed on to the screen that all soldiers must return to their billets immediately. When the couple reached home, he discovered that the invasion code word had been phoned through. He seized his rifle and kit and reported to army headquarters.

She was about to wash her hair before the midnight news when the doorbell rang. Outside she found a 'very young, very solemn soldier'. He had been told to use their phone to deliver a message, then await further orders for his unit, which had taken up a defensive position nearby. She suggested he put his kit in the hall but he insisted on piling his rifle, tin hat and gas mask by the telephone. He admitted he had never used a phone before so she explained which way to hold the receiver, how to dial and what the engaged tone sounded like. 'He obviously considered that the safety of Britain hung on his every act.'

When she returned at about twelve thirty, having listened to the news, she found him 'clutching the telephone with sweat pouring down from his head and not a thing happening'. She connected him to his headquarters, then stood by, coaxing the right words out of him. After that the phone trilled all night and busloads of troops arrived; Phil returned at 7 a.m.

Frank O'Brien, the Glaswegian soldier, had been on guard duty for six nights that week and was feeling tired and 'fed up'. He seemed conscious that an important moment was approaching but was not quite ready for it. 'I hope everything up in Glasgow is OK,' he wrote to Mary. 'It's very bad up here with air raids. Southampton and Portsmouth are getting it very hard. I don't want to do any fighting in England; I would hate to see any German landing in this country. I would rather fight in France.'

Frank's subdued approach to the crisis is in marked contrast to the reaction of many Home Guard units. Several who received the code word did not realise it was for information only. They believed their time had come. The following account of what happened to the 5th Battalion (Caernarvonshire) Home Guard gives some idea of the panic it caused. Training was officially over for the night in Llandudno, and most members had wandered home, to the pub or the working-men's club. A few of the keener members lingered at the British Legion even though the bar had closed several hours before. A corporal from the Royal Corps of Signals was demonstrating the correct procedure for a slow march when the phone rang.

'Good Lord. Who's ringing up at this time o'night?' said Bartle, as the telephone bell rang.

'Yes?' he said, irritably, as he lifted the receiver. 'Oh, I'm sorry,' he continued, with a complete change of tone, 'I didn't know it was you, Colonel. Anything the matter?'

He held up his hand for silence.

'Glad to find you, Bartle. The Zone Commander's been ringing.'

'Yes?'

'Yes. I'm damned if I can make him out. All he'd say was "Cromwell".'

'Good Lord. What's he mean by that?'

'That's what I want to know,' the Colonel exploded. 'I asked him but all he'd say was "Cromwell".'

Stott [the Royal Corps of Signals corporal] had stopped his demonstration and the men were half listening to what Bartle was saying.

'I don't know,' mused Bartle aloud. 'Cromwell? Cromwell?'

'Cromwell,' cried Stott, 'Good grief, I'm off. Good Lord, "Cromwell".' He reached for his cap and was gone in a trice.

'What's bitten him?' shouted Bartle. 'No, sir. I was referring to a soldier who was here. Ran off like a startled rabbit the moment I mentioned "Cromwell".'

'It must be a code word,' fumed the Colonel. 'You can't expect me to remember the damned things.'

'By Heavens, you're right, sir,' cried Bartle, the light suddenly dawning. 'It's the ruddy invasion.'

He dropped the phone and told the few remaining men in the room to report to their posts while he moved on to another club. There he whispered, 'Cromwell,' to another Home Guard member who 'looked at him pityingly and remarked, "The feller's crackers."'

Slowly the men trickled into the headquarters, one lieutenant wearing his uniform over pyjamas. D Company patrolled the seafront and golf links. It was a tense, physically uncomfortable night as several men fell into ponds and got bogged down in marshland. Patrols crept over a wide area of Caernarvonshire, many armed with live ammunition. 'The men were in uniform. They were soldiers. They had had some training and felt ready to deal with the enemy if he came. It was the occasion for which they had been preparing,' the unit's official history recorded.

Other units reacted in a less excitable manner. The alert took longer to spread in rural areas where few Home Guard members had telephones. The delay meant that the units did not start to gather until well into the night. In Buckinghamshire E Company 'stood to' from 1 a.m. until 10 a.m. – a stint of duty that the battalion's history recorded as noteworthy because it led to the payment of its first subsistence allowance. In the Outer Hebrides the code word was telegraphed to Harris, North and South Uist; the Home Guard took to the beaches with thirty rifles near the Lochboisdale Hotel and at other points in the islands. But the censor's office at Inverness suspected that the word might be helpful to the enemy and delayed sending the message to Barra so that Compton Mackenzie and other members of the Home Guard there received both 'Cromwell' and 'All Clear' on Monday morning.

In other parts of the country the Home Guard and the army did not wait for proof of parachutists but rang the church bells without delay. In the lonely, rolling farmland of Lincolnshire, where the defenders felt particularly vulnerable to attack from the North Sea, a dispatch rider spread the alarm, and the bells rang out from five Lincoln churches. A series of explosions shook the night as the army destroyed bridges to slow the Germans' advance. Peter Parnham was manning a Lewis gun for the Home Guard when the army blew up Simmon House bridge, which crosses Hobhole Drain. That ditch, which runs for over a hundred miles, had been built originally to protect the area from flooding but now it offered a strategic coastal defence against the invader. Roads in the area were also mined and a twenty-year-old gunner in the Royal Artillery was killed when one exploded at nearby Midville. He was not the only casualty that night.

Two army officers called out the district superintendent of the London and North Eastern Railway and told him that the Germans had landed and that he should put into action the plan to disrupt the area's railway network. This would have meant blowing up railway bridges and smashing parts of the infrastructure that had already been marked with red paint for easy identification. Fortunately he was not convinced and rang Southern Area Central Control for verification. They told him to carry on as normal.

Across Britain, those whose sleep had been untroubled by a siren shifted in their beds as traces of the panic ricocheting around the country entered their world: the half-heard slamming of a car door as a member of the Home Guard drove off to meet others from his unit, the fumbling of an ancient key into the door of a moonlit church tower, a garden gate squeaking as someone who had no business to be out in the middle of the night stole towards their hideout. Vera Brittain heard the bells and wondered whether the moment had come. Another author wrote to a friend in America: 'It was absolutely medieval being awakened by all the church bells ringing to warn us the Germans were here, just as hundreds of years ago we warned of the Danes! I wish I could tell you the exciting things that happened but must not.'

The bells rang out at Witney, north-west of Oxford, and a roadblock clanged into place. A small crowd gathered to quiz the air-raid warden about what was going on. When someone asked how they would sound the all-clear, the warden's reply brought home the significance of the moment: 'There won't be any more all-clears.'

Bells at five or six churches around Woking in Surrey tolled urgently at about 10 p.m. for two hours, during which householders grabbed brooms, garden forks and spades to patrol outside their homes, as the *Daily Telegraph* said, 'intent on giving the invaders a warm reception'.

In the West Country the sound of bells rolled out from the south coast of Cornwall to Bristol. At about 11 p.m. someone – probably a fisherman or member of the Home Guard – at a place *The Times* later described, with the deliberate, security-conscious vagueness of the moment, as a 'coastal town', but which was almost certainly Polperro, spotted unfamiliar boats creeping through the sea mist. It was the wrong time of night for the fishing fleet to be returning and, besides, there were other factors to take into account: air raids at nearby Plymouth, and Eden and Churchill's warnings about the threatened invasion. In this climate of suspicion a moonlit ripple out to sea easily transmogrified into landing barges and someone shouted, 'Here come the—s by the thousand.' A member of the Home Guard recalled, 'Up at the automatic telephone exchange I waited with my fellow guards, expecting hordes of Germans to scramble on the cliff-top fields at any moment.' When dawn came some of them decided that, 'Germans or no Germans', the cows needed milking. Those who stayed felt rather foolish and went home for breakfast.

Elsewhere, the anti-invasion plan sprang into action. Saboteurs disappeared into their underground hideouts and waited to carry out the murderous acts for which they had been training. In Scotland some auxiliary units 'stayed put' for five days, and a few men on the north coast only agreed to return to normal life when their commander, Eustace Maxwell, turned out in person to convince them that the invader had not appeared.

Civilians who realised that the moment had come prepared to put in place long-held plans, or to revert to primeval instincts. When Margery Allingham experienced her first 'invasion scare' she made herself a mug of 'farmer's tea' – fortified with whisky and lots of sugar – then found the biscuit tin with her precious manuscript and went back to bed. Others reached for handmade weapons. When the bells rang out in the Cotswolds a small boy caught sight of the chimney-sweep's wife sharpening a carving knife on the stone sill of their cottage. Molly Smith, who lived in Farnborough and had a small baby, described hearing the church bells ringing as 'the most hair-raising experience'. Her father banged on the door and shouted, ' "Come on, the beggars are dropping!" We were expecting an invasion and knew we were a prime target. My husband grabbed his rifle and I always had the leg of a chair handy!' A few – mainly those who had been bombed – did exactly what the government had feared: they abandoned their homes and headed west; for many Londoners this meant taking the train from Paddington to Oxford.

SITUATION REPORT

	Area	Patrols	Patrols forming	Men	Dumps distributed	Instruction Patroling	Technical
1a	Caithness and Sutherland	20		60	22	(x)	40
1	East Highlands and Aberdeen	35		230	40	100 (x)	200
3	East Riding	37	4	110	37	74	
4.	Lincolnshire	23		112	43	80	100 ∅
5	Norfolk	23		120	25	20	75 ∅
6	Suffolk and Essex	42	3	282	42	150	282 ∅ x
7	Kent	25		120	17	56	120 x @
8	Sussex	11		118	15	118	118 @
8a	Isle of Wight East Hampshire	13) 13)		70) 40)	10	25 30	30 ∅ 30
9	Dorset and West Hampshire	40	8	320	65	101	150 @
10	Somerset	40		180	7 out 38 in store	35	180 @
11	Devon and Cornwall	34	50	266	34	80	200 @
12	South Wales	15		150	25	35	80 ∅ Majority already acquainted with use of explosives

x - More advanced state of training than average.
@ - 6 Patrol Leaders attended demonstration course, Coleshill
∅ - 3 Patrol Leaders attended demonstration course, Coleshill
(x) - most of these are gillies and keepers and are expert in fieldcraft.

4.9.40.

H.Q. Auxiliary Units,
G.H.Q. Home Forces.

This 'most secret' report offers a rare insight into the state of readiness of Britain's network of resistance fighters. A few days after it was typed many patrols went to ground, believing the Germans had landed.

They left behind fires that burned so fiercely that the moon appeared to turn blood red. Heavy black smoke spread a canopy over the Thames but the flames acted as a flare path for each subsequent wave of bombers. The air was heavy with a rich mixture of smells from the burning docks: caramelised sugar, which hardened on the pavements to be picked off later by dockers and taken home to sweet-starved children, noxious gas and woodsmoke. Gunfire rattled the remaining windows, and falling shrapnel made a metallic click as it hit the ground. The slow, deliberate tolling of church bells contrasted with the clang of ambulances and fire engines. In Shaftesbury Avenue at around midnight a bomb landed on the Queen's Theatre, where Celia Johnson and Margaret Rutherford were starring in *Rebecca*. The cast had left for the night but the direct hit brought the run to an abrupt end and the Edwardian theatre went dark for nearly twenty years.

The BBC radio reporter Charles Gardner watched the attacks from high up on Hampstead Heath and broadcast a report on Sunday at 1 p.m.: 'From the Heath I could see, far away, the Thames estuary barrage flicking up and down on the horizon like a continuous display of lightning, and every now and then there would be a blue and white flash on the ground, as the Germans dropped more bombs. At first they seemed to be adding more bombs to the fire in the east, but as the night drew on, the bombing became more general and more promiscuous. It was during this second period that most of the damaged working-class houses in the east and south-east areas received their hits.'

Those people who were caught in the midst of the bombing reacted with a mixture of emotions. A few watched in something close to awe as the great German planes opened their bomb-racks and discharged their deadly load. The bombs dropped with such grace that some eyewitnesses did not realise what they were until the after-shock of the blast. Then the East End was transformed into a crazy, fun-fair world in which the air compression pushed and pulled people around in a manic dance. One young man felt his eyeballs being sucked out of their sockets and put his hands over them to try to resist the force. He described the air-raid shelter as lifting and rolling like a ship in rough seas, its steel door banging backwards and forwards against the wall. Children whimpered and adults cried; others were sick and lost control of other bodily functions.

When the raid was at its height Gardner visited the fire brigade headquarters to see how they were coping. The government had set up an Auxiliary Fire Service (AFS) as back-up to the brigade before the war had started but so far it had remained largely untested. The force was unpopular with some sections of the public: they viewed its members as 'army dodgers', who had secured an easy ride through the war. Saturday, 7 September 1940, gave the AFS the chance to silence even its most vociferous critics.

Frank Hurd was one of the AFS firemen called out. He and his crew had become impatient with the endless alerts in which they had to dress up in full fire gear, complete with respirator, and stay 'rigged' until they heard the all-clear – which might be six hours later. That Saturday the siren had sounded at 4.30 p.m.; the firemen heard aeroplanes approaching to the east and assumed the attack was 'over the Thames again'. They settled down in their shelter at Euston to wait for the alert to pass and for supper, which was to be served at 6.30 p.m. 'We were getting a bit fed up with this sort of things [*sic*],' he wrote later, 'and I think a few of us (I know I did) half-hoped for "something to happen" and then felt ashamed for letting the monotony "get us down". Then suddenly it came!'

The alarm went at 6.15 p.m. Four heavy units and four trailer pumps hurtled towards a fire station at Kingsland Road (the A10, which dissects Islington and Hackney in north London). As he clung to the side of one of the fire engines Hurd could see a vast column of smoke rising into the sky in the direction of the docks. At the station they were ordered on to East Ham. Since this was outside the London County Council area and a long way from their base, they knew that something unusual had happened. Once they had entered the East End they began to see evidence of the raids: wrecked houses, roads torn to pieces and a surface shelter destroyed. Ambulance and rescue crews struggled to help survivors while fires burned all around. For most of the AFS crew this was their first experience of a large blaze. At about 9 p.m. they dashed off to Beckton gasworks, close to the Thames.

> . . . chaos met our eyes. Gasometers were punctured and were blazing away, a power house had been struck rendering useless the hydraulic hydrant supply (the only sources of water there). An overhead gantry bearing lines of trucks communicating with the railway siding was also well alight. And then overhead, we heard 'Jerry'. The searchlights were searching the sky in a vain effort to locate him. Guns started firing, and then I had my first experience of a bomb-explosion. A weird whistling sound and I ducked beside the pump together with two more of the crew. The others, scattered as we were, had thrown themselves down wherever they happened to be. Then a vivid flash of flame, a column of earth and debris flying into the air, and the ground heaved. I was thrown violently against the side of the appliances. As 'he' still concentrated his attentions on our fire we were forced to take shelter in the works 'dug-out'. After a time things quietened down, and we went out again.

The raid had given the fire a chance to take hold and the firemen were hampered by lack of water, caused by damaged water mains and the low level of the tidal Thames. A fire engine set off half a mile away to collect water from three pumps that were in turn being supplied by hydrants. Hurd and his team trained the water on the blaze and tried to stop cars bursting the hoses as they sped over the junction.

> What a sight. About a mile away to our right was the river front. The whole horizon on that side was a sheet of flame. The docks were afire! On all other sides it was much the same. Fires everywhere. The sky was a vivid orange glow. And all the time the whole area was being mercilessly bombed. The road shuddered with the explosions. A-A shells were bursting overhead. A Royal

Navy Destroyer berthed in one of the docks was firing her A.A.
equipment, as were other ships. The shrapnel literally rained
down. It was now about midnight and still this incessant racket
kept on. It surprised me how quickly one got used to sensing
whether a bomb was coming our way or not. At first we all lay flat
everytime we heard anything but after an hour or so we only dived
for it if one came particularly close. Even so I had a funny feeling
inside each time I heard it coming. It took quite a time to overcome that. It wasn't exactly fear, but I don't know now just what it
was.

A canteen van arrived at about 3.30 a.m. and served them tea
and sandwiches. It was the first time that many had eaten for
nearly fifteen hours.

Just then the bombing became more severe and localised. A
brighter glow was in the sky immediately over us, then we saw
the flames. They had started another fire in the gasworks, which
by now, after about 6 hours concentrated work by us on it had
been got well under control. Then a huge mushroom of flame shot
into the air from the docks followed by a dull rolling roar. An oil
container had exploded. The whole atmosphere became terrible
again with the noise of gunfire . . . Then, quite suddenly, it
ceased. The silence was almost overpowering for a time. Then,
about 5 o/c a.m. the 'All Clear' went. We had been subjected,
without any real cover, to 8 hours' bombing!

Relief crews arrived, but Hurd and his team were not allowed to
leave until mid-morning when firemen from Brighton took their
place. '. . . what a scene of desolation we passed through. Debris
everywhere confined to the East End though. I was too tired to care
much what I saw then.' The final blow came when, instead of being
allowed the usual twenty-four hours' leave, they were back on duty
at 9 p.m. on that Sunday night.

Another observer, Desmond Flower, at nearby Surrey Docks,
described 'fire hoses along the side of the road, climbing over one
another like a helping of macaroni, with those sad little fountains

spraying out from the leaks, as they always seem to do from all fire hoses' and noticed fire engines from as far away as Sheffield, Birmingham and Bournemouth. In peacetime a major fire was one that needed thirty pumps; by midnight on 7/8 September, fire crews were struggling to contain nine 'hundred-pump' blazes. Around 430 civilians died on the first night of the Blitz, 1600 were seriously injured and countless families were made homeless.

22

Sunday, 8 September 1940,
A National Day of Prayer

———————◆◆◆———————

The three American journalists spent Saturday night at a hotel in
Gravesend. It was almost morning before the all-clear sounded
and they drove back to London. Police guided them round time
bombs, and they dodged craters in the streets until they reached
the devastation of the East End. There, a few children gave the
thumbs-up as they had seen the survivors of Dunkirk do three
months earlier.

Sunday, 8 September, the first Sunday after the anniversary of
the start of the war, had been designated a National Day of Prayer
long before the need for divine intervention had become quite so
pressing, and churches were full. The previous National Day of
Prayer had taken place on 26 May, just before what newspapers
now referred to as 'the successful evacuation of Dunkirk'. General
Alan Brooke spent the morning in his office, where he found
'further indications of impending invasion. Everything pointing to
Kent and E. Anglia as the two main threatened points.' He tried to
restore calm by making it clear that a member of the Home Guard
should only ring the church bells if he had personally seen at least
twenty-five parachutists. The sound of other bells or second-hand
reports of Nazis were not sufficient reason to raise the alarm. He
also cleared up the misunderstanding over what 'Cromwell'
meant.

The code word stayed in place until 19 September but it never
again produced the raw panic of that first Saturday night.

It was a bright, early-autumn Sunday morning, but as the day
progressed cloud descended, mimicking the fug of tiredness that
enveloped Londoners. Saturday's bombardment represented the
most severe night attack on the capital so far, but the nocturnal

disturbances had started a week earlier. The increase in warnings, before the night-time bombings became regular, gave a new rhythm to the day: snatching a few hours' sleep became a priority and catnapping an art form. Londoners dozed on buses or spent their lunch-hour snoozing in the park. Night time was a period of intense activity. Even if they did not make the journey outside to the shelter, people tossed and turned in their beds or wandered round the house trying to find a spot that seemed quieter or safer. Only the rich, who could escape to the country at weekends, had the luxury of 'going upstairs to bed'. Parents spent fitful nights comforting their children and emerged in the morning rubbing red-rimmed eyes. An American radio report described how British beauty parlours were attracting female customers who wanted 'tiredness lines' around their mouth and eyes massaged away. Some 'beauty specialists' advertised air-raid treatments, which helped to relax nerves and muscles that ached from constant strain and lack of sleep.

The first night of the Blitz left behind a raw, exposed city. For the next fifty-seven consecutive nights London shook with explosives; sometimes the Germans came by day too. New sights and sounds became commonplace – the tinkle of glass being swept up, the hammering of boards over gaping windows, and bomb-disposal experts chatting to one another 'like plumbers'. The air was thick with dust and grit. Shops and offices closed an hour earlier, and theatres adjusted their schedules to give customers a chance to get home before the bombing started. As night fell, people clutching bedding, Thermos flasks and babies lined up to take their places on Underground platforms or squeezed in beside the metal tracks.

London's landscape moved to the next stage of war. It felt less like a highly fortified capital and more like a battered and bandaged battlefield. At St Giles's Church in Cripplegate, Milton toppled off his plinth and Virginia Woolf described the damage near her home as 'like a tooth knocked out'. Another brand of euphemism evolved: bomb victims were said to have died 'very suddenly', and targets were reduced to crossword clues – 'a nursery rhyme church associated with oranges and lemons' or a 'famous public school'. Explosives that blew off the victims' clothes also exposed their private lives: silk stockings and underwear snagged on telegraph poles, and bedrooms were open to view, as if, like a doll's house, the front wall of the house had been folded back.

In the countryside people wondered what was happening to city dwellers. Every night those who lived close enough watched the red glow spread across the horizon and those with friends and relatives in London tried desperately to reach them on the telephone. Snettisham continued to suffer raids, as Muriel wrote that weekend:

> Woke up in middle of night with a terrific noise of bombs dropping. J was calling out and I tore out of bed and rushed downstairs not stopping for dressing gown or slippers. Somehow fell into bathroom where mother and J and I sat in dark disgussing [*sic*] how near it was this time. Decided it was nearest yet within 5 miles anyway. After about 10 mins and nothing further, a plane which seemed over the house at time of explosion had gone, we ventured out and looked in the garden. No one about on road so J and I went up to bed and I slept in about 15 mins until this morning. Everyone this morning is asking where the bombs fell last night.

But they were aware that London was in the middle of something much worse – the most obvious indication was that the newspapers did not arrive until mid-afternoon. 'I am jolly glad I am not in London,' Muriel wrote. 'Everybody here talks about the raids there and wonders what their friends and relations are doing. Mr M is worried ever so much about his relations.' Later that week they learnt that two evacuees who had returned to London for the school holiday had been killed by bombs.

But terrible though the bombing was, it was a relief to know that if this was the worst the Germans could throw at Britain there was a chance of survival. General Lee celebrated the start of the 'real' war by opening a magnum of champagne with Somerset Maugham, who was about to leave for America. The subtle change in mood was also evident in a new and powerful rumour that circulated shortly after the weekend when so many people had responded to 'Cromwell'. An officer in Eastern Command, who had received the 'Cromwell' signal on the Saturday night, later summed up, 'Generally supposed that this was the German full dress rehearsal for the invasion of Britain and was a flop owing to our bombs and the acute seasickness of German forces.'

'Is the rumour true, I wonder, that invasion was actually attempted and withstood on September 16?' Vera Brittain wrote. The tale expanded as the likelihood of a German invasion became more remote. In its most elaborate form, some highly secret weapon capable of setting fire to the sea had put paid to the threat. Margaret Kennedy's dentist told her how a sailor patient claimed to know all about a covert device that had 'burnt them all up'. As if to confirm the tale, friends told her they knew someone who had arrived from France where the hospitals were full of burnt Germans. Kennedy was not taken in: she compared it to the First World War myth of Russians who were 'spotted' in various parts of Britain, wearing snow-covered boots, on their way to relieve the Allies on the Western Front.

The speculation about a failed invasion was particularly strong in East Anglia – perhaps because the region was viewed as a 'front line'. A diarist in Ipswich wondered, 'What is the secret of last Saturday's [7 September] affair?' He had heard that rumours in New York suggested that 30,000 'Jerry corpses' had been washed up on the Suffolk coast, although he wondered why their heavy equipment had not sunk them.

The myth that the Germans had attempted an invasion but were burnt to death persists to this day and has settled around the desolate spot of Shingle Street, twelve miles east of Ipswich on the Suffolk coast. The tiny beach settlement was hastily evacuated in the summer of 1940 when it became part of the Defence Zone, but by then it already had a reputation for intrigue. Nearby Orford Ness had been used for secret military trials since the First World War and at Bawdsey, also close by, radar was helping to give the RAF a tactical advantage over the Luftwaffe, which went some way to counter its numerical shortfall. It was the perfect setting for a conspiracy theory. The most convincing explanation of the 'bodies on the beach' story is that at least one dead German pilot was washed up at Shingle Street and that this solitary victim multiplied into hordes during the 'Cromwell panic.' The flaming sea, which a few eyewitnesses reported, has been attributed to the RAF bombing raids on northern France, which reflected a crimson glow on the clear night sky of 7 September. The panic engendered by 'Cromwell' was real; the burning sea was not.

Even Churchill believed that the corpses of about forty German soldiers had been washed up along the coast between Cornwall and the Isle of Wight. He claimed they had been killed by British bombers while practising embarkation routines from barges on the other side of the Channel. This, he said, was the source of the rumour that the Nazis had tried to invade but had been driven back by a flaming sea or had drowned through simple ill-fortune. The government recognised the gruesome story's power and did its best to spread the 'black propaganda' in occupied Europe. In an attempt to unsettle the nervous invader, the RAF dropped thousands of leaflets written in the style of a tourist guide entitled, *Wir Fahren Gegen Engelland,* after the patriotic song about marching on England. The leaflet listed phrases in German, French and Dutch, such as, 'Is our boat capsizing – sinking – burning – blowing up?'; 'What is that strong smell of petroleum?'; 'What is setting the sea on fire?'; 'Does not the captain burn beautifully?'; 'Karl – Willi – Fritz – Johann – Abraham – is incinerated? Drowned? Sliced up by the propellers?'

The rumour appears to have touched a nerve – it combined the fear of water and fire – and quickly spawned connected tales. Churchill claimed that a shop in Brussels was displaying men's bathing-suits marked 'For Channel Swimming'; another rumour suggested that Germans were placing large orders with a Paris manufacturer for asbestos suits. In Berlin the American journalist William Shirer wrote in his diary that he had seen a Red Cross train that stretched for over half a mile. He wondered whether it was connected with a rumour he had heard in Switzerland that the

The RAF dropped thousands of these mock tourist guides, entitled 'We're on our way to England', over occupied Europe. Phrases such as 'What is setting the sea on fire?' reinforced rumours that Britain had a deadly, secret weapong

British had used a new weapon to set the sea alight and that many Germans had drowned or been badly burnt in an attempt either to cross the Channel or in a rehearsal for invasion.

Ten days after the 'Cromwell' scare Frank O'Brien had moved to Barton-on-Sea, Hampshire. He spent every night, from 6 p.m. until 9 a.m., on the beach waiting for the Germans. His battery had a new gun, a French 75, especially for the invasion – 'if it comes off'. It was bitterly cold and there was barely enough light for him to write the letters to Mary he did not have time to compose during the day when he caught up on sleep. The imminent threat induced a curious sense of elation:

> I'm right in the sea front line so I'll be very disappointed if the Germans don't come . . . And darling it's lovely to sit on the beach and look at the moon, it's so peaceful; you wouldn't think there was a war as everything is so nice and quiet. Yet the Germans are on the other side waiting to come over here at any minute, it's horrible to think of it. But they will never land in this country as long as the British troops are on the coast and are ready for any German who tries to land here.

He had no idea that, for him, the war was only just beginning.

Epilogue: No More Waiting

As large parts of Britain had been preparing for invasion, Ludwig Baruch was recovering from nearly two months aboard a floating prison.

The journey had started badly. The *Dunera*, with more than two thousand men on board, headed for the Atlantic via a circuitous route designed to outwit the German U-boats that prowled round the northern tip of Ireland. The ship sailed north, parallel with the Scottish coast, until on 12 July she was twenty miles west of the island of Barra – where some of the *Arandora Star*'s victims had been washed up. Just after eight o'clock in the morning passengers and crew heard an ugly grating noise, followed by a loud bang. To men like Ludwig and the crew of the *Adolf Woermann* the noise was horribly familiar, while the panic that followed was ominously similar to what had happened during the moments that preceded the sinking of the *Arandora Star*. Many prisoners rushed to the stairs only to find their way blocked by guards with fixed bayonets; others shrugged their shoulders and braced themselves for a replay of the nightmare that was seared into their memories. But the *Dunera* was lucky: the two torpedoes fired at her missed – one might have glanced off the hull without exploding.

Eventually prisoners disappeared back into the gloom below deck and the foetid slave-ship atmosphere. The *Dunera* was packed to almost twice its capacity. For two months men slept on the floor or on tables; nearly all of the portholes remained shut and the air was rank. Conditions worsened as the journey continued; slop buckets overflowed with vomit and human waste, while illness raged in the insanitary conditions and as the climate became tropical. Prisoners later complained about the lack of an emergency drill and of the constant pilfering by some soldiers who took wedding rings, wrist-watches and other valuables. Three internees died; one man committed suicide by jumping overboard when he discovered that his visa for entry into South America had been destroyed during looting. They had no idea of their destination or how long they would be imprisoned on the stinking ship, which intensified their agony. Only the changing length of the sun's shadow offered a clue as to where in the world they were heading.

On 3 September the *Dunera* reached Melbourne, Australia, and Ludwig and the other survivors from the *Arandora Star* were marched by armed guard on to a train for Tatura, 110 miles north. The prisoners were pale and undernourished, bemused Robinson Crusoe figures in their tattered clothes. Ludwig was still wearing the second-hand army uniform with a red cross daubed on the back, but he had shortened the trousers and secured them with a length of string. Back in Britain the *Daily Mail* reported how survivors of *Arandora Star* had quarrelled violently among themselves on board *Dunera*.

The soldiers sent to guard them were expecting dangerous Nazis and one, a member of the Communist Party in Melbourne, was startled to find his prisoners handing round books they had collected on the journey. When they began to discuss whose turn it was to read the socialist classic *The Ragged Trousered Philanthropist*, he knew his charges were not committed Nazis. It was this discovery that prompted the soldier to begin a campaign that would eventually lead to Ludwig's release.

Hilda received her first letter in four months on 11 November 1940. She was in bed when the post came and the whole family gathered round to hear her read it aloud. She dispatched her reply, not knowing how long it would take to reach Ludwig: 'You ask me whether I had any new plans. The only plans I have, darling, and the only thing I am concerned about is to finish Nazi-ism once and for all, so that when we are together again nothing will be able to separate us.'

Although the British public did not know it, Hitler had ordered the indefinite postponement of Operation Sealion on 17 September.

The Luftwaffe had failed to overpower the RAF – something that was always seen as a prerequisite to invasion – and the constant bombing seemed only to have hardened Britain's determination not to surrender. Instead, Hitler turned his attention to his former ally and in June 1941 invaded Russia. The Soviet Union quickly signed a mutual-assistance agreement with Britain; the shift in alliances meant that Communists – at least on paper – must be treated as friends. Ludwig and his fellow prisoners acknowledged this new order in November 1941 when they celebrated the anniversary of the Bolshevik revolution. They decorated their mess hall with slogans urging a closer bond with Russia and international solidarity; some banners were in German, others, like Churchill's 'Every Nation and Every Individual Who Wants to Fight Nazi-ism is our Ally', were in English. The prime minister's face glowered down beside Stalin's, and the Soviet emblem flew next to the Union flag. For Ludwig the celebrations held a bitter irony:

> I can't describe how much agony I felt still being imprisoned on November 7th, having to sing the 'Internationale' behind barbed wire! I am beginning to feel ashamed of Liverpool. Where is the solidarity I had a right to expect? Why am I still being left to rot? Last night we had a magnificent celebration commemorating the 24th birthday of the Revolution – which gave us for a short time the idea we are still part of the movement although we have been so shamefully let down . . . Were you not ashamed, Liverpool, that such celebrations are held behind barbed wire?

Hilda redoubled her efforts to have him freed before he was placed in a PoW camp for Germans. 'I cannot bear to think of the consequence of such a move for a well-known Anti-Nazi and a Jew,' she wrote, at the beginning of 1942. Ludwig returned to Britain in November and was held on the Isle of Man. 'We shall spend a lot of time together in our own room,' she wrote, once she knew he was back. 'I want to kiss you lots and lots, and there's a popular tune called "You're one in a million". For me you are the only one in the whole world.'

Ludwig was finally released in December 1942 but had to obey a curfew between 10.30 p.m. and 6 a.m. and, once more, was not allowed to ride a bicycle – until the Manchester and Salford Trades Council successfully appealed to the chief constable of Lancashire. After the war he moved to Bradford, where he worked for a manufacturer of babies' clothes until, in 1971, he became a director of trade-union studies at Leeds Polytechnic.

When the Soviet Union again became the enemy, Ludwig's political sympathies caused him trouble again. Visitors to his house told him that the police had asked them to spy on him and his numerous requests for naturalisation were rejected. When the UK joined the Common Market in 1974 he renewed his German citizenship and obtained a passport; in 1996 he was able to vote in a British election. Despite the hardship that his convictions had brought him he never faltered in his support for the Campaign for Nuclear Disarmament, or helping refugees from the first Gulf War, in 1990, who settled in Bradford.

Hilda and he had two children, John and William, but their marriage broke down in the mid-sixties. He met his second wife, Joyce, while he was organising a campaign against the Beeching cuts to railway services. They had two children, Miriam and Sean. Ludwig died in 2002 at the age of eighty-five.

Release was more straightforward for those who had not been deported. François Lafitte's *The Internment of Aliens* was published in November 1940 and sold nearly fifty thousand copies. The book opened the public's eyes to how men and women who should have been a great support to Britain had been imprisoned and suffered terrible hardship. He argued convincingly that most refugees usually brought with them a paper trail of references and personal reports that gave police more information on them than probably any other section of the community. He also pointed out that Quisling, the infamous Norwegian, was a home-grown traitor.

The first Category C men were released in August, and later that month Sir John Anderson, in a debate in the House of Commons, expressed his regret at the 'deplorable' things that had happened, for which he blamed the haste with which internment had been implemented and individuals' mistakes, 'stupidity and muddle'. By early October over four thousand men and women had been released – nearly all those in Category C, deemed the least dangerous – and releases continued at a rate of about a thousand a month. Some of the six thousand men who had been sent to Canada were allowed to return, the first leaving in December 1940 to brave the Atlantic crossing.

In north London, Renée kept vigil for several months in the hope that she would see her father, Decio Anzani, walking up the road – as she had been promised he would. Later in the war she and her mother were in the cinema one rainy day when the whole building shook violently. They walked home to find their house reduced to a single staircase climbing up through rubble. Today she is still angry, but not bitter, at the senseless loss of her father but she, too, has moved on and become a wife and mother.

Günther Prien, captain of the U-boat that sank the *Arandora Star*, was killed in March 1941 by British depth-charges in the Atlantic.

Churchill asked Lord Snell to investigate the *Arandora Star* case but its findings in November 1940 were restricted to the method of selection. A full version, which pointed out that Decio Anzani had been arrested in error and that he was not a member of the Fascist Party, was never made public.

After lying in wait for Hitler on the south coast, the following two years were relatively quiet for Frank O'Brien. Then, in March 1943, his regiment moved to North Africa where he fought in the battles of Oued Zarga, Medjez Plain and Tunis, exotic names that sounded even more so when pronounced with a Glaswegian lilt. On New Year's Day 1944, they moved to Egypt and then to Italy where the Allies pushed north to Florence. At the end of 1944 his regiment was poised to withdraw to Palestine when they were told instead to head for Greece to quell a civil war.

Frank and Mary continued to write to one another during their protracted separation. Like most epistolary relationships there were periods when theirs appeared to cool but once Frank had returned to Scotland the courtship resumed with all its old vigour. They married in 1947 and had four children; Frank worked as a postman until he retired in 1979 and retained close friendships with many of his army comrades. He died in 1989; Mary lived on until 1996. His elder son, Raymond, came across his father's letters stuffed into an old handbag of his mother's a few years after her death.

Frank, of course, was one of the lucky ones. Although he was thrown into some highly dangerous situations, he survived with no physical injury and returned to a family who were also unharmed. Many of those who cheated death in the summer of 1940 did so only once.

James Nicolson, the sole fighter pilot in the Second World War to win the Victoria Cross, was haunted by the need to 'earn' his medal. Although he nearly died from his injuries he was back in the air barely a year later. He served in the Far East and won the Distinguished Flying Cross while leading a squadron of fighters. In May 1945, less than four months before the war ended in the Pacific, he was on board a Liberator bomber that burst into flames 130 miles south of Calcutta. A flying-boat recovered two survivors but Nick's body was never found.

Frank Hurd, the auxiliary fireman who had been pushed beyond the point of exhaustion that first weekend of the Blitz, died three months later from injuries sustained while he was fighting a fire at West Smithfield. He was twenty-four.

Ben Robertson, the American reporter who had witnessed the build-up to invasion, died on a return flight to London in 1943. His plane crashed into the sea while it was attempting to land at Lisbon. Ed Murrow, the colleague with whom he had sheltered on the first day of the Blitz, went on to become one of the most famous voices in radio. On at least one occasion he broadcast from a rooftop, and many of his London reports were punctuated by sirens. While photographers showed America what the Blitz looked like, Murrow supplied the soundtrack.

Joseph Kennedy was replaced as ambassador to Britain early in 1941 by the less flamboyant John Winant, who served until 1946. Pearl Harbor finally gave President Roosevelt the mandate he needed officially to take sides. Kennedy, who had been so vociferous in his support of appeasement, suffered the cruellest personal vindication of his views when Joe, his eldest son, who had carried with him the weight of his father's hopes, was killed in August 1944. He had volunteered to take part in a highly dangerous mission to knock out the Belgian launch site for the Germans' V-1 bombs that were terrorising London, but his plane exploded over the Suffolk countryside.

For many people the code word 'Cromwell' provided a full stop. It was as if, having survived the tension of that summer and the immediate threat of bombs and invasion, they felt free to wander further afield. Although Churchill continued to urge vigilance it became less likely that the Germans would come. The weather stepped in to help Britain: high winds and rain made it impossible for the Nazis to cross the Channel in the late autumn and winter. By the time the sea had calmed, Germany had more pressing concerns. When Hitler declared war on Russia, he gave his countrymen enemies to consider on two fronts; if he could subdue this new foe Britain might surrender voluntarily.

After he had helped to set up the first auxiliary unit, Peter Fleming left Britain to put the ethos of the 'unorthodox warrior' to Allied use. He trained saboteurs and helped to spread misinformation and confusion among the enemy in Greece, India and Burma, ending the war as head of Strategic Deception in South East Asia Command. He died of a heart-attack in 1971 while on a shooting trip in Scotland.

★   ★   ★

Leonard Marsland Gander, who had complained about the cut-throat world of London journalism, went on to file reports for the *Daily Telegraph* from some of the most dangerous war zones. Although he was denied the chance to report on the spies who landed on the south coast of England in September 1940, he later witnessed the Germans' last successful invasion when élite troops took the Greek island of Leros. His eyewitness account was a worldwide exclusive.

The nature of their job meant that those who had been selected to form auxiliary units rarely left Britain. Many would-be saboteurs never spoke of their other life, believing that the Official Secrets Act bound them to perpetual silence. Some of their 'ammo dumps' were discovered after the war and a few hideouts were uncovered, but most had retreated into the undergrowth.

Charlie Mason was never called upon to kill a German but the war left its scars on him. In September 1940 he received a message that his twenty-one-year-old friend Stanley, who had fulfilled Charlie's dream of flying with the RAF and who had escaped injury in the débâcle of Norway, had been killed, ironically during an uneventful patrol. His Hurricane had stalled in a steep turn then crashed on to the ground. Charlie collected his friend's belongings from Stapleford Tawney, in Essex. The airfield was bruised after the Battle of Britain: the ground crew had hastily filled in huge bomb craters and the tail of a crashed aeroplane – Charlie could not tell whether it was German or British – poked out of a building's roof. 'I looked at the Hurricanes all ready for take-off. They had patching on their sides and wings, red daubs that made them look like they were bleeding,' he remembers. 'They looked as though they had been bandaged up ready to go, as though they were looking, watching. I felt, these Hurricanes are going to take off if they get the alarm.'

Muriel and Jenny both left Snettisham in 1941 and spent a few years engaged in 'land work': growing vegetables in the grounds of stately homes and market gardens around the country. Jenny married a former Japanese prisoner-of-war and lived to be nearly ninety. Muriel met her future husband on a youth-hostel ramble in 1943; they were married for forty-seven years. She settled by the sea on the south coast and is now a grandmother in her mid-eighties but has not been back to her former home for fifty years. Matthew worked in one of the local aerodromes, which had fascinated him so much, and lived into his sixties.

Snettisham's most exciting moments occurred after the sisters had left. Several hoards of Roman treasure were discovered, most notably a two-thousand-year-old gold necklace. Tragedy also struck: in 1953 floods claimed the lives of twenty-five people – ten more than had died in the Second World War.

Lord Haw-Haw, who amused and sometimes horrified listeners in Snettisham and elsewhere, made his final broadcast in April 1945, a drunken, slurred version of his former rantings. In 1946 William Joyce was executed – the last man to be hanged in Britain for high treason. His death was as controversial as his life had been: as an American-born citizen he should not – strictly speaking – have been found guilty of treason. Joyce's true crime was in having lied about his nationality in an application for a British passport in 1933. Usually the penalty for such a false statement was a two-pound fine.

The trial of the 'Four Men in a Boat' was held at the Old Bailey in November 1940. It lasted a week and there was debate as to how much should be made public once a verdict was reached. Eventually it was decided to release a brief statement because large parts of Kent had already caught a whiff of the story. The authorities also felt the news might boost morale and act as a deterrent to any would-be fifth columnists. The news story differed from the truth in a few telling details, which were designed to confuse the SS. The report spoke of the men's 'surreptitious arrival' and omitted to mention that they had come by sea; it also included a few misleading details about the radios that were discovered. But, most significantly, it failed to say that one man was acquitted. Such was the secrecy surrounding the case that there was even debate about whether or not a notice of execution should be fixed to the prisoners' cell doors. Eventually it was decided that it would be illegal not to: the public had the right to know that three men had been hanged.

As the immediate threat of invasion receded, the government gradually relaxed some of its more Draconian measures. In October 1942 signposts returned to towns and, the following May, to the countryside although place-names remained obscured until October 1944. In 1943 church bells rang out once more after Churchill admitted they were a poor warning system and that the prospect of an invasion was 'bound to leak out'. The Home Guard was officially stood down on 31 December 1944.

Ury, Ludwig's youngest brother, qualified as a doctor in Canada before he returned to Britain in 1948. Walter, the middle son, came home in 1942 and completed his studies in Liverpool. Their mother, Hedwig, was released from internment in 1941 and rejoined Daniel, her husband, in London where she worked in a factory, sewing shopping-bags. Hilda Froom and the Quakers helped them to find a house in Manchester, where Hedwig did more factory work, and Daniel taught himself to mend watches. She died in 1973 at the age of eighty-three; her husband lived to be nearly ninety-seven, despite the heart trouble that had persuaded the authorities to release him from internment. His youngest sister, Gertrud, and Hedwig's sister and brother-in-law died in Auschwitz; another of Daniel's sisters disappeared during the Nazi invasion of the Soviet Union.

After the war Margaret Kennedy wrote several successful books, and a film adaptation of her best-selling novel, *The Constant Nymph*; its star, Joan Fontaine, was nominated for an Academy Award for Best Actress. Kennedy's husband, a barrister, was knighted in 1952. She died in Oxfordshire in 1967, aged seventy-one.

In September 1940 Margaret Kennedy wrote: 'The weather has broken and we are getting those equinoctial gales we have been waiting for. For some reason they seem to think the invasion will be off for some months once the big gales start . . . The leaves are beginning to turn and today I have rinsed through and dried our bathing dresses and put them away till next year. The summer is over. What a summer!'

On the night of 1 August German aeroplanes dropped leaflets in which Hitler urged Britons to surrender. Many were later auctioned to raise money for the Red Cross.

Notes

1: Jenny and Muriel – All Quiet in Norfolk

p.3 Muriel and Jenny's diaries form part of the Mass-Observation (MO) Archive at the University of Sussex. Muriel and Jenny were among hundreds of volunteers around Britain who kept diaries or completed open-ended questionnaires about their everyday lives. As specified by MO, their names and the names of the people they mention have been changed to protect their identity. For anyone who would like to consult the archive, 'Muriel' is diarist 5324 and 'Jenny' is diarist 5323.

p.3 'The nation groped', shops took advantage of people's need to be seen and sold 'blackout accessories': collars, walking-sticks, badges, lapel pins and raincoats that made their owner more visible to vehicles and other pedestrians. There was even a blackout coat for dogs.

p.10 'Around 400,000 cats and dogs', Philip Ziegler, *London at War, 1939–1945*, p.74.

p.10 'The Duchess of Gloucester', Theo Aronson, *The Royal Family at War*, p.179.

p.10 'An advertisement in *The Times*'. This may not be as far-fetched as it sounds since scientists have long suspected that animals possess a kind of 'radar' for detecting various forms of danger before it arrives. Thousands of animals survived the tsunami that devastated parts of Asia in December 2004 and might have been alerted to the approaching tidal wave by barometric changes that humans were unable to detect.

p.10 'Vera Brittain pointed out that', Vera Brittain, *England's Hour* p.5.

p.13 'an old-fashioned schoolmaster, loaded with sarcasm', George Beardmore, *Civilians at War, Journals 1938–1946*, p.59.

p.13 'A gent I'd like to meet', quoted in J. A. Cole, *Lord Haw-Haw, The full story of William Joyce*, p.115.

p.14 'A secret report by the BBC', Ian McLaine, *Ministry of Morale, Home Front Morale and the Ministry of Information in World War II*, p.55.

p.15 'The wife of a former mayor', Cole, *Lord Haw-Haw*, p.181.

2: Ludwig and Hilda – Life as an 'Enemy Alien'

p.17 The correspondence between Hilda and Ludwig is part of the Ludwig Baruch Internment Archive, Special Collections, University of Bradford. I am also very grateful to Ludwig's son, Dr John Baruch, for allowing me access to unpublished chapters from Ludwig's autobiography, notes on the family's history and his unpublished obituary of Ludwig.

p.21 'Jack remembers him as a small but spirited', interview with the author.

p.23 'Ludwig was one of around three hundred "aliens" classified as "Category A",' Peter and Leni Gillman, '*Collar the Lot!*': *How Britain interned and expelled its wartime refugees*, pp.43–6.

p.23 '30,000 refugees had flooded into', ibid., pp.24–5.

3: Listening to Hitler

p.28 I am indebted to Ewald Osers for allowing me to see an English translation of chapter six of his memoirs, *Loňské sněhy* (Snows of Yesteryear). After the war Osers became a literary translator of over 140 books and maintains that his work at Wood Norton provided an excellent schooling for his future life as a professional translator.

p.28 See also Lesley Chamberlain, 'War Across the Airwaves', *Financial Times Magazine*, 3 May 2003.

p.28 'polyglots in their own right'. Other talented monitors who went on to glittering careers include the art historian Ernst Gombrich (later Sir) and Martin Esslin, who became head of BBC Drama, a producer, and a professor of modern drama in the United States.

p.28 'Somewhere in the country', Olive Renier and Vladimir Rubinstein, *Assigned to listen: the Evesham experience 1939–43*, p.26.

p.30 'shaggy White Russian', Geoffrey Grigson, *The Crest on the Silver, An Autobiography* p.213.

p.30 'by his landlady's malapropisms', 'Weidenfeld was baffled' George Weidenfeld, *Remembering My Good Friends, An Autobiography*, p.96.

p.30 'Wuthering Heights', Renier and Rubinstein, *Assigned to Listen*, p.31.

p.31 'After all, the Germans', Osers, *Loňské sněhy*.

4: Jenny and Muriel, April – Hitler Catches Two Buses

p.37 'As Ed Murrow, the celebrated American radio broadcaster, told listeners', Edward Murrow, *This is London*, p.83.

p.38 'We gasped over Denmark and Norway', Diana Forbes-Robertson and Roger Straus (eds), *War Letters from Britain*, p.18.

p.38 'being forgotten by the men in Whitehall'. A retired policeman was employed to sit just inside the door of the local bank, a pistol at the ready. But, rather than reassuring customers, visitors became convinced that he was eavesdropping on their business. Jenny blamed his intrusive presence on the bank's decision in April to close due to lack of business.

p.39 'Georgie, it's going to be all right, isn't it?' George Beardmore, *Civilians at War, Journals 1938–1946*, p.49.

p.41 'Let's walk through the park and 'ave a look at the vegetables', *Punch*, 24 July 1940.

p.41 'Vegetables grew in the moat', Gilda O'Neill, *Our Street, East End Life in the Second World War*, p.132.

p.42 'an estimated 1196 wartime broadcasts on food', Asa Briggs, *The History of Broadcasting in the UK, Volume III*, p.36.

p.42 '*Woman's Own* told its readers', November 1939; quoted in Jane Waller and Michael Vaughan-Rees, *Women in Wartime, The Role of Women's magazines, 1939–45*, p.45.

p.43 '*Picture Post* portrayed a model sporting a necklace of discarded corks', 24 August 1940.

p.43 'anti-concussion bandeau of aerated rubber', Peter Fleming, *Invasion 1940*, p.111.

p.43 'England is gradually turning khaki', Forbes-Robertson and Straus (eds), *War Letters from Britain*, p.18.

p.43 'Elizabeth Arden advised', William Shawn (ed.), *Mollie Panter-Downes, London War Notes, 1939–1945*, p.24.

p.43 'Vera Brittain reported', Vera Brittain, *England's Hour*, p.14.

p.44 'Yet the women of England still', Naomi Royde Smith, *Outside Information, Being a Diary of Rumours*, p.32.

p.44 'Cinema managers', Shawn (ed.), *Mollie Panter-Downes*, p.52.

p.44 'hiding for weeks', *The Times*, 27 April 1940.

p.46 'That word "invasion" ', Beardmore, *Civilians at War, Journals*, p.50.

5: Jenny and Muriel, May – Scanning the Skies

p.49 'The perfection of the weather is getting on our nerves', Frances Partridge, *A Pacifist's War*, p.41.

p.49 'Just before nine', Nigel Nicolson (ed.), *Diaries and Letters, 1939–1945*, p.83.

p.49 'most dramatic and the most far-reaching', Roy Jenkins, *Churchill*, p.577.

p.50 'nothing particular up his sleeve', Margery Allingham, *The Oaken Heart*, p.154.

p.50 'the man driving', ibid., p.155.

p.50 'One hundred and forty years ago', quoted in Jenkins, *Churchill*, p.578.

p.50 'You have sat too long', ibid., p.579.

p.51 'felt a grip of fear', Partridge, *A Pacifist's War*, p.38.

p.51 'Hell had broken loose', Richard Buckle (ed.), *Self Portrait with Friends, The Selected Diaries of Cecil Beaton, 1936–1974*, p.73.

p.51 'Perhaps the darkest day', Robert Rhodes James (ed.), *Chips, The Diaries of Sir Henry Channon*, p.10.

p.51 'crunched and crumbled', Allingham, *The Oaken Heart*, p.154.

p.51 'theatrical props', ibid., p.154.

p.52 'primarily charming', ibid., p.167.

p.55 'Officially women'. It was illegal for women to join the Home Guard until 1943.

p.55 'Press photos', *War*, 2 August 1940, p.1086.

p.55 'If the Germans invade Britain', *War*, 2 August 1940.

p.56 'I've got a butcher-knife myself', Ben Robertson, *I Saw England*, p.63.

p.56 'She is reported to have added', *Hereford Times*, Flashback series, n.d.

p.56 'and one [soldier] joined up at the age of', S. P. Mackenzie, *The Home Guard, A Military and Political History*, p.38.

p.57 'Why do we in this country', Alan Danchev and Daniel Todman (eds), *War Diaries 1939–1945, Field Marshal Lord Alanbrooke*, 29 June 1940, p.89.

p.57 'It won't matter now', *'We also Served': The Story of the Home Guard in Cambridgeshire and the Isle of Ely 1940–1943*, p.81.

p.57 'rifles from the Indian Mutiny', Peter Fleming, *Invasion 1940*, p.200; Philip Ziegler, *London at War*, p.104.

p.57 'packets of pepper', *'We also Served'*, p.64.

p.58 'A cartoon in the *Tatler*', 17 July 1940.

p.58 'likely to serve no useful purpose', George Beardmore, *Civilians at War, Journals 1938–1946*, p.61.

p.60 'Cricket clubs', *The Times*, 2 July 1940.

p.61 'The *Daily Express* informed', *Daily Express*, 13 May 1940.

p.61 'the Dutch Foreign Minister told a London press conference'. See *The Times*, 22 May 1940. A Home Office circular confirmed that the parachutists might land disguised as policemen or ARP wardens; see Mackenzie, *The Home Guard*, p.22.

p.61 'Noël Streatfeild confided to her brother', 13 June 1940, Mrs U. Streatfeild 87/1/1, Imperial War Museum. This is quoted with the kind permission of Bill Streatfeild.

p.61 'A report from the Air Ministry', quoted in Fleming, *Invasion 1940*, p.54, from Charles Graves, *The Home Guard of Britain* (1943).

p.63 'Overnight he became the most hated man in Britain', William Shawn (ed.), *Mollie Panter-Downes, London War Notes, 1939–1945*, p.63.

p.63 'In Hammersmith and Dulwich', Philip Ziegler, *London at War, 1939–1945*, p.94.

p.63 'Does he not realise how small nowadays', F. Tennyson Jesse and H. M. Harwood, *London Front, Letters Written to America (August 1939–July 1940)*, p.401.

p.63 'Lloyd George ranted, 2 June 1940, quoted in Joseph P. Kennedy and James M. Londis, *The Surrender of King Leopold*, p.1.

6: Springtime in London

p.65 'The Channel had now shrunk', William Shawn (ed.), *Mollie Panter-Downes, London War Notes, 1939–1945*, p.60.

p.65 'Even the organ', ibid., p.49.

p.65 'the BBC had used as an interval signal', Asa Briggs, *The History of Broadcasting in the UK, Volume III*, p.194.

p.66 'dark as a pocket', James Leutze (ed.), *The London Observer, The Journal of General Raymond E. Lee, 1940–41*, p.5.

p.66 'The symbolic Stone of Scone'. My thanks to Dr Tony Trowles, Librarian, The Muniment Room and Library, Westminster Abbey, for answering my queries about the Stone of Scone. See also Maureen Waller, *London 1945, Life in the Debris of War*, p.6.

p.66 'bags sprouted grass', Philip Ziegler, *London at War, 1939–1945*, p.72.

p.67 'great silver elephants . . . These captive', Charles Ritchie, *The Siren Years, Undiplomatic Diaries, 1937–1945*, p.42.

p.67 'Notices on the walls of train', Ben Robertson, *I Saw England*, p.34.

p.67 'tough-looking Norwegian seamen', Ritchie, *The Siren Years*, p.53.

p.67 'They have come', Alfred Draper, *Operation Fish, The Race to Save Europe's Wealth 1939–1945*, p.106.

p.68 'The Dutch foreign minister', ibid., p.138.

p.68 'snored so loudly', Robertson, *I Saw England*, p.113.

p.68 'I thought that was rubbish', quoted in Draper, *Operation Fish*, p.139.

p.68 'An even more undignified exchange', Theo Aronson, *The Royal Family at War*, p.175.

p.69 'sandbagged like a fort', Robertson, *I Saw England*, p.22.

p.72 'Anna de Wolkoff', KV2/ 840–843, National Archives.

p.73 'serious internal trouble', quoted in John Costello, *Ten Days That Saved the West*, p.103.

p.74 'the speculator's smartness', Leutze (ed.), *The London Observer*, p.x.

p.75 'the answer', Ralph F. de Bedts, *Ambassador Joseph Kennedy, 1938–1940, An Anatomy of Appeasement*, p.214.

p.75 'told George VI', Aronson, *The Royal Family at War*, p.76.

p.75 'fine two-handed drinker', quoted in de Bedts, *Ambassador Joseph Kennedy*, p.201.

p.75 'a very foul specimen', ibid., p.196; and Costello, *Ten Days That Saved the West*, p.130.

p.75 'Harold Nicolson attacked him', *Spectator*, 8 March 1940.

p.75 'I thought my daffodils', de Bedts, *Ambassador Joseph Kennedy*, p.214.

p.76 'From then until late in the', Robertson, *I Saw England*, p.16.

7: Frank O'Brien – The Soldier's Story

p.77 Frank O'Brien's letters are on long-term loan to the Kevin Morrison Collection at Glasgow Caledonian University. Extracts are reproduced here with kind permission of Frank's family. I am very grateful for additional material supplied by Frank's son, Raymond.

p.81 The War Diary of 77th (Highland) Field Regiment, RA (TA) 1939–45 is held at the National Archives, WO167/497.

p.83 'our soldiers in dire peril in France', Norman Gelb, *Dunkirk: The Incredible Escape*, p.83.

p.84 'a secret weapon', ibid., p.52.

p.84 'a crewless tank', ibid., p.70.

p.85 'tennis shorts', ibid., p.99.

p.86 'loading ships by the spoonful', Walter Lord, *The Miracle of Dunkirk*, photo caption.

p.86 'He saw a woman', E. Bliss (ed.), *In Search of Light*, p.24.

p.86 'Sitting in a crude wood O.P.', Spike Milligan, *Adolf Hitler, My Part in His Downfall*, p.30.

p.87 'With the distant booms', ibid., p.32.

p.87 'God had decided', Ben Robertson, *I Saw England*, p.50; Lady Astor was convinced of this.

p.87 'A rumour started ', Charles Ritchie, *The Siren Years, Undiplomatic Diaries, 1937–1945*, p.61.

p.87 'like a piece of polished steel', Milligan, *Adolf Hitler*, p.30.

p.88 'extension of the actual war zone', Ritchie, *The Siren Years*, p.54.

p.88 'laden, not funereal but weighty', Leonard Woolf (ed.), *A Writer's Diary, being extracts from the Diary of Virginia Woolf*, 30 May 1940.

p.88 'Only occasionally', Edward Murrow, *This is London*, p.122.

p.89 'desperately exhausted', Colin and Eileen Townsend, *War Wives, A Second World War Anthology*, p.20.

p.90 'Ironside wrote in his diary', Colonel Roderick Macleod and Denis Kelly (eds), *The Ironside Diaries, 1937–1940*, 30 June 1940, p.376.

p.91 'But now – look', J. B. Priestley, *Postscripts*, Wednesday, 5 June 1940, p.4.

p.91 'Like, son?', Milligan, *Adolf Hitler* p.33.

8: To Fight or Flee?

p.92 'for the brave boys', 'This flower, safety' appeared in the *New Yorker* on 6 July 1940 and is reproduced in Mollie Panter-Downes, *Good Evening, Mrs Craven: the Wartime Stories of Mollie Panter-Downes*.

p.92 'an estimated two million people', Angus Calder, *The People's War, Britain 1939–1945*, p.36.

p.93 'visited homes where the occupants', George Beardmore, *Civilians at War, Journals 1938–1946*, p.44.

p.93 'five-point action plan', Margaret Kennedy, *Where Stands a Wingèd Sentry*, p.52.

p.94 'absolutely foolish', Colin and Eileen Townsend, *War Wives, A Second World War Anthology*, p.24.

p.94 'Writer and Mass-Observation diarist Naomi Mitchison', Naomi Mitchison, *Among You Taking Notes*, p.61.

p.94 'According to one estimate'. Norman Longmate, *How We Lived Then, A History of Everyday Life During the Second World War*, p.74, suggests 2700 'official evacuees and 11,000 private ones had left'.

p.94 'stampede from this country', Roy Jenkins, *Churchill*, p.628.

p.94 'the prime minister sent', ibid., p.629.

p.94 'Pixie is frightened to death', Nancy Mitford, *The Pursuit of Love*, p.161.

p.95 'Eton College wrote to all parents', Peter Fleming Papers, July 1940, University of Reading.

p.95 'gallant pathetic courage', Vera Brittain, *England's Hour*, p.75.

p.96 'Celia Johnson and Peter Fleming', Kate Fleming, *Celia Johnson, A Biography*, pp.80 and 81.

p.96 'German radio', Monitoring Service, 5 September 1940, BBC Written Archives.

p.96 'Yes,' she said, 'I shall not', Nigel Nicolson (ed.), *Diaries and Letters, 1939–1945*, 10 July 1940, p.100.

p.97 'Hugh Dalton . . . visited', Ben Pimlott (ed.), *The Second World War Diary of Hugh Dalton 1940–1945*, Friday, 31 May 1940, p.31.

p.97 'Winston Churchill once discovered', Amanda Smith (ed.), *Hostage to Fortune – The Letters of Joseph P. Kennedy*, p.457.

p.97 'The Duke of Gloucester', Theo Aronson, *The Royal Family at War*, p.178.

p.97 'Coats Mission', David Lampe, *The Last Ditch*, p.33, and Peter Fleming, *Invasion 1940* pp. 144–5.

p.97 'The only time the Coats Mission', ibid., p.29.

p.98 'George VI persuaded his mother', Aronson, *The Royal Family at War*, pp. 59–64.

p.99 'According to one account', ibid., p.118.

p.99 'Banks were told', Alfred Draper, *Operation Fish, The Race to Save Europe's Wealth 1939–1945*, p.265.

p.99 'ballista', Sir Donald Banks, *Flame Over Britain, A Personal Narrative of Petroleum Warfare*, p.51. The Bank of England evacuated many of its staff to Overton in Hampshire.

p.100 'Over the next two years a total of £470,250,000', see Draper, *Operation Fish*, p.358. In Norway the country's wealth had been smuggled out by children who had loaded one bar of gold at a time on to a sledge, then swiped it past a sentry and on to a waiting freighter. The deception took six weeks.

p.101 'buried his drawings', Lampe, *The Last Ditch*, p.56.

p.101 'A friend of diarist Frances Partridge', Frances Partridge, *A Pacifist's War*, 15 May 1940, p.40.

p.101 'very precious', 'After all', Nigel Nicolson (ed.), *Diaries and Letters, 1939–1945*, p.88.

p.101 'buried his diaries', Robert Rhodes James (ed.), *Chips, The Diaries of Sir Henry Channon*, 24 May 1940, p.253.

p.102 'shipped his sixty volumes of diary', Colonel Roderick Macleod and Denis Kelly (eds), *The Ironside Diaries, 1937–1940*, p.356.

p.102 'He kept completed volumes locked', David Dilks (ed.), *The Diaries of Sir Alexander Cadogan O.M., 1938–1945*, p.17.

p.102 'A memo from the BBC', draft memo, 2 July 1940, BBC Written Archives.

p.102 'Public Record Office', John D. Cantwell, *The Public Record Office*, pp.425–30.

p.103 'The National Library of Wales', Lampe, *The Last Ditch*, p.36.

p.103 'The Tate Gallery'. Tate Gallery director Sir John Rothenstein closed the gallery on the same day that news came through of the German–Soviet pact on 22 August 1939 and the evacuation of art began two days later. The Natural History Museum moved many specimen jars full of strange pickled creatures to caves in Surrey for safe-keeping.

p.104 'The authorities are becoming pressing', Lady Helena Gleichen to Fincham, 20 February 1940, Tate Gallery Archive.

p.104 'Blenheim Palace in Oxfordshire', *The Guardian*, Monday, April 25 2005.

p.104 'I hope that Lady Valda's', Mr F? to Lady Helena Gleichen, 9 September 1939, Tate Gallery Archive.

p.105 'completely full', Lady Helena Gleichen, 12 January 1940, Tate Gallery Archive.

p.105 'loudly abused', letter from Senior Attendant Sergeant R. Beasley to director?, 23 June 1940, Tate Gallery Archive.

p.105 'White Park cattle'. Whether the cows were evacuated as a way of preserving the breed or for purely commercial reasons is open to debate.

p.106 'When Cecil Beaton visited 10 Downing Street', Richard Buckle (ed.), *Self-Portrait with Friends, The Selected Diaries of Cecil Beaton, 1936–1974*, p.75.

p.106 'Churchill told his friend, the minister for Air Production', see Joseph Kennedy Diary, in Smith (ed.), *Hostage to Fortune*, 24 June 1940, p.445.

p.106 '*The Times*'. My thanks to Eamon Dyas, Archivist, Times Newspapers Limited, and Judith Dunn, Director of Editorial Projects, News International, for supplying extra information.

p.106 'the Manchester Guardian and Evening News Ltd', see David Ayerst, *The Manchester Guardian, Biography of a Newspaper*, pp. 533–5. My thanks to Roger Browning for his help in finding this information.

9: Jenny and Muriel – 'If the Invader Comes . . .'

p.111 'All over Britain'. The law seemed to be on the side of the marksman. *The Times*, 18 June 1940, reported the opinions of Lord Mottistone, lord lieutenant of Hampshire, who said that since the attackers were expected to be disguised it was unlikely that any court of justice, and certainly no British court, would restrict an Englishman's rights and duties. He added that a member of the Home Guard was not a civilian but a member of the armed forces of the Crown.

p.111 'On an unusually warm evening'. For the Welsh incident see *The Times*, 18 June 1940 *Wrexham Leader*, 21 June 1940. For the sentry inquest, *The Times*, 6 June 1940.

p.112 'In July police shot dead a farmer', *The Times*, 31 July 1940.

p.112 'Lord North . . .', *The Times*, 26 August 1940.

p.112 A 'brilliant scientist', *The Times*, 10 June 1940.

p.112 'I was faintly perturbed', Compton Mackenzie, *My Life and Times, Octave Eight, 1939–1946*, p.87.

p.115 'A freelance journalist', MO Archive, diarist 5175.

p.115 'The spirit of France is not broken', Monitor's Report, 13 June 1940, BBC Written Archives.

p.116 'Le jour', Olive Renier and Vladimir Rubinstein, *Assigned to Listen, the Evesham experience, 1939–43*, p.53.

p.117 'tragic week for the British people', William Shawn (ed.), *Mollie Panter-Downes, London War Notes, 1939–1945*, p.66.

p.117 'macaroni joints', ibid., p.68.

p.118 'Damn and blast the ruddy French', Helen D. Millgate (ed.), *Mr Brown's War, A Diary of the Second World War*, p.48.

p.118 'I can't understand the French packing up', undated, Amy Johnson Archive, RAF Museum.

p.118 'The last minutes of France', Ben Robertson, *I Saw England*, p.31.

p.118 'We're in the final now', Philip Ziegler, *London at War, 1939–1945*, p.83; Michael Glover, *Invasion Scare 1940*, p.53; and Hugh Dalton, addressing the Home Guard on 23 June 1940, Ben Pimlott (ed.), *The Second World War Diary of Hugh Dalton 1940–1945*, p.46.

p.119 'from the addresses still to be found', David Lampe, *The Last Ditch*, p.3.

p.120 'jolly good mix-up', E. Bliss (ed.), *In Search of Light*, p.23.

p.120 'Madame X', *Punch*, 3 July 1940.

p.120 'In another cartoon, a boy said proudly', *Punch*, 24 July 1940.

p.120 'In the same July issue', 24 July 1940.

p.120 'muzzling', *The Times*, 22 June 1940.

p.121 'Tom Lock'. This is not his real name.

p.121 'Oh, just give it a good whacking', from a letter to the author.

p.121 'local crisis', Pimlott (ed.), *The Second World War Diary of Hugh Dalton*, 23 June 1940, p.46.

p.124 'plough, sow, cultivate', Peter Fleming, *Invasion 1940*, p.86.

p.124 'Ordinary people', Margery Allingham, *The Oaken Heart*, p.165.

p.124 'One woman, who had worked out', Diana Forbes-Robertson and Roger Straus (eds), *War Letters from Britain* p.73.

p.125 'Ben Robertson met a goldsmith's wife', Ben Robertson, *I Saw England*, p.63.

p.125 'Lord Beaverbrook', Anne Chisholm and Michael Davie, *Beaverbrook, A Life*, p.394.

p.125 'Hans Christian Andersen', Vere Hodgson, *Few Eggs and No Oranges, A Diary Showing How Unimportant People in London and Birmingham Lived Through the War Years 1940–1945*, p.40.

10: Frank's Story – The Soldier's Return

p.132 For further details of how the British landscape changed, see Bernard Lowry (ed.), *20th Century Defences in Britain, An Introductory Guide*, published by the Council for British Archaeology.

p.133 'plans to flood parts of Romney', Edward Carpenter, *Romney Marsh at War*, p.vi.

p.134 'breeches arse', *'We also Served'*: *The Story of the Home Guard in Cambridgeshire and the Isle of Ely 1940–1943*, p.78.

p.134 'In one suggestion', *War*, 26 July 1940.

p.134 'even less sophisticated plan', Angus Calder, *The Myth of the Blitz*, p.28.

p.135 'The parish invasion committee at Barton'. This document is held in the Cambridgeshire Collection, Cambridge. Its date is unclear but was probably late 1940 or 1941.

p.136 'Our defences', Colonel Roderick Macleod and Denis Kelly (eds), *The Ironside Diaries, 1937–1940*, 28 June 1940, p.373.

p.136 'alien elements introduced as refugees', ibid., 9 June 1940, p.360.

11: Decio Anzani – The Italian's Story

p.138 I am very grateful to Alfio Bernabei for putting me in touch with Decio Anzani's daughter, Renée Chambers. A full account of Decio's life story appears in Alfio Bernabei, *Esuli ed emigrati Italiani nel Regno Unito, 1920–1940*. See also the magazine, *il punto*, number 80. Further information comes from an interview and correspondence between Mrs Chambers and the author. Peter and Leni Gillman, *'Collar the Lot!'*: *How Britain Interned and Expelled its Wartime Refugees*, and François Laffitte, *The Internment of Aliens* are both valuable on the subject.

p.139 'In the space of a fortnight over four thousand Italians', Peter and Leni Gillman, *'Collar the Lot!'*, p.155.

p.139 'Cadogan wrote in his diary', David Dilks (ed.), *The Diaries of Sir Alexander Cadogan O.M. 1938–1945*, 29 May 1940, p.292.

p.139 'A neat device for catching wops', *Tatler*, 28 August 1940.

p.141 'An Italian organ-grinder in Leeds', Robert Winder, *Bloody Foreigners, The Story of Immigration*, p.239.

p.141 'Isle of Man – it had the capacity to take ten thousand inmates', see Gillman, *'Collar the Lot!'*, p.225.

p.142 'They used whatever scraps of material', Jessica Feather, *Art Behind Barbed Wire*, p.15.

p.142 'A Jewish engineer, an expert in designing machine tools', Anne Chisholm and Michael Davie, *Beaverbrook, A Life*, p.386.

p.142 'About thirty candidates', R34/316 Policy, Controller (Administration's Papers) 1938–1941, 1944, BBC Written Archives.

p.143 'In Hampstead', Philip Ziegler, *London at War, 1939–1945*, p.96.

12: The Nun with the Hairy Arm and Other Rumours

p.150 'If you thought anything', Margery Allingham, *The Oaken Heart*, p.192.

p.150 'existence of a fifth column'. Fifth columnists were also blamed for a fire in north London. *The Times* reported that police had found a mysterious note on the door of a storage building in Barnet. It was signed in pencil with the letter 'C' and contained the words 'guess where?' The building had caught fire on Saturday evening and was badly damaged; the implication was that this was no ordinary case of arson. *The Times*, 28 May 1940.

p.150 'curious cryptograms', '*We also Served*': *The Story of the Home Guard in Cambridgeshire and the Isle of Ely 1940–1943*, p.52.

p.151 'General Ironside reported', Colonel Roderick Macleod and Denis Kelly (eds), *The Ironside Diaries, 1937–1940*, 31 May 1940, p.347.

p.151 'dingy quarter of dockland', Colonel H. R. V. Jordan, IWM 79/2/3. He left a full account of his work but failed to expand on his initials.

p.155 'held an anti-gossip week', *The Times*, 28 May 1940.

p.156 'Virginia Woolf', Leonard Woolf (ed.), *A Writer's Diary, Being Extracts From the Diary of Virginia Woolf*, 25 May 1940, p.333.

p.156 'face tattooed', F. Tennyson Jesse and H.M. Harwood, *London Front, Letters Written to America (August 1939–July 1940*, p.404. This version occurred in St John's Wood.

p.156 'At the beginning of June', *Lynn News*, 4 June 1940.

p.156 'Diana Cooper', quoted in Jenny Hartley (ed.), *Hearts Undefeated, Women's Writing of the Second World War*, p.65.

p.157 'those damned parachutists', Nancy Mitford, *The Pursuit of Love*, p.184.

p.157 'Naomi Mitchison', Naomi Mitchison, *Among You Taking Notes*, p.61.

p.157 'A cartoon in the *Daily Express*', 13 March 1941.

p.157 'a blind man', George Beardmore, *Civilians at Work, Journals 1938–1946*, p.59.

p.157 'Pen Ponds', ibid., p.35.

p.158 'supermorgues', Margery Allingham, *The Oaken Heart*, p.125.

p.158 'In Edinburgh', Angus Calder, *The People's War, Britain 1939–1945*, p.134.

p.158 'Arthur Greenwood', Compton Mackenzie, *My Life and Times, Octave Eight, 1939–1946*, p.94.

p.158 'In Cornwall', Margaret Kennedy, *Where Stands a Winged Sentry*, p.188.

p.159 'A nasty rumour', Tennyson Jesse and Harwood, *London Front*, p.427.

p.159 'toy balloons', Beardmore, *Civilians at War*, p.35.

p.159 'the *War* magazine warned', 10 June 1940.

p.159 'The novelist Naomi Royde Smith', Hartley (ed.), *Hearts Undefeated*, p.65.

p.160 'Specks of soot', *Lynn News*, 18 June 1940.

p.160 'cobweb-like material', Norman Gelb, *Dunkirk: The Incredible Escape*, p.70.

p.161 '*New York Times*', 29 May 1940, quoted in ibid., p.145.

p.161 'Almost as alarming', Naomi Royde Smith, *Outside Information, Being a Diary of Rumours*, p.8.

p.161 'the clock in Gayton', *Lynn News*, 4 June 1940.

p.161 'Orpington high street', J. A. Cole, *Lord Haw-Haw, The Full Story of William Joyce*, p.156.

p.161 'residents of Commercial Road', ibid., p.157.

p.161 'to have informers', ibid., p.155.

p.162 'easy to poke fun at'. A revue, *Haw Haw!*' ran at the Holborn Empire.

p.162 'A cartoon in *Punch* showed two women gossiping', *Punch*, 10 July 1940.

p.162 'Cholmondeley-Plantagenet out of Christchurch', quoted in Asa Briggs, *The History of Broadcasting in the UK, Volume III*, p.129.

p.162 'Vere Hodgson', Vere Hodgson, *Few Eggs and No Oranges, A Diary Showing How Unimportant People in London and Birmingham Lived Through the War Years 1940–1945*, p.33.

p.163 When 'Ed Murrow stopped for a drink', Ed Murrow, *This is London*, p.128.

p.163 'A clergyman's daughter', Hartley (ed.), *Hearts Undefeated*, p.65.

p.164 'In one of his *Postscripts* talks': Sunday, 8 September 1940.

p.164 'Churchill confided', Ben Pimlott (ed.), *The Second World War Diary of Hugh Dalton 1940–1945*, p.34.

p.164 'wife of the Speaker', Philip Ziegler, *London at War, 1939–1945*, p.98.

p.164 'spotted flycatchers', Tennyson Jesse and Harwood, *London Front*, pp. 428, 431.

p.164 'Margery Allingham experienced a similar', Allingham, *The Oaken Heart*, p.166.

p.165 'A friend of Frances Partridge', Frances Partridge, *A Pacifist's War*, p.47.

p.165 'the SS had worn', Michael Glover, *Invasion Scare 1940*, p.30.

p.165 'An RAF officer based in Norfolk reported', from R. D. V. Jones, *Most Secret War*, quoted in R. Douglas Brown, *East Anglia 1940*, pp.77–8.

p.166 'they might as well be occupied', Hodgson, *Few Eggs and No Oranges*, p.33.

13: Ludwig and Decio on Board the *Arandora Star*

p.171 The National Archives hold several documents about the sinking of the *Arandora Star*. See in particular HO 213/1834, *Sinking of SS Arandora Star: inquiry by Lord Snell into method of selection of aliens sent overseas*. PREM 3/49 concerns the decision not to publish a full report of the inquiry. Reasons included personal references and national security: 'It was, of course, always intended that while aliens should be interned in large numbers, and inevitably without much initial inquiry, at a later stage the sheep should be sorted from the goats.' HO 213/1721 covers the list of Italians missing.

p.173 'in error'. In early draft of Lord Snell's report, but later removed.

p.174 'Alfonzo Paolozzi's loyalties'. I am indebted to Sarah Mnatzaganian for pointing out the reference to Paolozzi. For obituaries of Paolozzi see *The Economist*, 30 April 2005, *Guardian*, Friday 22 April 2005, *Scotsman*, 23 April 2005.

p.176 According to an Admiralty document held in the National Archives, PREM 3/49, the ship was struck at 55 degrees 20 minutes north 10 degrees 33 minutes west.

p.176 This description of the sinking of the *Arandora Star* is taken from a number of sources including an unpublished account by Ludwig Baruch and an interview with his son, Dr John Baruch. One survivor professor Rainer Radok, wrote about his experiences in *Before and After the Reichkristallnacht, The History of a Königsberg Family*, which he published on the internet. Witnesses differ over exact times.

p.179 'Keep your chins up. Help coming', Jim Arnison, *Hilda's War*, p.31.

p.181 'Hilda was also consumed with worry', ibid., p.36.

p.183 'drifted almost to his home', Compton Mackenzie, *My Life and Times, Octave Eight, 1939–1946*, p.97.

p.184 'Neapolitan tenor'. Compton Mackenzie and his wife refer to the Italian tenor as Mario Serena but they are almost certainly using a false name for Enrico Muzio, an opera singer whose death was registered in Inverness-shire.

p.184 'herringboned the sand around him', Mackenzie, *My Life and Times*, p.281.

14: Leonard Marsland Gander –
Family Life on the South Coast

p.185 Leonard Marsland Gander's diary is held at the Imperial War Museum, in L. Marsland Gander, 76/62/1, and is reproduced with the kind permission of Nigel Gander.

p.187 'Sir Alexander Cadogan', David Dilks (ed.), *The Diaries of Sir Alexander Cadogan O.M. 1938–1945*, p.319.

p.187 'The only nice thing', Nigel Nicolson (ed.), *Diaries and Letters, 1939–1945*, 23 May 1940, p.88.

p.188 'as though left by drunken drivers', Ed Murrow, *This is London*, p.120.

p.188 'There is no colour of any sort', James Leutze (ed.), *The London Observer, The Journal of General Raymond E. Lee 1940–1941*, 7 July 1940, p.13.

p.190 'Some Home Guard units', Peter Fleming, *Invasion 1940*, p.203; and R. Douglas Brown, *East Anglia 1940*, p.119.

p.190 'Joseph Kennedy was said', Fleming, *Invasion 1940*, p.91. Kennedy, in a letter to Peter Fleming, 1957, Peter Fleming papers, University of Reading, queried this assessment.

p.191 'They [the Germans]', Margaret Kennedy, *Where Stands a Wingèd Sentry*, p.58.

p.191 'Always before', ibid., p.120.

p.193 '*Boy's Own*', May 1940.

p.193 'Get your Nazi!', Kevin Morrison Collection.

p.194 'An eight-year-old girl', Diana Forbes-Robertson and Roger Straus (eds), *War Letters From Britain*, p.89.

p.194 'Heil Hitler!' Margaret Kennedy, *Where Stands a Wingèd Sentry*, p.114.

p.195 'Bring me my carpet', ibid., p.149.

p.195 'One hotelier', *Lynn News*, 16 July 1940.

p.195 'By mid-July half the population', Angus Calder, *The People's War, Britain 1939–1945*, p.128.

p.195 'the population of Folkestone shrank', Norman Longmate, *How We Lived Then, A History of Everyday Life During the Second World War*, p.74.

p.195 'Hunstanton's asked its bank', *Lynn News*, 6 August 1940.

p.196 'Railway stations which', Vera Britain, *England's Hour*, p.121.

p.196 'Everything was there', J. B. Priestley, *Postscripts*, 14 July 1940, p.30.

15: The Defence of Southern England –
Jenny, Muriel and Frank

p.200 'The whole thing' Sir Donald Banks, *Flame over Britain*, p.29.

p.200 'At the end of June Churchill', Dan Cruickshank, *Invasion –Defending Britain From Attack*, p.170.

p.200 'Alan Brooke had also decided', Alex Danchev and Daniel Todman (eds), *War Diaries 1939–1945, Field Marshal Lord Alanbrooke*, p.94.

p.203 'Everyone echoes Bottom', Mollie Panter-Downes, *London War Notes, 1939–1945*, p.28.

p.203 'The actor Anthony Quayle', Anthony Quayle, *A Time to Speak*, p.209.

p.204 'General Lee noted in his diary', James Leutze (ed.), *The London Observer, The Journal of General Raymond E. Lee 1940–1941*, p.29.

p.204 'As the moon got full', Ben Robertson, *I Saw England*, p.52.

p.204 '1940 was a peak year for recruitment', Angus Calder, *The People's War, Britain 1939–1945*, p.119.

p.206 'I realise that I have never', Margaret Kennedy, *Where Stands a Wingèd Sentry*, p.152.

p.208 'If your knees knock kneel on them', Vera Brittain, *England's Hour*, p.214.

p.208 'lugubrious prayers for courage', ibid., p.39.

p.208 'put the Lord into an awkward position', Kennedy, *Where Stands a Wingèd Sentry*, p.22.

p.208 'jolly good', Vere Hodgson, *Few Eggs and No Oranges, A Diary Showing How Unimportant People in London and Birmingham Lived Through The War Years 1940–1945*, p.36.

p.208 'The *Lynn News* called it a 'revolting broadcast', 16 July 1940.

p.209 'whether he had a German blitzkrieg', George Beardmore, *Civilians at War, Journals 1938–1946*, p.58.

p.209 'shrewd woman', Charles Ritchie, *The Siren Years, Undiplomatic Diaries, 1937–1945*, p.56.

p.209 'One elderly woman', Leutze (ed.), *The London Observer*, p.359.

p.210 'growing exhilaration', quoted in Ian McLaine, *Ministry of Morale, Home Front Morale and the Ministry of Information in World War II*, p.63.

p.210 'Biggest raid ever', Vera Brittain, *England's Hour*, p.115.

p.210 'little white lice, Margery Allingham, *The Oaken Heart*, p.213.

p.210 'heavy, massive hum', Vera Brittain, *England's Hour*, p.79.

p.210 'Pumph-er, Pumph-er', Simon Garfield, *We Are at War*, p.357.

p.210 'zoomzazoomzazoomzazoomza', Kennedy, *Where Stands a Wingèd Sentry*, p.199.

p.213 'One woman gave birth', Colin and Eileen Townsend, *War Wives, A Second World War Anthology*, p.281.

p.214 'I'd be the first to agree', Diana Forbes-Robertson and Roger Straus (eds), *War Letters from Britain*, p.65.

p.214 'The number of legitimate births'. For figures on birth rates see *Office of Population Censuses and Surveys, Birth Statistics, Historical series of statistics from registrations of Births in England and Wales 1837–1983, Series FM1 no. 13.*

16: Peter Fleming –
Training Britain's Underground Resistance

p.219 'He cleaned his plump backside by scraping', Peter Fleming, *The Flying Visit*, p.35.

p.219 'His padded flying boots suggested', ibid., p.40.

p.219 'could not face a war on two fronts', ibid., p.62.

p.220 'only one eye, only one arm', quoted in Duff Hart-Davis, *Peter Fleming, A Biography*, p.224.

p.221 'Hitler had missed the bus in Norway', quoted in ibid., p.228.

p.221 'Phlegm'. For the account of Fleming's experience at Southend, see *Spectator*, 28 May 1965.

p.223 'One thing is clear', Monitors' Notes, NBBS 21. 30 BST, 14 August 1940, BBC Written Archives.

p.224 'A *Daily Telegraph* reader', Michael Glover, *Invasion Scare 1940*, p.128.

p.224 'The incident probably fanned', Kennedy, *Where Stands a Winged Sentry*, p.226.

p.224 'Can't find him', David Dilks (ed.), *The Diaries of Sir Alexander Cadogan O.M. 1938–1945*, p.321.

p.225 'We poked about', Ralph Arnold, *A Very Quiet War*, p.53.

p.226 'tact, and patience, and friends at court', MS 1391, reference 14/1, University of Reading; notes from uncompleted book on strategic deception in the Second World War, 1971.

p.229 'Anthony Quayle', *Newcastle Evening Chronicle*, 23 April 1968.

p.229 'ancient domed stone huts', David Lampe, *The Last Ditch*, p.99.

p.229 'In Berwickshire', ibid., p.102.

p.229 'Coleshill'. For more on Coleshill see *Sunday Times*, 12 August 2001, and Dr B. Lawton, *A History of Highworth*, part three, published by Highworth Historical Society, Swindon, 1992. The millionaire Ernest Cook, of Thomas Cook, bought the house in 1946 but it was destroyed by a fire sparked by a workman's blowtorch in 1952. The National Trust now owns the land.

17: Charlie Mason – The Resistance Fighter

p.231 Interview with the author, November 2004. Although Charlie did not join his auxiliary unit until later in 1940 his experiences are typical of the recruitment work of the organisation.

18: Leonard Marsland Gander
and the Best Spy Story Never Told

p.239 'Yes, but with mists come storms and rough seas', James Leutze (ed.), *The London Observer, The Journal of General Raymond E. Lee 1940–1941*, p.36.

p.240 'take its death dive', ibid., p.38.

p.240 'It seemed queer', ibid.

p.240 'three-minute channel', Ben Robertson, *I Saw England*, p.94.

p.241 'Just after midnight'. The account of the spies is taken from trial notes, an unpublished newspaper report in KV2/1452, the National Archives, and Gander's notes. In some reports Charles van den Kieboom is 'van der'. There are also alternative spellings for 'Sjoerd Pons' and 'Meier' is also spelt 'Maier'.

p.246 'the *Lynn News* posed the question', 6 August 1940.

p.246 'the first of mine', Robert Hewison, *Under Siege, Literary Life in London, 1939–1945*, p.142.

p.248 'In September the novelist', Naomi Royde Smith, *Outside Information, Being a Diary of Rumours*, p.66.

p.248 'Vera Brittain', Vera Brittain, *England's Hour*, p.206.

19: Better Dead than Nazi?

p.249 There are various accounts of Nicolson's experience, some, no doubt, embellished over time. One of the most accurate is in Chaz Bowyer, *For Valour, The Air VCs*.

p.250 'So great was the fear'. Mr Menzies Sharpe, officer commanding Newgate Street (Herts) Home Guard, offered £5 for every German parachutist captured alive; *War*, 6 September 1940.

p.251 'Rebecca West summed', quoted in Jenny Hartley (ed.), *Hearts Undefeated, Women's Writing of the Second World War*, pp 75–6.

p.251 'Would you rather die', Margery Allingham, *The Oaken Heart*, p.170.

p.251 'I should count it a privilege', David Dilks (ed.), *The Diaries of Sir Alexander Cadogan O.M. 1938–1945*, 19 May 1940, p.287.

p.251 'Cecil Isaacs' for 'Cecil Cecil'. My thanks to Veronica Forwood for sharing this with me.

p.251 'many Jewish servicemen'. My thanks to Martin Sugarman, Archivist of the Association of Jewish Ex-Servicemen and women of the UK, AJEX Museum.

p.252 'One mother told her daughter', *Ely Standard*, Thursday, 5 May 2005.

p.252 'Victor Gollancz', David Lampe, *The Last Ditch*, pp.56–7.

p.252 'On June 9 Virginia wrote', Leonard Woolf (ed.), *A Writer's Diary, Being Extracts From the Diary of Virginia Woolf*, p.336. When she killed herself in the river near their home in the spring of 1941 it was more likely to have been for reasons of depression than fears for the outcome of the war, although many people reacted angrily to her decision to take her life when so many were risking theirs to save Britain.

p.252 'Rose Macaulay wrote to her sister', Constance Babington Smith (ed.), *Letters to a Sister from Rose Macaulay*, p.99.

p.252 'But I fear the Gestapo will be up to that', ibid., p.99.

p.254 'That is all right. I had them on my list too', *Guardian*, Friday, 14 September 1945.

p.254 'My dear – the people we should have been seen dead with'. Noël Coward in *Future Indefinite*, quoted in Walter Schellenberg, *Invasion 1940, The Nazi Invasion Plan for Britain*, p.148.

p.254 'MI5's list eventually stretched', article by Ben Fenton, see news. telegraph, 12 October 2004.

p.254 '12th Duke of Bedford', KV2/793 and PREM 4 39/1, National Archives. The secret services had been building up a file on the Duke since the 1920s. He was described as 'a pacifist and believer in monetary reform . . . a vegetarian and a strong supporter of the Society for the Prevention of Cruelty to Animals'. In 1940 he retreated to his Scottish home where he produced anti-war pamphlets. The government decided not to arrest him because of the publicity this would give his views.

p.255 'A friend of Partridge', Frances Partridge, *A Pacifist's War*, p.44.

p.255 'A mother of a well-to-do family': this was told to the author in confidence.

p.255 'I can imagine circumstances', Margaret Kennedy, *Where Stands a Wingèd Sentry*, p.104.

p.255 'What I dread is', Nigel Nicolson (ed.), *Diaries and Letters, 1939–1945*, 26 May 1940, p.90.

p.256 'And there is always the bare bodkin', ibid., 5 June 1940, p.93.

p.256 'It all looks very simple', ibid., 19 June 1940, p.97.

p.256 'Female weavers in Huddersfield', Mass-Observation, diarist 5035, 21 and 25 May 1940.

p.256 'George Beardmore recorded how typists', George Beardmore, *Civilians at War, Journals 1938–1946*, p.55.

p.256 'The fear of internment', François Lafitte, *The Internment of Aliens*, p.149.

p.257 'I shall slightly regret', Constance Babington Smith (ed.), *Letters to a Sister from Rose Macaulay*, p.101.

p.257 'It is a pity that', F. Tennyson Jesse and H. M. Harwood, *London Front, Letters Written to America (August 1939–July 1940)*, p.398.

p.257 'Lytton Strachey's niece, Julia', Frances Partridge, *A Pacifist's War*, p.42.

p.258 'That Very Little Nazi', Words & Music by Eric Spear, Gordon Crier & Vernon Harris © Copyright 1996 Noel Gay Music Company Limited. Used by permission of Music Sales Limited. All Rights Reserved. International Copyright Secured.

p.258 'the only safe address in the world', Margery Allingham, *The Oaken Heart*, p.169.

p.259 'anticipated fleeing to the hills', Angus Calder, *The People's War, Britain 1939–1945*, p.130.

p.259 'a door close to the defence room', Asa Briggs, *The History of Broadcasting in the UK, Volume III* pp.267–8.

p.260 'When Gilbert Harding', Gilbert Harding, *Along My Line*, p.139.

p.260 'Everything is all right, Bill', R34/316/1 Controller (Administration) Papers (1938–41), BBC Written Archives.

p.260 'There are practically always two or three artists', memo from Mr Allport, 23 May 1940, BBC Written Archives.

p.261 'this happened twice in one day 13 May', Briggs, *The History of Broadcasting*, p.188.

p.261 'unauthorised interpolation', confidential brief for Ministry of Information, June 1940, BBC Written Archives.

20: Muriel, Jenny and Frank – Summer's End

p.266 '*Punch* claimed that Germany', *Punch*, 28 August 1940.

p.267 '*Lynn News*', 27 August 1940.

p.267 'When a valet told General Lee', James Leutze (ed.), *The London Observer, The Journal of General Raymond E. Lee 1940–1941*, p.14.

p.268 'On 29 August Sir Alexander Cadogan confided to his diary', David Dilks (ed.), *The Diaries of Sir Alexander Cadogan O.M. 1938–1945*, p.324.

p.269 'Virginia Woolf recorded', Leonard Woolf (ed.), *A Writer's Diary, Being Extracts From the Diary of Virginia Woolf*, 28 August 1940, p.344.

p.270 'night pirates', quoted in Ian Kershaw, *Hitler, 1936–1945, Nemesis*, p.309.

p.270 'On a cold-blooded', Leutze (ed.), *The London Observer*, p.x.

p.270 'The latest edition of the *War*', 6 September 1940.

21: Invasion Weekend, Saturday, 7 September 1940

p.272 'had been the driest since records', *Monthly Weather Report of the Meteorological Office for August, 1940*: 'Over the British Isles as a whole and over Ireland and England and Wales, considered separately, August 1940 was the driest August since comparable records are available, that is in 1870. In the long and reliable record at Oxford it was the driest August since registration began in 1815.'

p.272 'London had experienced only one rainy day in three months', Leutze (ed.), *The London Observer*, p.44.

p.272 'a perfect day', Ben Robertson, *I Saw England*, p.105.

p.273 'As the battle raged the bus-driver', ibid., p.106.

p.273 'others did exactly the opposite', Eric Sevareid, *Not so Wild a Dream*, p.171.

p.274 'These ships flew', ibid., p.106.

p.274 'as big as an elephant', Robertson, *I Saw England*, p.106.

p.274 'most appalling and depressing sight', ibid., p.106.

p.274 'London is burning', Ed Murrow, *This is London*, p.173.

p.275 'Someone's copping it', Spike Milligan, *Adolf Hitler, My Part in His Downfall*, p.58.

p.275 'disruption', ibid., p.58.

p.275 'They've all got Anderson Shelters', ibid., p.59.

p.275 'In Hauxton', Logbook of Hauxton Volunteer Defence Force, John Jopling, Cambridgeshire Collection.

p.276 'Hitler may at any hour give', quoted in Asa Briggs, *The History of Broadcasting in the UK, Volume III*, p.261.

p.276 'London scared stiff and drunk', BBC Written Archives, Monitors' Notes, Zeesen (Germany), in Afrikaans for SA, 6 September 1940.

p.277 'Everything seemed to point to invasion'. See *The Times*, 19 November 1946, for Clement Attlee's written reply to a question about the German invasion plans and why the invasion-imminent signal was given.

p.277 'The tides in the south-east'. The Admiralty provided the Cabinet Office with regular updates on the phases of the moon and tidal movements in the south-east. See CAB120/444, National Archives.

p.278 'According to some accounts', Paget's deputy, Brigadier (later Sir John) Swayne', see Basil Collier, *The Defence of the United Kingdom*, pp. 223–4. See also correspondence between General Sir John Swayne and Peter Fleming, September 1955, Peter Fleming Papers, University of Reading.

p.278 'Churchill wrote later', Sir Winston Churchill, *The Second World War, Volume II*, p.276.

p.278 'Alan Brooke stated in his diary', Alex Danchev and Daniel Todman (eds), *War Diaries 1939–1945, Field Marshal Lord Alanbrooke*, 7 September 1940, p.105

p.278 'Please, censor', Diana Forbes-Robertson and Roger Straus (eds), *War Letters from Britain*, p.80.

p.278 'very young, very solemn soldier', ibid., p.81.

p.279 'The following account', H. L. Wilson, *Four Years – The Story of the 5th Battalion (Caernarvonshire) Home Guard*, pp.39–41.

p.281 'In Buckinghamshire E, Company, L.W. Kentish, *Home Guard Bux 4 – Records and Reminiscences of the 4th Bucks Battalion Home Guard*, p.86.

p.281 'But the censor's office', Compton Mackenzie, *My Life and Times, Octave Eight, 1939–1946*, p.101.

p.281 'In the lonely, rolling'. According to Fred Hurt and Joan Barratt, *Lincoln War Diaries*, published by the authors in 1997, the five churches were St Faith's, St Martin's, St Mark's, St Peter at Gowt's and St Andrew's, p.25.

p.281 'destroyed bridges', *Sunday Times*, letters page, 28 October 1956. A. W. G. Harley said he was in a Field Company of Royal Engineers in Eastern Command which blew up twelve bridges.

p.281 'Peter Parnham'. My thanks to his son, Peter, for confirming this event.

p.281 'Two army officers', Norman Crump, *By Rail to Victory*, p.43.

p.282 'Vera Brittain heard', Vera Brittain, *England's Hour*, p.15.

p.282 'It was absolutely medieval', Forbes-Robertson and Straus (eds), *War Letters*, p.84.

p.282 'The bells rang out at Witney'. *Oxford Times*, 26 April 1957. W. F. Gibbons remembers hearing the bells in Oxford. See his account in the *Ringing World*, issue 3783, p.902: 'I remember seeing a church tower from my bedroom window, brilliantly lit by moonlight as I retired for the night. Some time later, I heard the tenor start to ring, so I counted the strokes to ascertain the time. At the 14th stroke, however, the significance of it all sank in! I leapt out of bed and dashed round to a friend's bedroom down the corridor, calling that the Germans were invading. The muffled reply from under the bedclothes indicated, amid expletives, that there was little that we could do about it! Undoubtedly he was right – we should only get in the way if paratroops were landing – so I went back to bed and settled down to sleep again.'

p.282 'intent on giving the invaders', *Daily Telegraph*, Monday, 9 September 1940.

p.282 'at a place *The Times* later described', *The Times*, 9 September 1940. See also *Sunday Times*, 21 October 1956, and *Sunday Times*, letters' page, 14 October 1956.

p.283 'Saboteurs disappeared'. For the auxiliary units' state of readiness on 4 September 1940, see CAB 120/241, National Archives. According to the 'Most Secret' 'Situation Report' there were 371 patrols. Suffolk and Essex had the most at forty-two; Sussex – surprisingly – the fewest at eleven. A total of 2178 men had been recruited.

p.283 'In Scotland some auxiliary units', David Lampe, *The Last Ditch*, p.108.

p.283 'When Margery Allingham experienced her first "invasion scare"', Margery Allingham, *The Oaken Heart*, p.186.

p.283 'a small boy caught sight of', Michael Glover, *Invasion Scare 1940*, p.164.

p.283 'the most hair-raising experience', Colin and Eileen Townsend (eds), *War Wives, A Second World War Anthology*, p.213.

p.283 'they abandoned their homes'. A Mass-Observation report mentioned in Angus Calder, *The Myth of the Blitz*, p.133.

p.285 'blood red', E. Bliss (ed.), *In Search of Light*, p.31.

p.285 'The BBC radio reporter Charles Gardner', BBC Written Archives, Sunday, 8 September 1940.

p.285 'Those people who were caught'. See 'September 7,1940: The First Day of the London Blitz. That story and does 9/11 change how we view it?' Lecture given by Professor Peter Stansky, Stanford University, at University of Texas, El Paso, March 2005, for a further discussion of the start of intense bombing.

p.286 'Frank Hurd was one', IWM, F Hurd 80/30/1.

p.288 'Another observer, Desmond Flower', quoted in John Carey (ed.), *The Faber Book of Reportage*, pp.537–8.

p.289 'by midnight on 7/8 September fire crews were struggling to contain nine "hundred-pump" blazes', Angus Calder, *The People's War, Britain 1939–1945*, p.157.

22: Sunday, 8 September 1940,
A National Day of Prayer

p.290 'further indications of impending', Alex Danchev and Daniel Todman, *War Diaries 1939–1945, Field Marshal Lord Alanbrooke*, p.105.

p.291 'An American radio report', CBS, in English for North America from London, 7 September, BBC Written Archives.

p.291 'like plumbers', William Shawn (ed.), *Mollie Panter-Downes, London War Notes*, p.100.

p.291 'like a tooth knocked out', Leonard Woolf (ed.), *A Writer's Diary, Being Extracts From the Diary of Virginia Woolf*, 10 September 1940.

p.293 'Generally supposed that', Major Sir Frank Markham P46 (where 'P' is a reference number), Imperial War Museum.

p.293 'Is the rumour true'. Vera Brittain, *England's Hour*, p.247.

p.293 'burnt them all up', Margaret Kennedy, *Where Stands a Winged Sentry*, p.224.

p.293 'A diarist in Ipswich wondered', Helen D. Millgate (ed.), *Mr Brown's War, A Diary of the Second World War*, p.61.

p.294 'The flaming sea'. See *The Battle of Shingle Street*, BBC Radio 4, Sunday, 30 January 2005.

p.294 '*Wir Fahren Gegen Engelland*', leaflet, Sir Donald Banks, *Flame Over Britain*, p.57.

p.294 'Shirer', William L. Shirer, *Berlin Diary. The Journal of a Foreign Correspondent, 1934–1941*, pp.396–7.

Epilogue: No More Waiting

p.298 'one man committed suicide by jumping overboard ', Peter and Leni Gillman, *'Collar the Lot!': How Britain Interned and Expelled its Wartime Refugees*, p.247.

p.298 'survivors of the *Arandora Star*', *Daily Mail*, 11 September 1940.

p.300 'After the war', unpublished obituary by John Baruch.

p.300 'François Lafitte's *The Internment of Aliens*'. Lafitte's father was American and his mother French; his stepfather was the sexologist Havelock Ellis. Lafitte was a one-time member of the Communist Party of Great Britain, and before the war he had helped many Jews to flee to Britain from Vienna.

p.300 Sir John Anderson, quoted in Gillman, *'Collar the Lot!'*, p.231. The debate took place on 22 August 1940.

p.301 'By early October', ibid., p.236.

p.305 'The trial of the "Four Men in a Boat" case'. On 23 May 1940, an Act of Parliament was passed to allow civilian courts to try people for spying. Known as the Treachery Act 1940, it was the only law passed in the twentieth century to increase the scope of the death penalty.

p.307 'The weather has broken', Margaret Kennedy, *Where Stands a Winged Sentry*, p.250.

Bibliography

Books

Adams, Jack, *The Doomed Expedition, The Norwegian Campaign of 1940*, Leo Cooper, London, 1989

Allingham, Margery. *The Oaken Heart*, Hutchinson, London, 1941

Arnison, Jim. *Hilda's War*, J. Arnison, Salford, 1996

Arnold, Ralph, *A Very Quiet War*, Rupert Hart-Davis, London, 1962

Aronson, Theo, *The Royal Family at War*, John Murray, London, 1993

Ayerst, David, *The Guardian: Biography of a Newspaper*, Collins, London, 1971

Banks, Sir Donald, *Flame Over Britain, A Personal Narrative of Petroleum Warfare*, S. Low, Marston, London, 1948

Barratt, Joan, and Hurt, Fred, *Lincoln War Diaries*, published by the authors, 1997

Beardmore, George, *Civilians at War, Journals 1938–1946*, John Murray, London, 1984

Bedts, Ralph F. de, *Ambassador Joseph Kennedy 1938–1940, An Anatomy of Appeasement*, Peter Lang, New York, 1985

Bennett, John C., *Christian Realism*, Student Christian Movement Press, London, 1941

Bernabei, Alfio, *Esuli ed emigrati Italiani nel Regno Unito, 1920–1940*, Mursia, Milan, 1997

Bliss, E. (ed.), *In Search of Light, The Broadcasts of Edward R. Murrow, 1938–1961*, Macmillan, London, 1968

Bowyer, Chaz, *For Valour, The Air VCs*, Kimber, London, 1978

Briggs, Asa, *The History of Broadcasting in the UK, Volume III*, Oxford University Press, Oxford, 1995

Brittain, Vera, *England's Hour*, Macmillan, London, 1941

Brown, Douglas R., *East Anglia 1940*, Terence Dalton, Lavenham, Suffolk, 1981

Buckle, Richard (ed.), *Self Portrait with Friends, The Selected Diaries of Cecil Beaton*, 1936–1974, Weidenfeld & Nicolson, London, 1979

Calder, Angus, *The People's War, Britain 1939–1945*, Jonathan Cape, London, 1969

————, *The Myth of the Blitz*, Jonathan Cape, London, 1991

Cantwell, John, *The Public Record Office, 1838–1958*, HMSO, London, 1991

Carey, D. John, *The Faber Book of Reportage*, Faber & Faber, London, 1987

Carpenter, Edward, *Romney Marsh at War*, Sutton Publishing, Stroud, 1999

Chisholm, Anne, and Davie, Michael, *Beaverbrook, A Life*, Hutchinson, London, 1992

Churchill, Winston, *The Second World War, Volume II, Their Finest Hour*, Penguin, London, 1985

Cole, J. A., *Lord Haw-Haw, The Full Story of William Joyce*, Faber & Faber, London, 1964

Collier, Basil, *The Defence of the United Kingdom*, Her Majesty's Stationery Office, London, 1957

Cornford, Stan, *With Wind and Sword, the Story of Meteorology and D-Day, 6 June 1944*, Meteorological Office, Bracknell, 1994

Costello, John, *Ten Days That Saved the West*, Bantam, London, 1991

Cruickshank, Dan, *Invasion – Defending Britain From Attack*, Boxtree, London, 2001

Dallek, Robert, *John F. Kennedy, An Unfinished Life*, Penguin, London, 2004

Danchev, Alex, and Todman, Daniel (eds), *War Diaries 1939–1945, Field Marshal Lord Alanbrooke*, Phoenix, London, 2002

Dear, I.C.B. (ed.), *Oxford Companion to the Second World War*, Oxford University Press, Oxford, 1995

Dilks, David (ed), *The Diaries of Sir Alexander Cadogan O.M., 1938–1945*, Cassell, London, 1971

Draper, Alfred, *Operation Fish: The Race to Save Europe's Wealth, 1939–1945*, Cassell, London, 1979

Feather, Jessica, *Art Behind Barbed Wire*, National Museums Liverpool, Liverpool, 2004

Fleming, Kate, *Celia Johnson, A Biography*, Weidenfeld & Nicolson, London, 1991

Fleming, Peter, *The Flying Visit*, Jonathan Cape, London, 1940

————, *Invasion 1940*, Rupert Hart-Davis, London, 1957; published as *Operation Sea Lion*, Pan, 1975

Forbes-Robertson, Diana, and Straus, Roger (eds), *War Letters from Britain*, Jarrolds, London, 1942

Garfield, Simon, *We Are At War, The Remarkable Diaries of Five Ordinary People in Extraordinary Times*, Ebury Press, London, 2002

Gee, H. L., *Don't Lose Heart*, Methuen, London, 1940

Geddes, G. W., *The Guildford Home Guard, 18th May 1940–31st December 1944*, Aldershot, 1945

Gelb, Norman, *Dunkirk: The Incredible Escape*, Michael Joseph, London, 1990

Gillies, Midge, *Amy Johnson, Queen of the Air*, Weidenfeld & Nicolson, London, 2003

Gillman, Peter and Leni, *'Collar the Lot!': How Britain Interned and Expelled its wartime refugees*, Quartet Books, London, 1980

Gleichen, Helena, *Contacts and Contrasts*, John Murray, London, 1940

Glover, Michael, *Invasion Scare 1940*, Leo Cooper, London, 1990

Gosling, Ted, *Colyton and Seaton in Old Photographs*, Alan Sutton, Stroud, 1994

Gosling, Ted, and Chapple, Roy, *East Devon at War*, Alan Sutton, Stroud, 1995

Grigson, Geoffrey, *The Crest on the Silver, An Autobiography*, Cresset Press, London, 1950

Harding, Gilbert, *Along My Line*, Putnam, London, 1953

Harding, Robert W., *A Tour of Snettisham*, Robert W. Harding, 1982

Hart-Davis, Duff, *Peter Fleming: A Biography*, Jonathan Cape, London, 1974

Hartley, Jenny (ed.), *Hearts Undefeated, Women's Writing of the Second World War*, Virago, London, 1994

Harvey, John (ed.), *The Diplomatic Diaries of Oliver Harvey, 1937–1940*, Collins, London, 1970

Hayward, James, *The Bodies on the Beach: Sealion, Shingle Street and the Burning Sea Myth of 1940*, CD41 Publishing, Dereham, 2001

Hennessy, Elizabeth, *A Domestic History of the Bank of England, 1930–1960*, Cambridge University Press, Cambridge, 1992

Hewison, Robert, *Under Siege: Literary Life in London, 1939–1945*, Weidenfeld & Nicolson, London, 1977

Highworth Historical Society, *A History of Highworth*, Part Three, Highworth Historical Society, Swindon, 1992

Hodgson, Vere, *Few Eggs and No Oranges, A Diary Showing How Unimportant People in London and Birmingham Lived Through the War Years 1940–1945*, Dennis Dobson, London, 1976

Iremonger, F. A. (compiler), *Each Returning Day. A Book of Prayers for Use in Time of War*, London 1940

Jenkins, Roy, *Churchill*, Pan, London 2002

Johnson, Derek E., *East Anglia at War*, Jarrolds, Norwich, 1992

Kennedy, Joseph P., and Londis, James M., *The Surrender of King Leopold*, New York, 1950.

Kennedy, Margaret, *Where Stands a Wingèd Sentry*, Yale University Press, New Haven, 1941

Kentish, L. W., *Home Guard Bux 4 – Records and Reminiscences of the 4th Bucks Battalion Home Guard*, Simpkin Marshall, London, 1946

Kershaw, Ian, *Hitler, 1936–1945, Nemesis*, Penguin, London, 2000

Kershaw, Roger, and Pearsall, Mark, *Immigrants and Aliens*, Public Record Office, Kew, 2000

King and Country, Selections from British War Speeches, 1939–1940, Chatto & Windus, 1940

Lafitte, François, *The Internment of Aliens*, Libris, London, 1988

Lampe, David, *The Last Ditch*, Cassell, London, 1968

Langdon, David, *Home Front Lines*, Methuen, London, 1941

Langdon-Davies, Major John, *Home Guard Training Manual*, John Murray and the Pilot Press, London, 1942

Leutze, James (ed.), *The London Observer, The Journal of General Raymond E. Lee 1940–1941*, Hutchinson, London, 1972

Liddell Hart, Basil, *Dynamic Defence*, Faber & Faber, London, 1940

Longmate, Norman, *How We Lived Then, A History of Everyday Life During the Second World War*, Hutchinson, London, 1971

Lord, Walter, *The Miracle of Dunkirk*, Allen Lane, London, 1983

Lowry, Bernard (ed.), *20th Century Defences in Britain, An Introductory Guide*, Council for British Archaeology, York, 2002

Lycett, Andrew, *Ian Fleming*, Weidenfeld and Nicolson, London, 1995

Mackay, Robert, *Half the Battle, Civilian Morale in Britain During the Second World War*, Manchester University Press, Manchester, 2002

Mackenzie, Compton, *My Life and Times, Octave Eight, 1939–1946*, Chatto & Windus, London, 1969

Mackenzie, S. P., *The Home Guard, A Military and Political History*, Oxford University Press, Oxford, 1995

McLaine, Ian, *Ministry of Morale, Home Front Morale and the Ministry of Information in World War II*, Allen & Unwin, London, 1979

Macleod, Colonel Roderick, and Kelly, Denis (eds), *The Ironside Diaries, 1937–1940*, Constable, London, 1962

Masterman, J. C., *The Double-Cross System in the War of 1939 to 1945*, Yale University Press, New Haven, 1972

Millgate, Helen D. (ed.), *Mr Brown's War, A Diary of the Second World War*, Sutton Publishing, Stroud, 1998

Milligan, Spike, *Adolf Hitler, My Part in His Downfall*, Penguin, London, 1971

Mitchison, Naomi, *Among You Taking Notes*, Gollancz, London, 1985

Mitford, Nancy, *The Pursuit of Love*, Penguin, London, 1945

Munthe, Malcolm, *Hellens, A Herefordshire Manor*, Duckworth, London, 1957

Murrow, Edward, *This is London*, Cassell, London, 1941

Nicolson, Harold, *Diaries and Letters, 1939–1945*, Collins, London, 1967

Ogley, Bob, *Kent at War*, Froglet Publications in association with Kent Messenger Group Newspapers, Westerham, 1994

O'Neill, Gilda, *Our Street, East End Life in the Second World War*, Viking, London, 2003

Osers, Ewald, *Lônské snĕhy*, Nakladatelstvi Karolinum [the Charles University Press], Prague, 2004.

Panter-Downes, Mollie, *Good Evening, Mrs Craven: The Wartime Stories of Mollie Panter-Downes*, Persephone Books, London, 1999

Partridge, Frances, *A Pacifist's War*, Hogarth Press, London, 1978

Pearson, Fiona, *Paolozzi*, National Galleries of Scotland, Edinburgh, 1999

Penguin Biographical Dictionary of Women, Penguin, London, 1998

Percival, John, *For Valour, The Victoria Cross, Courage in Action*, Methuen, London, 1985

Pimlott, Ben (ed.), *The Second World War Diary of Hugh Dalton 1940–1945*, Jonathan Cape, London, 1986

Plumb, J. H., *Royal Heritage: The Story of Britain's Royal Builders and Collectors*, published in association with the television series written by Huw Wheldon and J. H. Plumb, BBC, London, 1977

Priestley, J. B., *Postscripts*, William Heinemann, London, 1940

Quayle, Anthony, *A Time to Speak*, Sphere, London, 1990

Renier, Olive, *Before the Bonfire*, P. Drinkwater, Shipston-on-Stour, 1984

Renier, Olive, and Rubinstein, Vladimir *Assigned to Listen, the Evesham Experience, 1939–43*, BBC External Services, London, 1986

Rhodes James, Robert, *'Chips', The Diaries of Sir Henry Channon*, Weidenfeld and Nicolson, London, 1967

Ritchie, Charles, *The Siren Years, Undiplomatic Diaries, 1937–1945*, Macmillan, London, 1974

Robertson, Ben, *I Saw England*, Jarrolds, London, 1941

Rowbotham, Sheila, *A Century of Women: The History of Women in Britain and the United States*, Viking, London, 1997

Royde Smith, Naomi, *Outside Information, Being a Diary of Rumours*, Macmillan, London, 1941

Schellenberg, Walter, *Invasion 1940, The Nazi Invasion Plan for Britain*, St Ermin's Press, London, 2000

Sevareid, Eric, *Not so Wild a Dream*, Atheneum, New York, 1976

Shawn, William (ed.), *Mollie Panter-Downes, London War Notes, 1939–1945*, Longman, London, 1972

Shirer, William L., *Berlin Diary, The Journal of a Foreign Correspondent, 1934–1941*, Hamish Hamilton, London, 1941

Smith, Amanda (ed.), *Hostage to Fortune – The Letters of Joseph P. Kennedy*, Viking, New York, 2000

Smith Constance Babington (ed.), *Letters to a Sister from Rose Macaulay*, Collins, London, 1964

Spalding, Frances, *The Tate, A History*, Tate Gallery Publishing, London, 1998

Strange, Joan, *Despatches from the Home Front, The War Diaries of Joan Strange, 1939–1945*, Monarch, Eastbourne, 1989

Strategicus, *Can Britain Be Invaded?* Liberty Handbooks No. 2, J. M. Dent, London, 1941

Sunday Times Diary of the War, Cherry Tree War Special

Tennyson Jesse, F., and Harwood, H. M., *London Front, Letters Written to America (August 1939–July 1940)*, Constable, London, 1940

Townsend, Colin and Eileen, *War Wives, A Second World War Anthology*, Grafton Books, London, 1989

Vincent, Rodney H., *A Tanner Will Do – Village Life in the Nineteen Thirties and Forties*, Anchor Publications, Little Downham, 1997

Waller, Jane, and Vaughan-Rees, Michael, *Women in Wartime, The Role of Women's Magazines, 1939–1945*, Macdonald Optima, London, 1987

Waller, Maureen, *London 1945, Life in the Debris of War*, John Murray, London, 2004

Warwicker, John (ed.), *With Britain in Mortal Danger, Britain's Most Secret Army of WWII*, Cerberus, Bristol, 2002

Watts, Newman, *Britain's Secret Weapon*, Worthing, 1942

'We also Served': The Story of the Home Guard in Cambridgeshire and the Isle of Ely, 1940–1943, W. Heffer, Cambridge, 1944

Weidenfeld, George, *Remembering My Good Friends, An Autobiography*, HarperCollins, London, 1995

Williamson, Alan, *East Riding's Secret Resistance*, Middleton Press, West Sussex, 2004

Wilson, H. L., *Four Years – The Story of the 5th Battalion (Caernarvonshire) Home Guard*, Conway, Wales, 1944

Winder, Robert, *Bloody Foreigners, The Story of Immigration to Britain*, Little, Brown, London, 2004

Woolf, Leonard (ed.), *A Writer's Diary, Being Extracts From the Diary of Virginia Woolf*, The Hogarth Press, London, 1953

Ziegler, Philip, *London at War, 1939–1945*, Sinclair-Stevenson, London, 1995

Articles and Papers

Summerfield, Penny and Peniston-Bird, Corinna, 'Women in the Firing Line: The Home Guard and the defence of gender boundaries in Britain in the Second World War', *Women's History Review* (2000), vol. 9, no. 2

Tatler, July–September 1940

Picture Post, July–September 1940

Ely Standard

Cambridge Daily News

The Times

Daily Telegraph

Stansky, Professor Peter, lecture, 'September 7,1940: The First Day of the London Blitz. That story and does 9/11 change how we view it?' Stanford University, at University of Texas, El Paso, March 2005

'The Real Dad's Army', a *Lincolnshire Echo* Special Publication, Tuesday, 18 January 2005

Radio Programmes

The Battle of Shingle Street, BBC Radio 4
War in the Ether, BBC Radio 4
Germany Calling, BBC Radio 4

Acknowledgements

This book is about voices from the past, but it would have been impossible without the help of so many people whose busy lives I have interrupted to drag them back to a time of blackouts and shortages. I am profoundly grateful to everyone who has allowed me to include their story, or their relative's, in this book.

Jenny and Muriel's exuberant and insightful diaries represent a tiny fraction of the treasure trove of Mass-Observation's Archive at the University of Sussex. I am grateful to the trustees for allowing me to reproduce extracts and to Dorothy Sheridan, Director of the Mass-Observation Archive, Sandra Koa Wing, Development Officer for the Mass-Observation Project, and other staff at the archive for their patience and kindness. I was very fortunate that 'Muriel' was able to answer my questions about what happened to her family after the war and that, forty years on, she still seems to be just the sort of person who would take the terror and tedium out of an air raid.

Raymond O'Brien helped me to understand his parents and their lives, and never failed to answer my countless questions in great detail. I would like to thank him and Frank's other children: Frances Stobbs, Geraldine McWilliams and Christopher O'Brien for allowing me to quote from their father's letters. Kevin Morrison was most helpful when I visited the fascinating wartime cornucopia that he has assembled and which is held at Glasgow Caledonian University.

I am also indebted to Dr John Baruch, Department of Cybernetics, Internet and Virtual Systems, University of Bradford, for allowing me to quote from his parents' correspondence and for providing me with other material that enabled me to piece together the Baruch family's early history. He was endlessly patient and helpful, despite the demands of his busy job. Alison Cullingford, Special Collections Librarian, and John Brooker, Special Collections Assistant at the J. B. Priestley Library, University of Bradford, also went out of their way to answer my queries in great depth. I am grateful to Jack Jones MBE, for sharing his memories of Ludwig with me.

Alfio Bernabei was kind enough to put me in touch with Renée Chambers. Talking to her and her daughter, Carole Storey-Tennant, was one of those occasions when it seems impossible to think of research as 'work'; I only regret that the ultimate reason for our meeting was tragic.

No invader would have enjoyed meeting Charlie Mason but, unarmed and in peacetime Hull, he was fascinating on the role of the auxiliary units. I am grateful to David Smith, Senior Local Studies Librarian at the Local Studies Library in Hull, for putting me in touch with him, and to Jo Edge for arranging our meeting.

Peter Parnham and Thomas Priestley both shed light on their fathers' activities in 1940, and Leonard Marsland Gander's son, Nigel Gander, very kindly allowed me to quote from his father's diary, held in the Imperial War Museum, London.

I am very grateful to the many experts whose brains I have picked during the course of my research. Peter Elliott, Senior Keeper, Department of Research & Information Services, Royal Air Force Museum, answered a myriad queries with patience and wisdom. Max Tyler, Historian of the British Music Hall Society, proved as helpful as ever, and the Society of Authors offered support in countless different ways.

Ewald Osers very kindly allowed me to see an English version of part of his memoirs, which gave me a vivid insight into the life of a BBC monitor, and Lesley Chamberlain drew my attention to two radio programmes on the subject.

David Palmer shared his knowledge of Eduardo Paolozzi; Richard White enthused about bell-ringing; and Alicia Foster reminded me of the joys of Nancy Mitford's work. Chris Jakes of the Cambridgeshire Collection showed me some fine wartime photos and was also kind enough to read my manuscript; any errors that remain are entirely mine.

Rowena Webb, my editor at Hodder & Stoughton, was everything an author could ask for: a source of inspiration and a steady hand from start to finish. Her assistant, Fenella Bates, has been a great help. Hazel Orme performed her usual magic as copy-editor – a title that fails to do justice to her many, varied talents. Juliet Brightmore was most helpful in answering my queries about illustrations and in suggesting alternative sources.

My agent, Faith Evans, provided her customary incisive suggestions when they were most needed and helped in so many ways, large and small. Her assistant, Lucie Sutherland, made some extremely valuable comments on the final manuscript.

I am, yet again, grateful for the generosity and kindness of friends and relatives. Ann-Janine Murtagh, Richard Scrivener, John and Dinah Kelly, Veronica Forwood, Roger Browning and Ruby Mackie gave me a bed – in some cases for several nights – in my travels round Britain, and showed an interest in the book that went beyond the bounds of friendship. Bridie Pritchard, Veronica Forwood and Roger Browning read early drafts of the book and their comments were both helpful and heartening. Sarah Mnatzaganian, Jenny Burgoyne and Kathryn Hughes each offered encouragement when I most needed it.

Jim Kelly, my husband and 'the man at the other end of the corridor', helped in endless different ways; I hope he knows how grateful I am. My daughter, Rosa, went camping without me and learnt to live with my obsession with the strange man with the funny moustache.

In September 1940 my mother was working for the Ministry of Supply and my father had just joined the Scots Guards. I owe them the biggest debt of all – which is why this book is dedicated to them.

A Note on Sources

Without exception, every archive and library I contacted was most helpful and I would like to thank the following people by name: Ted Gosling, Curator, The Axe Valley Heritage Museum; Erin O'Neill,

Archives Researcher, BBC Written Archives Centre; John Warwicker and the Museum of the British Resistance Organisation; Martin Lubowski, Archivist of Bunce Court School & Landschulheim Herrlingen Archive; Stephanie Clarke, Archivist, Imperial War Museum; Lindsay Campbell, Team Librarian (Local Studies), King's Lynn Library; Adrian Wilkinson, Archivist, Lincolnshire Archives; Eleanor Nannestad, Community Librarian, Information and Local Studies, Lincoln Central Library; Sara Basquill, Keeper of Collections Management, Museum of Lincolnshire Life; Hugh Alexander, Image Library Deputy Manager Enterprises, and Darragh McElroy, Press and Publicity Officer, The National Archives; Katherine Boyce, Department of Printed Books, National Army Museum; Polly Tucker, Archivist, The Natural History Museum; Dianne Yeadon, Norfolk Heritage Centre; Mike Bott, Keeper of Archives & Manuscripts, and Verity Andrews, Archives Assistant, University of Reading; Dr Tony Trowles, Librarian, The Muniment Room and Library, Westminster Abbey; Joy Thomas, Local Studies Librarian, A. N. Palmer Centre for Local Studies and Archives, Wrexham County Borough Museum.

I am equally grateful to staff at the following institutions whose names I do not know: Bank of England; British Library; British Library National Sound Archive; British Postal Museum and Archive; County Record Office, Cambridge; Ely Library; Euston Fire Station; HM Tower of London; House of Lords Record Office (The Parliamentary Archives); Hyman Kreitman Research Centre for the Tate Library and Archive; Ipswich Record Office; Met Office; National Museums Liverpool; Office for National Statistics; Rare Breeds Survival Trust; The Royal Archives; University Library, Cambridge; The Women's Library.

Permissions

Extracts from *Where Stands a Winged Sentry* are reproduced with kind permission of Curtis Brown Ltd, London, on behalf of the Estate of Margaret Kennedy. Copyright Margaret Kennedy 1941.

My thanks to the BBC Written Archives Centre, Caversham Park, Reading, for allowing me to quote from various documents.

Extracts from the diaries of Jenny and Muriel are reproduced with permission of Curtis Brown Group Ltd, London, on behalf of the Trustees of the Mass-Observation Archive. Copyright © Trustees of the Mass-Observation Archive.

The Oaken Heart written by Margery Allingham and reproduced with the kind permission of Rights Limited. *The Oaken Heart* © 1941 Rights Limited, a Chorion company. All rights reserved.

Every effort has been made to contact copyright holders. Should anyone believe I have failed to acknowledge the proper sources I will be happy to rectify this in future editions.

Picture Acknowledgements

Doctor John Baruch: 2 top left. Renée Chambers: 14 top right. Fraser Darrah: 15 top. Getty Images: 7 top, 8 top right, 14 top left. Imperial War Museum, London: 1 (HU93104), 2 bottom (63693), 3 bottom (HU 93107), 4 top (HU73594), 4 bottom (HU 73545), 5 bottom (HU36270), 6 bottom (PL13456c), 7 bottom left (F4824), 7 bottom right (F4799), 8 top left (HU93105), 8 bottom (HU93103), 9 top (HU85534), 9 bottom (HU85538), 10 top left (D3918), 10 top right (H5850), 10 bottom (HU36167), 11 top (H3034), 11 centre (H2177), 11 bottom (H2181), 12 top (2278), 12 bottom (HU93100), 13 top (D22932), 14 bottom (HU88699), 15 centre (AP8165), 16 top left (HU93102), 16 top right, 16 bottom (HU36222). Kevin Morrison Collection, Glasgow Caledonian University (The War 2nd August 1940): 5 top, 13. bottom. Raymond O'Brien: 6 top left and right. Private Collection: 3 top right. Vladimir Rubinstein: 2 top right. University of Sussex: 3 top left. Walker Art Gallery, National Museums Liverpool: 15 bottom.

Illustrations within the text
Cambridgeshire Collection: 262. Illustrated London News Picture Library: 59, 140.
Imperial War Museum, London: 122 (Dept of Documents), 123 (Dept of Printed Books, Ephemeral Collection), 295 (Dept of Printed Books, Leaflet Collection), 308 (E65881). Ministry of Information/COI: 7. National Archives of the UK: 192 (INF 13/171), 205 (INF3/219), 227 (WO199/738), 233 (WO199/738), 236 (WO199/1517), 245 (KV3/76), 284 (CAB120/241). Reproduced by permission of Punch Limited/www.punch.co.uk: 41, 119, 163.

Index